The Path to

Contentment

in Islam

Published by Fercan Corporation

Waterloo, Ontario, Canada

www.fercan.ca

ISBN: 978-1-7750670-8-5

First Edition 2021

Printed in Canada

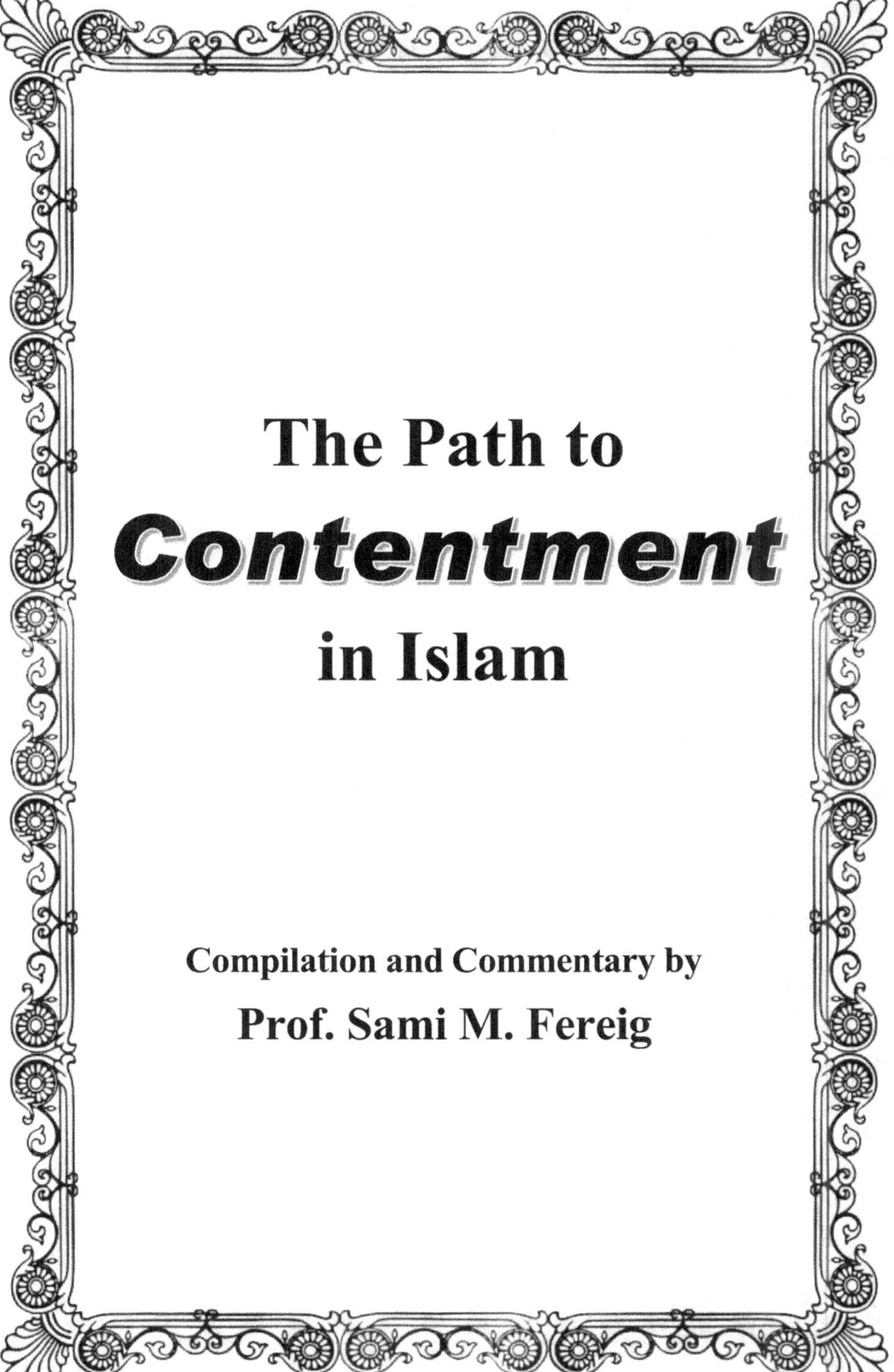

The Path to **_Contentment_** in Islam

Compilation and Commentary by

Prof. Sami M. Fereig

This is a translation of the 'Approval to Publish' Letter, in Arabic,
issued by Al-Azhar in Cairo, Egypt in 2016.

Al-Azhar   **20984   /   22/2016**
Council for Islamic Research
General Administration
Research, Authorship and Translation
Mr. Sami Mohamed Fereig

As per your request to inspect and review the book 'El-Rida' (Contentment), 258 pages, the author is Sami Mohamed Fereig.

We confirm that nothing in the book prevents it from being published, and there is no objection to it being printed and published at your own expense.

You should take good care when writing the Qur'anic verses and Hadith, and deliver five (5) copies to Al-Azhar Public Library after printing the book.

This approval is limited to this edition, and should be renewed for any subsequent edition, or five (5) years from the date of this letter. This approval should not be used for another edition. Also, you should adhere to the relevant laws. In case of addition or deletion, this approval will become null and void.

Glory be to Allah and He knows the intentions.

Dated: 1437 AH / 2016 AD

General Manager
General Administration
Research, Authorship and Translation
24 May 2016
(Signature)

Assistant Secretary General for Culture

26 May 2016

(Signature)

General Secretary
27 May 2016
(Signature)

Official Seal of Al-Azhar

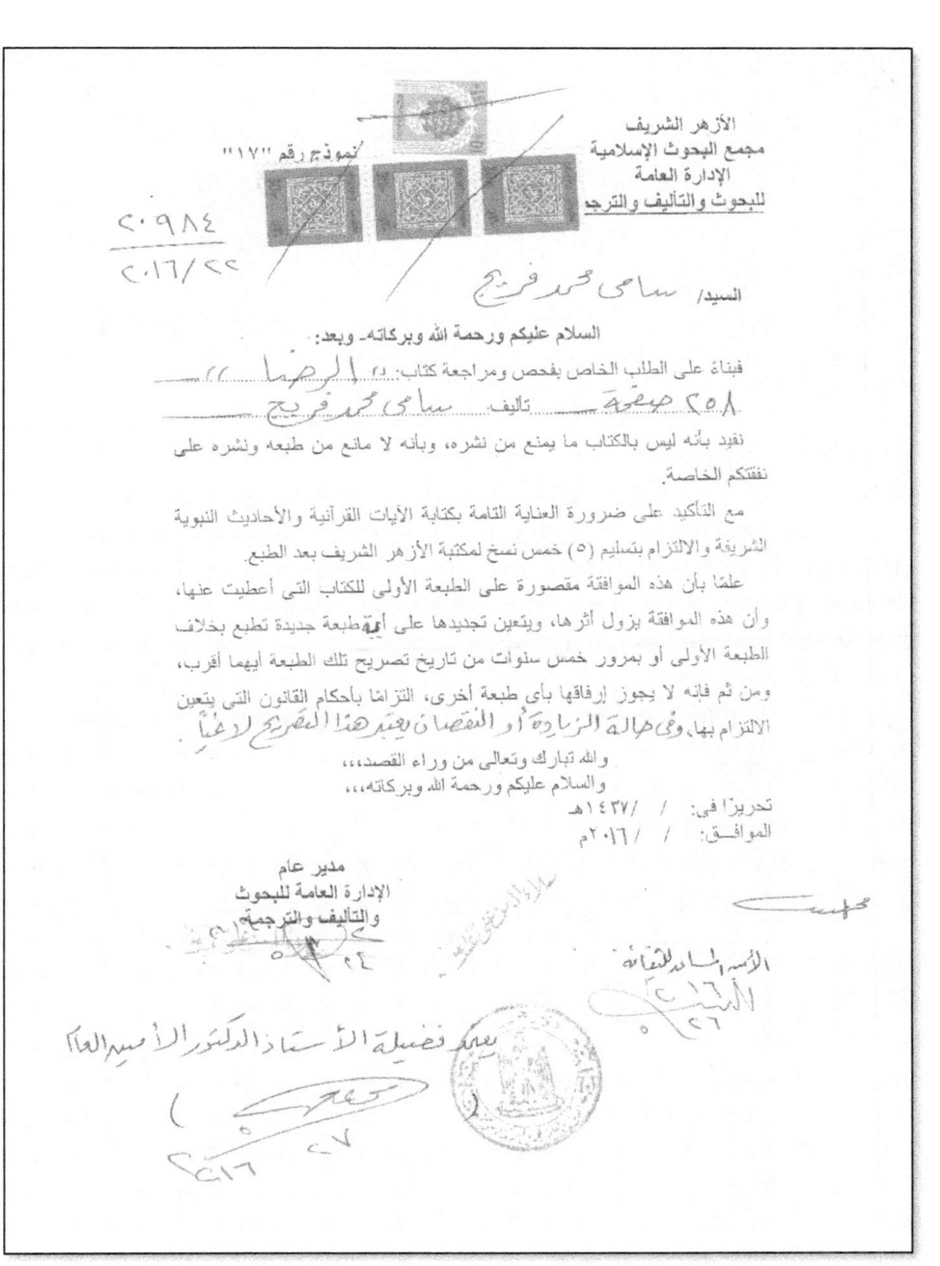

نموذج رقم "١٧"

الأزهر الشريف
مجمع البحوث الإسلامية
الإدارة العامة
للبحوث والتأليف والترجمة

٢٠٩٨٤
٢٠١٦/٢٢

السيد/ سامى محمد فريح

السلام عليكم ورحمة الله وبركاته. وبعد:

بناءً على الطلب الخاص بفحص ومراجعة كتاب: د؟ " الرضما "
تأليف ــ سامى محمد فريج

نفيد بأنه ليس بالكتاب ما يمنع من نشره، وبأنه لا مانع من طبعه ونشره على نفقتكم الخاصة.

مع التأكيد على ضرورة العناية التامة بكتابة الآيات القرآنية والأحاديث النبوية الشريفة والالتزام بتسليم (٥) خمس نسخ لمكتبة الأزهر الشريف بعد الطبع.

علمًا بأن هذه الموافقة مقصورة على الطبعة الأولى للكتاب التى أعطيت عنها، وأن هذه الموافقة يزول بزول أثرها، ويتعين تجديدها على أية طبعة جديدة تطبع بخلاف الطبعة الأولى أو بمرور خمس سنوات من تاريخ تصريح تلك الطبعة أيهما أقرب، ومن ثم فإنه لا يجوز إرفاقها بأى طبعة أخرى، التزامًا بأحكام القانون التى يتعين الالتزام بها، وفى حالة الزيادة أو النقصان يعتبر هذا التصريح لاغياً

والله تبارك وتعالى من وراء القصد،،،
والسلام عليكم ورحمة الله وبركاته،،،

تحريرًا فى: / ١٤٣٧/هـ
الموافق: / ٢٠١٦/م

مدير عام
الإدارة العامة للبحوث
والتأليف والترجمة

Dedication

❈*... say, "To God we belong, and to Him we will return."*❈ *[Q 2:156]*

Praise be to God for His Compassion and Mercy,
and for what He has ordained and willed.

On the evening of 8th July 2008 (5th Rajab 1429 AH), our son Omer was reading a book while sitting under a maple tree in Christie Pits Park, Toronto. At about 7:30 pm, this tree was struck by lightning and Omer departed this life. He was 28 years old.

He was a graduate of Civil Engineering at the University of Waterloo, and had recently married. All his family and friends greatly miss him, and we pray that he is now in paradise.

This book has been compiled in Omer's memory, hoping that others might benefit from its contents, especially those who have gone through similar experiences and difficult circumstances. We hope that they will keep Omer and us in their prayers.

❈*... call upon Him in reverence and in hope. Surely the Mercy of God is ever near to the virtuous.*❈ *[Q 7:56]*

❈*Their supplication therein shall be, "Glory be to Thee, O God!" And therein their greeting shall be, "Peace." And the conclusion of their supplication shall be, "Praise be to God, Lord of the worlds!"*❈ *[Q 10:10]*

إهـــداء

الحمد لله وإنا لله وإنا إليه راجعون

الحمد لله على قضاء الله وقدره وهو الرحمن الرحيم، ماضٍ فيَّ حكمه عدلٌ فيَّ قضاؤه، موقنٌ بأن رحمة الله أَجَّلُ من حبنا لفلذات أكبادنا وألطف. ولعل تقديم هذا العمل يمثل إضاءة في طريق الواصلين إلى الرضا والنور الإلهي وسبيلاً لرحمة الله على روح نجلي المرحوم بإذن الله تعالى

المهندس/ عمر سامي محمد فريج

((ونسأل القارئ الدعاء له ولنا ولسائر المسلمين بالرحمة والمغفرة))

قال تعالى ﴿ إِنَّ رَحْمَتَ اللَّهِ قَرِيبٌ مِّنَ الْمُحْسِنِينَ ﴾

[الأعراف: ٥٦]

وآخر دعوانا أن الحمد لله رب العالمين

ACKNOWLEDGEMENTS

I wish to express my deep gratitude to my wife (Um Omer) for her help in editing this book. I also want to thank Dr. Abdelaziz Hamdy, professor of Arabic Translation at the American University in Cairo, for translating the Most Beautiful Ninety-Nine Divine Names of God and the prayers of Sidi Ibn Arabi that are associated with the Ninety-Nine Names.

I give my sincere thanks to two of Omer's closest friends, Dr. Atif Khalil, Associate Professor in the Department of Religious Studies at the University of Lethbridge, Alberta and Dr. Mohammad Rustom, Associate Professor of Islamic Studies at Carleton University in Ottawa, Ontario. Dr. Khalil wrote the Preface and Dr. Rustom wrote the Foreword, and they also reviewed all of the text, giving helpful feedback and comments.

I also acknowledge the efforts of Mr. Abdelhamid Salim, Mr. Fady Mohammad, Mr. Mohamed El-Nshrtawy and Mr. Ahmed Radwan of Dar Al-Rida Corporation in Cairo, Egypt for their help in gathering the Quranic verses and Prophetic Hadith used in this book.

Preface

In the *Nourishment of Hearts*, Abu Talib al-Makki (d. 996 CE) notes that the *'ulama'* have debated among themselves the ranks of three people. One of them anticipates and even yearns for death, because death, for him, opens the gate for an encounter with the divine Beloved. Another desires a prolonged life in order to accumulate as many virtuous deeds as possible over his brief journey through the world. The third person leaves the matter entirely to God, saying to himself, "if He wills, He can give me life for as long as it pleases Him; and if He wills, He can give me death tomorrow." Where do each of these people stand, asks Makki, both in relation to God, and in relation to each other? Without reservation, he confers the supreme degree upon the final of the three, on the one who leaves the decision to God, since he occupies, according to Makki, the *maqam* or station of *rida*, being content, satisfied and well-pleased with what God decrees for him. His state is like that of the soul before it entered the world: just as one did not choose to come into the *dunya*, let alone when to enter it, likewise, the *radi* (the one marked by *rida*) foregoes the decision, returning to an almost primordial state of complete and total surrender to God. The second rank, continues Makki, belongs to the one who longs for death, not because of the toils and hardships of life, let alone suicidal inclinations, but out of a pining to return to God, to the ultimate object of his love and existential affection. Such a man stands at the station of *tashawwuq*, at the station of longing, desire, and yearning, consumed as he is by a love for his Maker. Finally, the lowest rank belongs to the one who wishes for a long life. The nobility of this rank—and it is still a noble rank—rests on the man's desire to accumulate as many beautiful deeds as possible, before the final accounting, and not out of a wish to delay the return simply to enjoy the transient pleasures of this world. Such a person stands at the station of hope or *raja'*, since he hopes for a grace through which God will enable him to live a life of holiness and piety. Makki goes on to declare that there is no fourth rank, and that the spiritual aspirant should aim to stand on one of the three rungs. That Makki unhesitatingly accords the supreme state to the *maqam al-rida* illustrates the centrality of the character trait in Islamic spirituality. After all, the Prophet himself would pray to God, "I ask for *rida* from You, after the passing of decree."

As many of the virtues of the Quran, *rida* is a quality which both God and the human being share. In other words, both may be qualified by it. The Quran states on more than one occasion, describing the righteous, that *He has rida with them, and they have rida with Him* (Q 5:119, 9:100; 57:22. 98:8). There is no question that the human being is summoned by Muslim revelation to seek God's satisfaction and good-pleasure. On at least one occasion, after describing the delights of

Paradise, the Quran moves on to declare that *the ridwan of God is greatest* (Q 9:72) — *ridwan* being an intense form of *rida*. In other words, the final, saving experience of God's acceptance of and satisfaction with the soul will surpass, according to Revelation, the delights of the Garden promised to its inhabitants. Now, how is one to obtain God's *rida*, and beyond that, divine *ridwan*? In the contemplative tradition, as enunciated by the authorities of Muslim spirituality, the virtually unanimous answer was that it is a consequence of the human being's fulfillment of the commands of God, one the one hand, and the result of human *rida*, on the other. In other words, if the human being meets God with *rida* for His decree, then God will meet the human being with His own *rida*, since a hadith has God declare, "He who has *rida* (with Me) encounters My *rida* when he meets Me, and he who is displeased (with Me) encounters my displeasure when he meets Me." Elaborating on the nature of the virtue demanded by God, one authority would state that there are in fact two kinds of *rida* made incumbent on the human being: *rida* with God in so far as He is the Arranger (*mudabbir*) of affairs, and *rida* with what comes from God by way of His decree. The implications of this apparently inconsequential distinction would be elaborated in significant ways in the later tradition.

In this fine book, Dr. Sami Fereig has brought together the most relevant verses from the Quran and the traditions of the Prophet on the theme of *rida*. Almost encyclopedic in its scope, it will serve as an invaluable resource for those desiring, in a single volume, what the sacred sources of Islam have to say about contentment and satisfaction. Compiled in memory of Omer Fereig (d. 2008) —with whom my relationship blossomed into a deep, spiritual friendship over the course of the last five years of life—it is a testament to a father's love for a son whose sudden death came as a shock to all of us. It also serves as a meditation of sorts (through the manner and style in which the work has been structured) on what the foundational texts of Islam teach us about how to cope with loss, suffering and the tribulations of life. Indeed, it is a curious feature of the Quran that when it speaks of "happiness" or *sa'ada,* it is described exclusively as an experience reserved for Paradise. In this world, however, the human being is invited to cultivate the virtues of patience, gratitude, trust, and *rida* as a response to the fluctuating circumstances of the human condition. And this is in order to create an inward stability, the fruits of which will be fully born in the afterlife, but the tranquility of which can be tasted even here, in the now, in the Garden of the Heart.

Atif Khalil
August 2020
University of Lethbridge

Foreword

The famous Egyptian spiritual master Dhu'l-Nun al-Misri was once asked about the meaning of the great Islamic virtue of contentment (*rida'*). In response to this question, he said, "Contentment is when a person's heart is happy with the passing of the Divine decree." This kind of happiness of heart can only be the state of someone who understands that God is in control of all things and that the outcome of every predicament that a believer may find himself in will always be good. And how can it not be good, seeing that we come from the One Who is All-Good, and that we are returning to Him?

A book that explains the nature and significance of contentment, from the words of the Quran and sayings of our beloved Prophet Muhammad, is therefore of the utmost importance for our lives today, especially in these odd times of uncertainty and unease. Learning to be content with God's decree and rejoicing in His promise that He will manage our affairs for us is one of the best things we can do, both for ourselves and others.

Our dear friend and teacher, who is the author of this book, shares with us the wisdom of Islam's teachings on contentment. At the same time, this work represents his journey along the path of contentment, which took on new meaning for him when his son Omer, who was my close friend, passed away at a young age exactly twelve years ago today. May God grant Omer His Good-Pleasure (*ridwan*) and increase his family in their love, patience, and contentment. And may this book aid all of us in our own search for contentment until that day when God says to each of us, "O thou soul at peace! Return unto thy Lord in utter contentment. Enter among My servants, and enter My Garden" (Quran 89:27-30). Amin.

Mohammed Rustom
Saadiyat Island, AD
July 8, 2020

TABLE OF CONTENTS

INTRODUCTION

Attaining the contentment of God, described in the Holy Qur'an as 'the supreme triumph,' leads to peace of mind, tranquility of heart and soul, a virtuous and good life, and ultimate contentment in the Hereafter. Believers who submit themselves to God, seek His guidance in the Holy Qur'an, and follow the example of His final messenger, Prophet Muhammad (peace and blessings of God be upon him) are on a straight path, one that leads to attaining His contentment.

❁This is the Book in which there is no doubt, a guidance for all who are conscious of God. ❁ [Q 2:2]

As believers seek contentment by following the straight path, they should guard themselves against Satan and his party. Satan's mission is to cause believers to stray from the straight path and misguide them to ingratitude and discontentment.

❁Truly Satan is an enemy to you, so treat him as an enemy … ❁ [Q 35:6]

Believers should know that what brings contentment to them is abiding by what God wants them to do, and refraining from what God does not want them to do. We rely on God's Grace and Guidance in His Book to clearly show the message and the means to guide all believers to the path of contentment. This work is divided into the following seven chapters.

Chapter 1 - Contentment: What the Holy Qur'an and Prophetic Traditions Tell Us

The Holy Qur'an states that contentment has to come first from God and that it is a gift from Him. When God is content with you, this will make you content with Him. With such mutual contentment between God and the believer, there will also be peace of mind, tranquillity of heart, a fulfilled life and, of course, the attainment of ultimate contentment in the Hereafter. To seek such Grace from God, we need to look for guidance throughout the Holy Qur'an and Traditions (Sunnah) of the Prophet, peace be upon him (pbuh).

❁God is content with them, and they are content with Him: this is the supreme triumph. ❁ [Q 5:119]

Believers must also be aware of Satan (the devil) and his party, who advocate a path ultimately leading to discontentment and punishment, and this is illustrated in many Qur'anic verses which explain that Satan is man's arch-enemy and how he will always try to lead us astray. To counter this, believers should seek refuge in God and ask Him to purify their souls so that they can be closer to Him.

Chapter 2 - Love of God and being Conscious of Him are Keys to His Contentment

This chapter explains how Islam is based on love. The mutual love between God and believers will lead to contentment. This love has three levels: between God and the believer, between believers and the Prophet (pbuh), and among believers themselves. It further explains that the way to God's love is through our consciousness of God and His Presence (Taqwa), and this takes the form of Taqwa of the heart through belief, and Taqwa through one's deeds.

Say, "If you love God, follow me, and God will love you and forgive you your sins. And God is Forgiving, Merciful." [Q 3:31]

God Almighty, in His Holy Qur'an, explains which actions and deeds of His servants that He loves, so they can obey Him and continue performing these actions. They include constantly remembering Him, putting one's full trust in Him, being just in one's dealings with others, doing good, turning to Him in repentance, purifying oneself, keeping one's promises, and being patient and steadfast.

But those who believe are more ardent in their love of God. [Q 2:165]

Similarly, there are many verses in the Holy Qur'an which clearly explain what God does not love, and the actions that will separate us from His love. These actions or characteristics include overstepping the limits, such as being arrogant, conceited and boastful, being extravagant and wasteful, being ungrateful, corrupt, untrustworthy, treacherous, persistently sinful, and talking openly about evil (which should be done only when you are the victim of an evil act). It can be seen from these verses that the path to God's love is through performing those deeds that He loves, and abstaining from those actions and attitudes which cause us to lose His love.

But as for those who strive for Us, We shall surely guide them in Our ways. Truly God is with the virtuous. [Q 29:69]

❀Surely those who believe and perform righteous deeds, for them shall the Compassionate ordain love. ❀ [Q 19:96]

Chapter 3 – Achieving Contentment by Accepting God's Will (Qader and Qadaa)

In this chapter, we discuss how the believer should understand and accept Qader (the measures set by God) and Qadaa (the manifestation of these measures) to have peace of mind and tranquillity of heart. These two terms are explained in light of the concept that our life is a series of tests or trials that can take the form of ease and prosperity or difficulty and adversity. Such tests are needed to strengthen our faith and belief so that God can reward us. They are explained in the form of three levels. The parts played by God's Measures and their Manifestation are shown in the different forms of sustenance bestowed upon us by God to try us and then see how we manage these trials.

❀"Indeed, everything have We created in due measure and proportion"❀ [Q 54:49]

A very important aspect of belief is Qader (God's measures) and Qadaa (when God makes His measures become manifested). A series of trials – of good and bad, of ease and difficulty, of health and sickness, of wealth and poverty – can take many different forms. Our performance during these trials forms the basis of where we will end up in the Hereafter; and also testify to the strength of our belief, the closeness we feel towards God, and how many lessons we have learned.

Chapter 4 - Sincerity and Putting Our Trust in God

The focus of this chapter is on the deeds that are loved by God, done only for His sake and with devotion to Him, which lead to earning God's contentment. Firstly, be dedicated only to God. Believers should not set up any partner with God for their deeds, and their work should be sincerely for the sake of God alone. He promises that such deeds will be rewarded with contentment, as mentioned in so many verses of the Holy Qur'an. As well, many hadiths, which will be given, also show the same.

❀And whosoever trusts in God, He suffices him. ❀ [Q 65:3]

The deeds accepted by God are those that are done sincerely for Him alone. This is the sign of someone who puts their whole trust in

God. When we put all our trust in God and rely on Him alone, He will reward us with His contentment.

... "Indeed, I have been commanded to worship God, [being] sincere to Him in religion." [Q 39:11]

Chapter 5 - Remembrance of God is Key to Contentment

The comprehensive concept of Dhikr (remembrance of God) is addressed in this chapter. It includes Dhikr through our actions and Dhikr through our remembrance of Him, and how it should be a continuous activity and way of life. Remaining conscious of God can be through one's heart, tongue, and actions. In Islam, every action or deed a believer does, with God in his heart, and done for God's contentment, is in essence a Dhikr or remembrance of Him. The Holy Qur'an is the largest collection of Dhikr, and God has promised to preserve it, as shown in the following verse.

Truly it is We Who have sent down the Reminder, and surely We are its Preserver (from all corruption). [Q 15:9]

God Almighty gives glad tidings of a great reward for those who are continuously conscious of Him, as shown in the following verse.

You only warn whomsoever follows the Reminder and fears the Compassionate unseen. So, give such a one glad tidings of forgiveness and a generous reward. [Q 36:11]

God also warns those who turn away from His remembrance and His guidance that they will have a hard life and will be raised up as blind people at the Resurrection.

But whosoever turns away from the remembrance of Me, truly his shall be a miserable life, and We shall raise him blind on the Day of Resurrection. [Q 20:124]

God, the All-Knowing, is aware of everything on the Earth and in Heaven; by remaining conscious of Him at all times, one's heart will be at peace. Those who keep remembering God are close to Him and, as He promised in His book, "If you remember Me, I will remember you." God opens so many avenues for Dhikr [Remembrance of Him], which lead to contentment. This will be elaborated upon in Chapter 5.

Chapter 6 – Thankfulness for what you have and overlooking what others have of worldly splendour

Contentment with God's sustenance includes feeling gratitude for His Grace, and detachment from the bounty given to others. Being thankful for God's Grace will result in being rewarded by more Grace. The Grace of God is limitless, seen and unseen. When believers are thankful for God's Grace, and do not turn their eyes towards others' bounty, they will surely be rewarded with contentment, as God has promised in the Holy Qur'an:

❈... If you give thanks (to Me), I shall surely grant you increase ....❈ [Q 14:7]

❈So bear patiently whatever they (who deny the truth) may say, and exalt your Lord's limitless glory, and praise Him before the rising of the sun and before its setting; and exalt His glory, too, during some of the hours of the night as well as during the hours of the day, so that you might attain contentment. [130] And never turn your eyes (with longing) towards whatever splendour of this world's life We may have allowed so many others to enjoy in order that We might test them thereby: for the sustenance which your Lord provides (for you) is better and more enduring. [131] And bid your people to pray, and persevere therein. (But remember:) We do not ask you to provide sustenance (for Us): it is We Who provide sustenance for you. And the future belongs to those who are conscious of God. [132] ❈ [Q 20:130-132]

One form of contentment is to be detached from this worldly life and not to wish for, or be envious of, what others have. This will increase our feelings of gratitude to God for everything He has blessed us with and, if God wills, protect our hearts from evil. He is the best Protector.

❈ "... The Day on which neither wealth nor sons will be of any use, [88] (and when) only he (will be happy) who comes before God with a heart free of evil!"[89] ❈ [Q 26:88-89]

Chapter 7 – A Path to Contentment: Being Forgiving and Patient, and Repelling Evil with Good

The Forbearing and the Patient are two of the Most Beautiful Divine Names of God, and believers should adopt these high values, to forgive as God wants us to forgive, to control our anger, be patient, and be good to those who are bad to us. These pinnacle values were most amply demonstrated in the behaviour of the Prophet (pbuh), who was exemplary in such behaviours as being forgiving and patient, having a pure heart, withholding anger, never holding a grudge, and never seeking revenge. Cultivating such virtues will lead to peace of mind and tranquillity, which will benefit believers and lead them to contentment.

❖... and who are patient in adversity out of a longing for their Sustainer's countenance, and are constant in prayer, and spend on others, secretly and openly, out of what We provide for them as sustenance, and (who) repel evil with good. It is these who shall find their fulfilment in the Hereafter. ❖ [Q 13:22]

The previous chapters have addressed the means, methods, ways and keys to contentment. All of them can be realized with patience and perseverance. Continuous obedience to God's orders and following His guidance requires perseverance, as well as patience and steadfastness when we are tested. Sincerity, putting one's full trust in God, continuous remembrance of Him, thankfulness, and forgiveness of others – all these key qualities are a great blessing from God, and will enable us to gain the contentment of God. The early believers regarded contentment as being on a higher level than patience, since people can be patient because they have no other choice, but the one who is content is the one truly at peace with his Lord.

❖God is content with them, and they are content with Him: this is the supreme triumph. ❖ [Q 5:119]

❖O you soul at peace! [27] Return to your Lord, contented (with Him) and (He) content (with you). [28] Enter among My servants. [29] Enter My Garden.[30] ❖ [Q 89:27-30]

Chapter 1

Contentment:

What the Holy Quran and Prophetic Traditions Tell Us

❖God is content with them, and they are content with Him: this is the supreme triumph. ❖ [Q 5:119]

بِسْمِ اللَّهِ الرَّحْمَنِ الرَّحِيمِ

﴿رَضِيَ اللَّهُ عَنْهُمْ وَرَضُوا عَنْهُ أُولَئِكَ حِزْبُ اللَّهِ أَلَا إِنَّ حِزْبَ اللَّهِ هُمُ الْمُفْلِحُونَ﴾

لَقَدْ رَضِيَ اللَّهُ عَنِ الْمُؤْمِنِينَ إِذْ يُبَايِعُونَكَ تَحْتَ الشَّجَرَةِ فَعَلِمَ مَا فِي قُلُوبِهِمْ فَأَنْزَلَ السَّكِينَةَ عَلَيْهِمْ وَأَثَابَهُمْ فَتْحًا قَرِيبًا

رَضِيَ اللَّهُ عَنْهُمْ وَرَضُوا عَنْهُ ذَلِكَ الْفَوْزُ الْعَظِيمُ

رضي الله عنهم ورضوا عنه

صدق الله العظيم

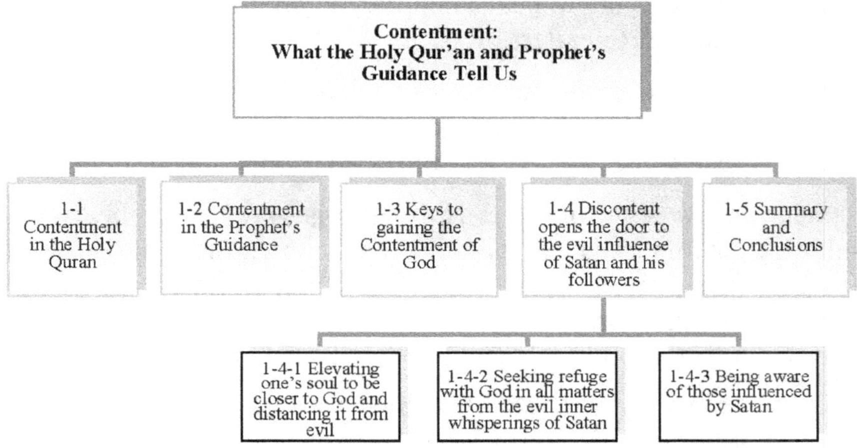

Fig. 1: The Structure of Chapter 1

1-1 Contentment in the Holy Qur'an

All true believers strive for God's contentment, which is the greatest blessing and grace from Him. For those with whom He is content, their hearts are at peace and they enjoy a righteous, fulfilling life here and in the Hereafter.

Believers who receive this blessing also have peace of mind and a life with which they can be content in this world and in the Hereafter; this is the greatest blessing of all – the eternal contentment of God.

Selected *verses* from the Holy Qur'an are given below that emphasize the importance of gaining God's contentment, and how God considers it the greatest achievement ('the supreme triumph') a believer can attain in this world. These verses also point out the wonderful rewards that God promises He will give to such believers.

Each verse shown is identified by a reference to its Chapter (in Arabic: 'Surah') and Verse (in Arabic: 'Ayat,' meaning a Sign) in the Holy Qur'an. The first quotation below is Verse 119 of Chapter 5. Hadiths are sayings of Prophet Muhammad, peace be upon him (pbuh) which have been narrated or reported by his companions and his family.

God is content with them (sincere believers) and they are content with Him: this is the supreme triumph. [Q 5:119]

One's constant awareness of God's Presence at all times leads to His contentment, and this awareness is a central spiritual virtue in the Quran.

… God (is) content with them, and they (are content) with Him: this is for whosoever is conscious of their Lord. [Q 98:8]

And He has promised those with whom He is content, spiritual prosperity in this life and in the life to come.

God is content with them and they with Him. They are on God's side, and God's side is the one to prosper! [Q 58:22]

God has promised believers mercy from Him and eternal contentment in the Hereafter.

Their Lord gives them glad tidings of Grace from Himself, and His Contentment (with them), and of Gardens wherein they will have enduring joy. [Q 9:21]

❦*Whosoever does righteous deeds, be it male or female - and is a believer - We will most certainly give them a good life; and most certainly shall We grant them their reward in accordance with the best of that which they used to do.* ❦ *[Q 16:97]*

This contentment will be the source of peace and tranquility for the soul and rest for the heart.

❦*Content was God with the believers when they pledged their allegiance to you (Muhammad) under the tree, for He knew what was in their hearts, and bestowed inner peace upon them from on high, and rewarded them with a victory soon to come.* ❦*[Q 48:18]*

Such a wonderful reward will not only be enjoyed in this world but also be extended to the Hereafter, as shown in the verses below.

❦*And goodly dwellings in Gardens of perpetual bliss. But contentment from God is greater* ❦ *[Q 9:72]*

❦*O you soul at peace! [27] Return to your Lord, contented (with Him) and (He) content (with you). [28] Enter among My servants. [29] Enter My Garden.[30]* ❦*[Q 89:27-30]*

That was the way of the early believers who emigrated from Mecca with the Prophet (pbuh), and those who supported, helped and protected him in Medina. These are the people of contentment, and we pray to Almighty God that He will also be content with us and we will be content with Him.

❦*(As for) the foremost, the first among the Emigrants and the Supporters, and those who followed them with virtue, God is content with them, and they are contented with Him.* ❦ *[Q 9:100]*

1-2 Contentment in the Prophetic Traditions

The life of the Prophet (pbuh) provides an outstanding example of contentment with God's Will and thankfulness to Him. The Prophet (pbuh) also urged Muslims to do the same.

Saad ibn Abi Waqqas (may God be pleased with him) narrated that the Prophet (pbuh) said, "The contentment of people is in their contentment with what God has bestowed upon them, and people's suffering is in their abandoning prayer for God's guidance, and being discontent with what God has decreed for them." [1]

For believers who seek God's contentment, He shall truly bestow on them contentment and happiness in this world and in the Hereafter, through their obedience to Him and commitment to the guidance of the Prophet (pbuh) in all circumstances.

Al-Abbas ibn Abd al-Muttaleb (may God be pleased with him) narrated that the Prophet (pbuh) said, "He has tasted the sweetness of faith who is content with God as his Lord, Islam as his religion and Muhammad as the Prophet of God." [2]

Abu Hurairah (may God be pleased with him) narrated that the Prophet (pbuh) said, "Be content with what God has bestowed upon you, and you shall be the richest of the people." [3]

Abu Sa'id al-Khudri (may God be pleased with him) narrated that the Prophet (pbuh) said, "God shall address the people of Paradise: 'O people of Paradise!' They will answer, 'Yes, our Lord, all good is in Your Hands!' God will then ask, 'Are you contented?' They will say, 'Why should we not be contented, our Lord, as You have given us what You have not given to any of Your created beings?' He will ask, 'Shall I not give you something better than this?' They will say, 'Our Lord! What else could be better than this?' He will then say, 'I bestow My Goodly Contentment on you and will never be displeased with you after this.'" [4]

Abu Hurairah (may God be pleased with him) narrated: "The Prophet (pbuh) said, 'Be on guard against the unlawful and you shall be the most worshipping among the people; be content with what God has allotted for you and you shall be the richest of the people; be kind to your neighbor and you shall be a believer; love for the people what you love for yourself and you shall be a Muslim (fully submitted to

---

(1) The speaker Tirmidhi – Source: Sunan al-Tirmidhi – page or number: 2151. Conclusion of the speaker: strange – that we only know from the saying of Muhammad ibn Abi Hameed. It is not that strong.

(2) The speaker: Tirmidhi – Source: Sunan al-Tirmidhi – page or number: 2623. Conclusion of the speaker: fair and sound.

(3) The speaker: Tirmidhi – Source: Sunan al-Tirmidhi – page or number: 2305. Conclusion of the speaker: strange that we only know from the saying of Jaffar ibn Soliman. The fair was not heard from Abu Hurairah

(4) The speaker: Al-Bukhari – Source: Sahih al-Bukhari – page or number: 6549. Conclusion of the speaker: fair.

God), and do not laugh too much, for much laughter hardens the heart." [1]

The Prophet (pbuh) urged believers to be conscious of God by day and by night for its great value in gaining the contentment of God, the Glorious.

A man was serving the Prophet (pbuh), and the Prophet (pbuh) said to him, "If anyone says in the morning and in the evening, 'I am content with God as my Lord, with Islam (submission to God) as my religion, and with Muhammad as my Prophet,' God will certainly make him content." [2]

We should remember this and repeat it daily and nightly, in the hope that our hearts will be full of the blessings of contentment with, and submission to, the One God.

1-3 Keys to Gaining the Contentment of God

Those who seek contentment should follow the Quranic and Prophetic guidance through which there will be healing for all the ills in one's heart. Following such guidance and adhering to the way of life of the Prophet (pbuh) is emphasized in the Quranic verses shown below. The rest of this book will outline how to follow such guidance in a more detailed way.

Reading the Holy Quran and reflecting on the wisdom of its verses is a healing for whatever distresses a believer, and a key to gaining the contentment of God.

❋ *O mankind! There has now come to you a teaching and good advice from your Lord, and a healing for all that lies within hearts, and a guidance and a mercy to all who believe (in Him).* ❋ *[Q 10:57]*

❋ *This is the Book in which there is no doubt, a guidance for all who are conscious of God ...* ❋ *[Q 2:2]*

❋ *Truly, this Quran guides toward that which is most upright, and gives the believers who do righteous deeds the glad tiding that theirs will be a great reward.* ❋ *[Q 17:9]*

---

(1) The speaker: Al-Albani – Source: Sahih Tirmidhi – page or number: 2305. Conclusion of the speaker: fair.

(2) The speaker: Abu Dawood – Source: Sunan Abu Dawood – page or number: 5072. Conclusion of the speaker: Did not comment [He wrote in his letter to the people of Mecca that whenever he did not comment, it is accepted].

❆Had We made it a Quran in a foreign tongue, they would surely say, "If only its signs were made clear. What! A foreign tongue and an Arab (messenger)." Say, "It is a guidance and a healing for all who believe."❆ [Q 41:44]

We can be rightly guided by following the outstanding example of the Prophet (pbuh), obeying him and being committed to his Sunnah (deeds and sayings); this will bring contentment.

❆O Prophet! Truly, We have sent you as a witness (to the Truth), and as a bearer of glad tidings and a warner, [45] as one who calls (all people) to God by His leave, and as a luminous lamp. [46] ❆ [Q 33:45-46]

❆Say: "Obey God and obey the Apostle." If they turn away, then truly God does not love the disbelievers. ❆ [Q 3:32]

❆… whereby God guides all who seek His Contentment to the ways of peace and, by His Grace, brings them out of darkness into light, by His leave, and guides them onto a straight path. ❆ [Q 5:16]

Believers, as they seek such contentment from God by praying for His Help and Guidance, and learning from the example of the Prophet (pbuh), should be aware that a part of the trials which Almighty God puts mankind through is resisting the temptations of Satan and his followers who always seek to divert believers from the path of contentment. We should therefore be alert to these trials in order to counter Satan's evil influence, as is explained in the following section.

1-4 Discontent opens the door to the evil influence of Satan and his followers

Believers should always be on guard against the Devil's attempts to divert them from the straight path, and realize that this is a test from God. They should also avoid becoming discontent or ungrateful, since that will lead to God's displeasure.

❆Is one who pursues God's Contentment like one who has brought God's wrath upon himself, and whose home will be Hell? An evil journey's end!❆ [Q 3:162]

God warns us against harboring feelings of dissatisfaction, the opposite of contentment. He names Satan as an example, for Satan earned the anger of God. Satan showed arrogance and ingratitude by disobeying God and rejecting His Will, choosing instead to disseminate corruption. The exact status of Satan is explained in verses shown below, where we are told that he is a Jinn (unseen being created from fire), and is not one of the angels (who are created from light).

The Holy Quran, in Verses 30 to 39 of Chapter 2, describes how Iblīs (Satan) was discontent and arrogant, and refused to obey God. Satan thus corrupted his own soul because of his disobedience. This was the path Satan chose for himself and his followers, until the end of time, and it resulted in God's rejection and being thrown out of Paradise, thus earning torment in the Fire of Hell. In this story are the lessons that are outlined below.

Believers should seek refuge with God from Satan and his followers who are dedicated to turning believers away from the straight path. Believers should also keep in mind that, as mentioned in the Holy Quran, Satan will be able to possess many of mankind who will follow him. We should learn these lessons, and know that our own discontentment can result in God's displeasure. The story begins when God ordained that Adam would be His vicegerent (trustee) on earth.

And when your Lord said to the angels: "I am placing a trustee upon the earth," they said: "Will you place therein one who will spread corruption there, and shed blood, while we glorify and praise You, and call You Holy?" He said, "Truly I know what you do not know." [30] And He taught Adam the Names, all of them. Then He brought them before the angels and said: "Tell Me the Names of these, if you are truthful." [31] They replied: "Glory be to You! We have no knowledge save what You have taught us. Truly You alone are the All-Knowing, the Most Wise." [32] He said: "Adam, tell them their Names." And when Adam had told them their Names, He said, "Did I not say to you that I know the Unseen of the heavens and the earth, and that I know what you reveal and what you conceal?" [33] And when We said to the angels, "Prostrate to Adam," they prostrated, except Iblis. He refused and became arrogant, and was among the disbelievers. [34] We said: "O Adam, dwell you and your wife in the Garden and eat freely thereof, wheresoever you will. But do not approach this tree, lest you be among the wrongdoers." [35] Then Iblis (Satan) caused them to slip therefrom, and thus brought about the loss of their previous state, and We said: "Get down, each of you an enemy to the other. On the earth you shall have a dwelling place and a livelihood for a while." [36] Then Adam received words from his Lord, and He relented to him. Indeed, He is the Relenting, the Merciful. [37] We said, "Get out, all of you. If guidance should come to you from Me, then whosoever follows My Guidance, no fear shall come upon them, nor shall they grieve." [38] But those who disbelieve and deny Our signs, it is they who are the inhabitants of the Fire, abiding therein."[39] ❧ *[Q 2:30-39]*

When God informed the angels that Adam would be His trustee on earth, they expressed their concern to Him that Adam's offspring would shed blood and spread corruption on earth. God willed to reveal to the angels the wisdom of His decision, so He taught Adam all the Names, which made him capable of such a task. God, the All-Knowing, willed that these names were not taught to the angels, and they acknowledged His Wisdom and obeyed Him. They glorified Him and accepted that their knowledge is limited to what He bestows upon them. Only God knows who should be entrusted with His message.

❧ *God knows best upon whom to bestow His message.* ❧ *[Q 6:124]*

God, in His Mercy and Wisdom, establishes the proofs, arguments and signs for mankind to strengthen their faith and put their hearts at rest, as mentioned in the story of Abraham.

❧ *And when Abraham said, "My Lord, show me how You give life to the dead," He said, "Do you not believe?" Abraham answered, "Yes, indeed, but just to put my heart at rest." So God said, "Take four birds and train them to come back to you. Then place a piece of them on every hill (around you). Then call them: they will come to you in haste. And know that God is Almighty, Wise."* ❧ *[Q 2:260]*

God has sent signs for believers to prevent doubts from arising in their hearts and minds, and for them to feel greater trust in Him. When God ordered the angels to bow down to Adam, they obeyed and accepted what He had ordained; they recognized and accepted that their knowledge is limited and that it is God alone Who has unlimited knowledge. He is the All-Knowing, Most Wise. It was only Iblīs (Satan) who became arrogant, rejected God's command, openly disobeyed Him, and went astray.

The Qur'an tells us that Iblis's nature is not angelic. He was created from fire (a smokeless flame) and is one of the Jinn (unseen beings) to whom God gave the ability to obey or not obey Him, and thus Iblis's true nature allowed him to disobey God. The angels, who are created from light, do not have this ability to disobey God.

God told Adam and Eve to dwell in the Gardens of Paradise and bestowed upon them His Grace. He ordered them only to avoid one tree, so that they would not become transgressors.

Satan envied them for what God had bestowed upon them, and he plotted to get them thrown out of God's Gardens of Paradise. He tricked and deceived them into disobeying God's order. Almighty God, the Forgiving and the Relenting, spoke words of forgiveness to Adam and ordained that he and his wife go down from Paradise. But He promised Adam and his offspring that if they followed His guidance they would have no fear, nor would they grieve.

The Holy Quran explains in detail in Chapter 7, Verses 11-25, shown below, what actually led Iblīs to be arrogant and disobedient, and why God caused him to be humiliated and disgraced.

Indeed, We created you, then We formed you, then We said to the angels, "Prostrate yourselves before Adam." And they all prostrated, save Iblis; he was not among those who prostrated. [11] God addressed Iblis: "What prevented you from prostrating when I commanded you?" Iblis said, "I am better than him. You have created me from fire, while You have created him from clay." [12] He said, "Get down from this! It is not for you to show arrogance here. So go forth! You are surely among those who are humbled." [13] Iblis said, "Grant me respite until the Day they are resurrected." [14] God said: "Truly you are among those granted respite." [15] Iblis said, "Because You have caused me to err, I shall surely lie in wait for them on Your straight path. [16] Then I shall come upon them from in front of them and from behind them, and from their right and from their left. And You will not find most of them thankful." [17] God said, "Go forth from here, disgraced and banished! Whosoever among them follows you, I shall surely fill Hell with you all." [18] "O Adam! Dwell you and your wife in the Garden, and eat from wheresoever you two will, but approach not this tree, lest you two be among the wrongdoers." [19] Then Iblis (Satan) whispered to them, so as to cause them to wrong themselves. And he said, "Your Lord has only forbidden you this tree, lest you should become angels, or immortals." [20] And he swore to them, "Truly I am a sincere adviser to you." [21] Thus he lured them on through deception. And when they approached the tree, they became wrong-doers. They then began to sew together the leaves of the Garden to cover themselves. And their Lord called out to them, "Did I not forbid you from that tree, and tell you that Satan is a manifest enemy to you?" [22] They said, "Our Lord! We have wronged ourselves. If You do not forgive us and have Mercy on us, we shall surely be among the losers!" [23] He said, "Get down, each of you an enemy to the other! There will be for you on earth a dwelling place, and enjoyment for a while." [24] He said, "Therein you shall live, and therein you shall die, and from there shall you be brought forth. [25]" ❧ *[Q 7:11-25]*

Iblīs went astray because he was under the delusion that he was better than Adam since he had been created from fire, while Adam was created from clay. One of the Prophetic Hadiths, narrated by 'Aisha, one of the wives of the Prophet (pbuh), tells us from what the angels and jinn were created.

'Aisha (may God be pleased with her) reported that the Messenger of God (pbuh) said, "The angels are created from light, just as the jinn are created from smokeless fire and mankind is created from what you have been told about." [1]

In his arrogance, Iblīs ignored the fact that God had created them with His infinite Wisdom and Knowledge. This arrogance is a common thread among Iblīs and his followers, based on their fantasies and imaginings, which have no basis. This is what caused Iblīs to be banished from the Garden. Nevertheless, Iblīs requested God to give him respite, and He, the All-Knowing, granted his request until the Day of Resurrection, and in that was a great trial for Adam and his offspring.

Iblīs and all his followers believe, with no basis, that they are the privileged and best creation of God. They disobey and build barriers to prevent believers from following the straight path. Iblīs's arrogance prevented him from repenting for what he had done. Instead, he vowed

---

(1) The speaker: Muslim – Source: Sahih Muslim – page or number: 2996 . Conclusion of the speaker: sound.

to misguide Adam and his offspring by placing stumbling blocks on the straight path and doing that by all means and from all directions.

❖Then I (Satan) shall come upon them from in front of them and from behind them, and from their right and from their left. And You will find most of them unthankful."❖ [Q 7:17]

The above verses also clearly show that Satan finds an entry to the human soul through man's ingratitude to God and disobedience of His orders. God bestowed His Grace on Adam, and let him dwell in His Gardens, but prevented him from approaching a particular tree – if he approached it he would become one of the transgressors. Iblīs claimed to Adam that he was his sincere advisor and, through deceit and delusions, convinced him that approaching this tree would ensure him an eternal kingdom. The Holy Quran, in various locations, urges believers to seek refuge with God from Satan's evil temptations through continuous remembrance of Him, which is the best protection from Satan, as is shown in the following two verses.

❖And should a temptation from Satan provoke you, seek refuge in God. Indeed, He is the All-Hearing, All-Knowing. ❖ [Q 7:200]

❖Truly those who are conscious of God, when they are touched by a visitation from Satan, they remember (God); then behold, they see (clearly). ❖ [Q 7:201]

The verses of Chapter 20, shown below, mention some of the ways that Satan tempts mankind to disobey God and thus earn His displeasure. Satan will always try to prevent believers from gaining God's contentment through forgetfulness, not paying attention to God's remembrance, not being steadfast in obedience to His laws, being attached to worldly desires, and hoping for eternal life and an unlimited kingdom in this world.

❖And We indeed made a pact with Adam aforetime, but he forgot. And We found no firmness of purpose in him. [115] And when We said to the angels, "Prostrate yourselves before Adam," – they prostrated, save Iblis; he refused. [116] We said, "O Adam! Truly, this is an enemy to you and your wife. So let him not expel the two of you from the Garden, such that you would be most miserable. [117]

Behold, it is provided for you that you shall not hunger here or feel exposed, [118] and that you shall not thirst here or suffer from the heat of the sun." [119] But Satan whispered to him, saying: "O Adam! Shall I lead you to the tree of life eternal, and (thus) to a kingdom that will never decay?" [120] And so the two ate thereof: and thereupon they became conscious of their wrong-doing and began to cover themselves with pieced-together leaves from the Garden. And (thus) did Adam disobey his Sustainer, and thus did he fall into grievous error. [121] Thereafter, (however,) his Sustainer elected him (for His Grace), and accepted his repentance, and bestowed His Guidance upon him, [122] saying: "Down with you all from this (state of innocence, and be henceforth), enemies to one another! Nonetheless, there shall most certainly come to you Guidance from Me: and he who follows My Guidance will not go astray, and neither will he be unhappy. [123] But as for him who shall turn away from remembering Me – his shall be a life of narrow scope; and on the Day of Resurrection We shall raise him up blind. [124]" ⁂ [Q 20:115-124]

⁂ *So be patient, as the resolute among the messengers were patient.* ⁂
[Q 46:35]

God Almighty taught Adam remembrance to guide and protect him, but when Adam forgot and did not pay attention, he unwittingly opened the door to Satan. This is why the lessons here are so important, such as firmness of purpose, patience and perseverance, and constant remembrance of God - virtues exemplified by all of His prophets and messengers.

God bestowed His Grace on Adam and his wife, and they faced no hardship, hunger or thirst as an eternal bounty from Him. Satan, however, was able to get them thrown out of all this through their forgetfulness and his deceit. Then Adam remembered and repented, and God, in His Mercy, accepted his repentance as He is the Ever-Accepting of Repentance, which is one of His most beautiful divine Names. If the offspring of Adam follow God's guidance, they will live a righteous life, but those who ignore His remembrance will have a difficult life.

Continuous remembrance of God is the best way to close the door to Satan and his followers. Ignoring what God has ordained, being arrogant, looking down on others, openly disobeying God, and putting obstacles in the way of believers - this is the way of Satan, and following it will result in discontent and conflict.

God Almighty, in His Wisdom and Mercy, guides mankind to three actions that will protect them and keep them away from the cunning temptations of Satan and his followers, the first of which is:

1-4-1 Elevating one's soul to be closer to God and distancing it from evil

As for one who fears standing before his Lord and forbids the soul from caprice (frivolous desires) [40] truly the Garden is the refuge. [41] [Q 79:40-41]

Love of worldly desires, envying others for what they have, denying the inevitability of the Hereafter, and forgetting that God's reward is much greater and more enduring than any rewards this world can offer, are all distractions that can open the door to evil temptations. To counter this, and purify the self (one's soul), believers must practise continuous remembrance of God.

Indeed, the one who purifies his soul succeeds. [9] And the one who corrupts it fails. [10] [Q 91: 9-10]

Purifying the soul includes being ever-conscious of God, being aware that we will meet Him in the Hereafter, and avoiding feelings of superiority or arrogance. The best way to achieve this is through the remembrance of God the Glorious, abstaining from the temptations and desires of this worldly life, and remaining humble.

Abdullah ibn Mas'ud (may God be pleased with him) narrated that the Messenger of God (pbuh) said, "He who has in his heart the weight of a mustard seed of arrogance shall not enter Paradise." A person (among his hearers) said: 'Truly a person loves that his dress should be fine, and his shoes should be fine.' He (pbuh) remarked, 'Truly, God is Beautiful and He loves beauty. Arrogance is disdain for the Truth (out of self-conceit) and contempt for people.' [1]

---

(1) The speaker: Muslim – Source: Sahih Muslim – page or number: 91. Conclusion of the speaker: sound.

Jaber ibn Abdullah (may God be pleased with him) reported that a group of believers (who had just fought in a battle) visited the Messenger of God (pbuh), who said to them, "You have safely returned from the lesser struggle (jihad) to the greater struggle (greater jihad)." They asked, "What is the greater struggle?" He (pbuh) said, "The struggle against frivolous desires." [1]

In Islam, elevating one's soul is the greater struggle in this life.

1-4-2 Seeking refuge with God in all matters from the evil inner whisperings of Satan

Protection from Satan's evil promptings and temptations is gained through seeking refuge in God and praying for His Mercy, Guidance and Support.

And say, "My Lord! I seek refuge in You from the evil promptings of the satans. [97] And I seek refuge in You, my Lord, lest they should be present with me. [98]" [Q 23: 97-98]

Say, "I seek refuge in the Lord of the daybreak [1] from the evil of what He has created, [2] from the evil of darkness when it descends, [3] from the evil of those who blow on knots (practise magic), [4] and from the evil of the envier when he envies. [5]" [Q 113:1-5 – The Daybreak (Al-Falaq)]

Say, "I seek refuge in the Lord of mankind, [1] the King of mankind, [2] the God of mankind, [3] from the evil of the stealthy whisperer (Satan), [4] who whispers into the hearts of mankind, [5] and from jinn (unseen beings) and mankind. [6]" [Q 114:1-6 – Mankind (Al-Nas)]

It is known that the Prophet (pbuh) used to seek refuge in God every morning and night by reciting the above two Chapters "The Daybreak" (Al-Falaq) and "Mankind" (Al-Nas) – known as 'The Two Verses of Refuge' [in Arabic: Muᶜawwidhatain].

---

(1) The speaker: Ibn Hajar al-'Asqalani – Source: al-Kafi al-Shaf – page or number: 194. Conclusion of the speaker: [includes] Eissa ibn Ibrahim from Yehia ibn Ya'li from Laith ibn Abi Salim, and the three are weak.

Abdullah ibn Khabib (may God be pleased with him) narrated that the Prophet (pbuh) said, "Say, "He is God, the One' and the two verses of Refuge (Muᶜawwidhatain) three times at night and in the morning, and they shall keep you protected from harm." [1]

The Prophet recommended that all believers should seek refuge with God by reciting or reading these two Chapters [Muᶜawwidhatain] in all the affairs of their lives.

Uqba ibn Amer (may God be pleased with him) narrated that the Apostle (pbuh) said, "Have you ever seen verses that came down this night with no equal? Say, 'I seek refuge in the Lord of the daybreak, and say, 'I seek refuge in the Lord of mankind.' "[2]

We should also follow the guidance of the Household of Abraham (pbuh). When ᶜImrān's wife Ḥannah gave birth to their daughter Mary (mother of Jesus), she immediately sought refuge in God to protect the newborn baby from Satan.

And I have named her Maryam (Mary), and I seek refuge for her in You, and for her offspring, from Satan the outcast." [Q 3:36]

And should a temptation from Satan provoke you, seek refuge in God. Truly He alone is the All-Hearing, the All-Knowing. [Q 41:36]

1-4-3 Being aware of those influenced by Satan

Satan was so sure that some of mankind would follow him, that he arrogantly said to God he would take his due share of His servants. Satan accomplishes this by misleading people who will listen to and follow him, and then carry out Satan's evil mission in this life. It is the responsibility of all believers to avoid the followers and supporters of Satan – they are the losers in this life. They will place obstacles on the straight path to mislead and deceive believers and try to make them forget the remembrance of God, as shown in the following verses.

Thus have we made for every prophet an enemy - satans from among men and jinn, who inspire each other with flowery discourse in order to deceive. [Q 6:112]

---

(1) The speaker: Tirmidhi – Source: Sunan al-Tirmidhi – page or number: 3575.

(2) The speaker: Muslim – Source: Sahih Muslim – page or number: 814

❖... whom God has cursed is him who said, "Assuredly I shall take of Your servants my due share ...❖ [Q 4:118]

It is therefore very important for believers to be aware of and avoid Satan's followers and not take them as friends or partners. One of the signs of those who follow Satan is that they have forgotten the remembrance of God, as described in the verse below.

❖Satan has gained control over them and made them forget God. They are on Satan's side, and Satan's side will be the losers.❖ [Q 58:19]

If one takes such people as one's friends and companions, they will try to turn you away from the remembrance of God, as mentioned in the verse below.

❖"... Oh, woe is me! Would that I had not taken so-and-so for a friend! [28] He did indeed cause me to go astray from the Reminder after its having come to me, and Satan is ever a forsaker of man. [29]"❖   [Q25: 28-29]

Believers should thus avoid the followers of Satan so that they do not become like his supporters or like those on whom Satan has cast his evil influence.

1-5 Summary and Conclusions

Contentment is a great gift of divine grace to those with whom God the Almighty is content. They are the ones who are guided by Him, and who are rewarded with tranquility, peace of mind, and satisfaction of the heart - the greatest triumph in this world and the Hereafter. True believers know with certainty that the Holy Quran contains the true words of God, with which they seek His Protection and Guidance. They know that there is healing for what is in the heart, and the Prophet (pbuh) is the true guide to God's way. His guidance provides the light which guides us on the straight path to contentment.

Believers are aware that life is full of temptations, tests and trials, some of which come from one's lower self, with its attachment to earthly desires. We should therefore purify our soul by focusing on the goal of becoming closer to God and attaining a high rank in the eternal life of the Hereafter. Other temptations come from Satan, who is mankind's arch-enemy, and his evil followers. All believers must be constantly alert to the fact that Satan's avowed mission is to make us forget the remembrance of God, and on diverting us from the straight path which leads to God and eternal joy in the Hereafter.

❖*Truly Satan is an enemy to you, so treat him as an enemy. He only calls upon his followers that they may be among the inhabitants of the Fire.* ❖ *[Q 35:6]*

The Holy Quran tells us that Iblīs rejected God's command to bow down to Adam, and that his disobedience was a result of his own arrogance, ingratitude to God, and envy of Adam. Iblīs then, because of his hatred of Adam, became a denier of the Truth, and a deceitful and treacherous enemy to mankind. These are the characteristics of the people who are influenced by Iblis (Satan) and follow his evil ways.

❖*And You will find most of them unthankful.*❖ *[Q 7:17]*

As believers, we should always express our gratitude and thanks to God for all His blessings and bounty in our lives.

❖*Though few of My servants are thankful."*❖ *[Q 34:13]*

❖*Truly, those who are conscious of God, when they are touched by a visitation from Satan, they remember (God); then behold, they see (clearly).*❖ *[Q 7:201]*

Thus, the sincere and honest believer who wishes to remain on the straight path should protect himself from Satan's evil whisperings by remembering God and being thankful to Him, as explained in the verse below.

❖*God said, ''This is the Day wherein the truthful shall benefit from their truthfulness. For them shall be Gardens with rivers running below, abiding there forever. God is content with them, and they are content with Him. This is the supreme triumph."*❖ *[Q 5:119]*

In this chapter we have presented the Qur'anic verses and Prophetic hadiths regarding contentment and the keys to achieve contentment in light of the Holy Quran and guidance of the Prophet (pbuh).

In the next chapter we will present Quranic verses and Prophetic hadiths which highlight the importance of having a heart that is full of love for God and a mind that is ever-conscious of Him, (that is, the importance of practising 'Taqwa').

Chapter 2

Love of God and being Conscious of Him are Keys to His Contentment

❀Surely those who believe and perform righteous deeds, for them shall the Compassionate ordain love.❀ [Q 19:96]

❀... Truly, God loves those who are conscious of Him. ❀ [Q 9:4]

❀And worship God (alone) ... and do good to your parents ... ❀ [Q 4:36]

بِسْمِ اللَّهِ الرَّحْمَنِ الرَّحِيمِ

﴿ إِنَّ الَّذِينَ آمَنُوا وَعَمِلُوا الصَّالِحَاتِ سَيَجْعَلُ لَهُمُ الرَّحْمَنُ وُدًّا ﴾

أَلَا إِنَّ أَوْلِيَاءَ اللَّهِ لَا خَوْفٌ عَلَيْهِمْ وَلَا هُمْ يَحْزَنُونَ

وَالَّذِينَ آمَنُوا أَشَدُّ حُبًّا لِلَّهِ

إن الله يحب المتقين

صَدَقَ اللَّهُ الْعَظِيمُ

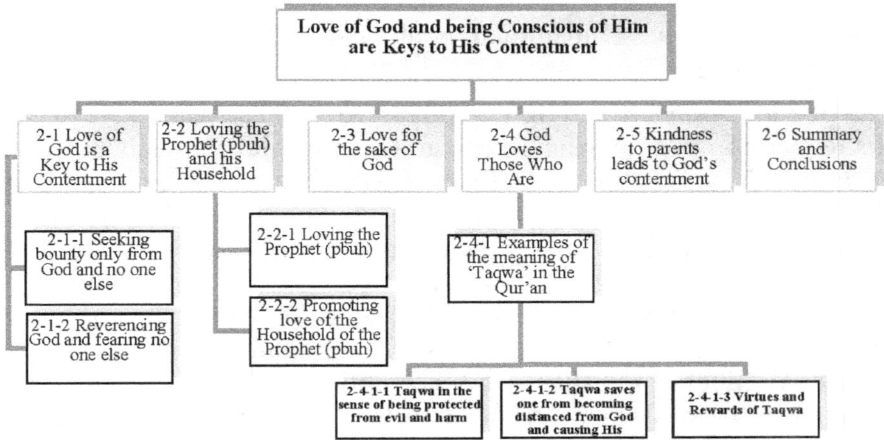

Fig. 1: The Structure of Chapter 2

2-0 Introduction

Almighty God, in His mercy, established His religion based on Love and being conscious of Him at all times, seeking His protection, and living one's life with humility, reverence and piety. In Arabic, this is known as 'Taqwa'. On the first level, there is love between God and His servants (believers). On the second level there is love between His servants and Prophet Muhammad (pbuh) and his Household, and on the third level there is love among all believers.

God loves sincere and righteous believers - those who strive to gain His love, through practising Taqwa at its various levels, such as Taqwa of faith and Taqwa of deeds. Through such means the believer gains God's love and closeness to Him. The Holy Quran (the Book) outlines the qualities that God loves in such believers – patience, humility, justice, and complete trust in Him. Believers should also be careful to stay away from those things that will cause them to earn the discontent of God, such as ingratitude, arrogance, extravagance, untrustworthiness, injustice, and corruption. All these have been outlined in various places in the Book as wrong-doing. The first and most important practice is to believe in God and do good deeds, as stated in the verse below.

❦Surely those who believe and perform righteous deeds, for them shall the Compassionate ordain love.❧ [Q 19:96]

God, the Compassionate, opens ways to His contentment with His servants. The first of these is the mutual love between Himself and His servants. This love is manifested in two ways - by doing what He orders you to do, obeying the injunctions given in His Book, and following the example of the Prophet (pbuh). The resulting elevated status is a great bounty from God. The believer should strive hard to reach this state. God has promised that whoever strives in His cause, He will guide them to the right way and they will always be with the righteous. The believers must also stay away from whatever God has ordered them to refrain from.

❦Among mankind there are some who take up equals apart from God, loving them like loving God. But those who believe are much stronger in their love of God ...❧ [Q 2:165]

❦O you who believe! Whosoever among you should renounce his religion, God will bring forth a people whom He loves and who love Him, humble toward the believers, stern toward the disbelievers, striving in the way of God, and fearing not the blame of any blamer.

That is the Bounty of God, which He gives to whomsoever He will. And God is the All-Encompassing, All-Knowing. [Q 5:54]

The meaning expressed in the above two verses is also shown in the Hadith (Prophetic Guidance) given below.

Abu Hurairah (may God be pleased with him) reported that God's Messenger (pbuh) said, "God says, 'Whosoever loves to meet Me, I love to meet him; and whosoever hates to meet Me, I hate to meet him.'" [1]

The proof of one's love for God is the love which exceeds the love of anyone or anything else, obeying His orders, following the example of the Prophet (pbuh), and refraining from doing anything that would diminish this love. Striving to reach this level of love for God will earn the ultimate bounty from God, since He has promised that He will guide those who strive hard in His cause.

But as for those who strive for Us, We shall surely guide them in Our ways. Truly God is with those who do good. [Q 29:69]

Their hearts are committed to God, the Ever-Forgiving, the Compassionate, and God will lead them to His ways which will strengthen their love for Him and they will be among those who do good.

2-1 Love of God is a Key to His Contentment

God urges believers, in the Holy Qur'an, to love Him. He also makes clear how believers can earn His love and which deeds will cause God to bestow on them His reward of contentment. The following verses show examples of the characteristics and deeds that God loves.

What God does not love ✗		What God loves ✓	
Truly, God does not love aggressors. [Q 2:190]	1	*Behold, God loves the doers of good.* [Q 2:195]	1
And God does not love corruption. [Q 2:205]	2	*Truly, God loves those who turn to Him in repentance, and He loves those who keep themselves pure.* [Q 2:222]	2

---

(1) The speaker: al-Bukhari – Source: Sahih al-Bukhari – page or number: 909 Hadith number: 7504. Conclusion of speaker: sound.

What God does not love ✗		What God loves ✔	
❧*And God does not love anyone who is stubbornly ungrateful and persists in sinful ways.* ❧ *[Q 2:276]*	3	❧*Truly, God loves those who are conscious of Him.*❧ *[Q 3:76]*	3
❧*Truly, God does not love those who deny the truth.*❧ *[Q 3:32]*	4	❧*God loves the doers of good;*❧ *[Q 3:134]*	4
❧*for God does not love evildoers.*❧ *[Q 3:57]*	5	❧*God loves those who are patient in adversity;*❧ *[Q 3:146]*	5
❧*God does not love evildoers.*❧ *[Q 3:140]*	6	❧*for God loves the doers of good.*❧ *[Q 3:148]*	6
❧*Truly, God does not love any of those who, full of self-conceit, act in a boastful manner;*❧ *[Q 4:36]*	7	❧*Truly, God loves those who place their trust in Him.* ❧ *[Q 3:159]*	7
❧*Truly, God does not love those who betray their trust and persist in sinful ways.*❧ *[Q 4:107]*	8	❧*Truly, God loves the doers of good.*❧ *[Q 5:13]*	8
❧*And God does not love the spreaders of corruption.*❧ *[Q 5:64]*	9	❧*Truly, God loves those who act equitably.* ❧ *[Q 5:42]*	9
❧*God does not love those who transgress the bounds of what is right.*❧ *[Q 5:87]*	10	❧*For God loves the doers of good.*❧ *[Q 5:93]*	10
❧*Truly, God does not love the treacherous!*❧ *[Q 8:58]*	11	❧*Truly, God loves those who are conscious of Him.*❧ *[Q 9:4]*	11

What God does not love ✗		What God loves ✓	
❈Truly, God does not love anyone who betrays his trust and is ungrateful.❊ [Q 22:38]	12	❈Truly, God loves those who are conscious of Him.❊ [Q 9:7]	12
❈Truly, God does not love those who exult (in vain things)!❊ [Q 28:76]	13	❈For God loves all who purify themselves.❊ [Q 9:108]	13
❈Truly, God does not love the spreaders of corruption.❊ [Q 28:77]	14	❈Truly, God loves those who act equitably!❊ [Q 49:9]	14
❈Behold, God does not love anyone who, out of self-conceit, acts in a boastful manner.❊ [Q 31:18]	15	❈Truly, God loves those who act equitably❊. [Q 60:8]	15
❈For God does not love any of those who, out of self-conceit, act in a boastful manner.❊ [Q 75:23]	16	❈Truly, God loves (only) those who fight in His cause in (solid) ranks, as though they were a building firm and compact❊. [Q 61:4]	16

As can be seen from the above verses, God makes clear whom He loves. They are, for example, those who remain conscious of Him, are doers of good, have a pure heart, are patient, just, and put their trust in Him. This is not a complete list, but includes many of the virtues that God loves in believers.

As God is the Most Merciful, and outlines what He loves, as a Grace from Him, He also outlines what He does not love. He warns believers to avoid the actions and characteristics not loved by Him: being ungrateful, proud, boastful, arrogant, self-conceited, miserly, extravagant, wasteful, untrustworthy, treacherous, corrupt, persisting in sinful ways, and transgressing the limits set by Him. Believers should thus safeguard their behavior from these things if they are sincere in pursuing His love, which is key to attaining His contentment.

❁And who is truer to his covenant than God?❁ *[Q 9:111]*

Abu Hurairah (may God be pleased with him) narrated: "The Prophet (pbuh) said, 'If God loves a person, He calls (Angel) Gabriel and says to him, 'God loves so and-so. O Gabriel! Love him.' Gabriel will then love him and make an announcement among the inhabitants of the heavens: 'God loves so-and-so, therefore you should also love him,' and all the inhabitants of the heavens will love him; he is then granted acceptance among the people on the earth.'" [1]

Aisha (may God be pleased with her) narrated: "The Prophet (pbuh) sent a unit of men under the command of a man who used to lead his companions in the prayers, and he would finish his recitation (of the Holy Qur'an) with Chapter 112: 'Say: "He is God the One God ..."' When the unit returned, they mentioned this to the Prophet (pbuh). He said (to them), 'Ask him why he does this.' They asked him and he said, 'I do so because it mentions the qualities of the Beneficent and I love to recite them (in my prayer).' The Prophet (pbuh) said (to them), 'Tell him that God loves him.'" [2]

2-1-1 Seeking bounty only from God and no one else

The believer should ask God for all his needs and not seek what other people possess. God is the All-Knowing and the Most Generous, so if you seek something, seek it from God.

❁... Call upon Him in fear and in hope. Surely, the Mercy of God is ever near to the virtuous.❁ *[Q 7:56]*

❁O you who believe! Shall I direct you to a commerce that will save you from a painful punishment? [10] (It is that) you believe in God and His Messenger and strive in God's cause with your wealth and your souls. That is better for you, if you but knew. [11]❁ *[Q 61:10-11]*

Believers should hope for what is in God's Hands and discard what is in people's hands, as what is with God is far better and more lasting, for He is the All-Encompassing and the Ever-Endowing. Whatever your

---

(1) The speaker: al-Bukhari – Source: Sahih al-Bukhari – page or number: 382 Hadith number: 3209. Conclusion of speaker: sound.

(2) The speaker: al-Bukhari – Source: Sahih al-Bukhari – page or number: 7375. Conclusion of speaker: sound.

needs are, ask God to provide them; He already knows what your needs are, before you even ask, since He is the All-Knowing, the All-Aware.

2-1-2 Reverencing God and fearing no one else

Revering God, placing all your trust in Him, and believing that He is the Ever-Near will free the believer from fears he may have, and make him feel safe and close to God. Fears can come from the evil whispering of Satan and his followers, or from a tyrant and his authority, or a perceived lack of provision, and other fears in this world. God, through His Mercy, Grace and Love, will keep believers safe.

❖That is only Satan sowing fear of his followers. So fear them not, but revere Me, if you are believers.❖ [Q 3:175]

In summary, we have spoken of three paths: one through love, another through righteous actions, and the third through remaining conscious of God. These are outlined in many places throughout the Holy Book, but the majority of the verses emphasize seeking God's contentment through love, and this should be the focus of every believer in order to increase and strengthen their faith in and love of God and become closer to Him, the Ever-Loving, the Ever-Near. The verses presented earlier in this chapter show clearly that God encourages us to do good deeds with love.

Believers' love for God leads to their eagerness to earn His love through performing good deeds. Believers should have no fear, and focus on remaining conscious of God and striving to gain His contentment.

2-2 Loving the Prophet (pbuh) and his Household

After addressing the love between God and His servants, we will now address the love between His servants - all believers - and the Prophet (pbuh).

2-2-1 Loving the Prophet (pbuh)

Since we have clarified the importance of loving God the Almighty, we now move to the importance of loving Prophet Muhammad (pbuh). This second level involves expressing our love for the Prophet (pbuh) who is

❖"... the Messenger of God, and the Seal of the Prophets ..."❖ [Q 33:40]

It is made abundantly clear, throughout the Holy Quran, that obeying the Prophet (pbuh) is the path to God's Mercy and Love, as shown in the Quranic verses given below.

Love of the Prophet (pbuh) is a foundation for faith and a path to contentment, and this love should be manifested in continuous prayer for the Prophet (pbuh), following his example, and adhering to his ways (the Sunnah), as God has ordered us to do.

Say (O Prophet): "If you love God, follow me, (and) God will love you and forgive your sins; for God is Ever-Forgiving, Most Merciful." [Q 3:31]

And obey God and the Messenger that you may obtain mercy. [Q 3:132]

As God mentions in the verses below, obeying the Prophet (pbuh) is part of one's obedience to God.

Say, "Obey God and obey the Messenger." And if you turn away (from the Apostle), know that he will have to answer only for whatever he has been charged with, and you for what you have been charged with; but if you obey him, you will be on the right path. The Apostle is not bound to do more than clearly deliver the message (entrusted to him). [Q 24:54]

... by your Lord! They do not (really) believe unless they make you (O Prophet) a judge of all on which they disagree among themselves, and then find in their souls no resistance to an acceptance of your decision and give themselves up (to it) in total self-surrender. [Q 4:65]

Whoever obeys the Apostle obeys God thereby; and as for those who turn away - We have not sent you to be their keeper. [Q 4:80]

In the traditions of the Prophet (pbuh) there are many sayings that urge the believer to love him more and more, and to obey him and abide by his traditions (the 'Sunnah' of the Prophet (pbuh)).

Anas ibn Malik (may God be pleased with him) said, "I never saw the Companions of the Messenger of God (pbuh) as happy about anything as I saw them happy about this thing: a man addressed the Prophet (pbuh), saying: 'O Messenger of God! A man loves another man for the righteous works he does, but he himself cannot do likewise.' The Messenger of God (pbuh) replied, 'A man will be with those whom he loves.'" [1]

---

(1) The speaker: Abu Dawood – Source: Sunan Abu Dawood – page or number: 5127. Conclusion of the speaker: Did not comment [He wrote in his letter to the people of Mecca that whenever he did not comment, it is accepted].

A sign of loving the Prophet (pbuh) is in keeping up continuous prayer for him (pbuh) and his Household. This demonstrates our sincere love for him (pbuh). Those who love the Prophet (pbuh) will be loved by God. If a believer prays once for the Messenger of God, God will pray for him ten times.

Love of the Prophet (pbuh) is not limited to Prophet Mohamed only, but should be extended to all of the Prophets, as shown in the Qur'anic verse below.

The Messenger believes in what has been revealed to him from his Lord, as do the believers. Each one (of them) believes in God, His Angels, His Books, and His Messengers. "We make no distinction (they say) between one and another of His Messengers." And they say: "We hear and we obey: (we seek) Your forgiveness, Our Lord, and to You is the end of all journeys." [Q 2:285]

2-2-2 Promoting love of the Household of the Prophet (pbuh)

'Ahl Al-Bayt' (meaning 'Family of the House') is an Islamic expression that refers to a group of believers who were very close to the Prophet (pbuh) and known to be very righteous. God purified them and gave them a special status. Scholars of Islamic history have a different definition for them depending on their school of thought. There are three spheres, or domains. The second sphere encompasses the first, and the third sphere encompasses the first and second. The third sphere is very general, and includes all the righteous followers of the Prophet (pbuh) to whom God promised they would enter Paradise without being called to account or being questioned.

The First Sphere ('Ahl Al-Kasa') includes the Prophet (pbuh) and the four immediate members of his family (his Household): Ali ibn Abi Taleb (the Prophet's cousin and son-in-law), Ali's wife Fatima El-Zahra (the Prophet's daughter) and their two sons Hassan and Hussein (peace be upon them all). They are mentioned in the 'Hadith of the Cloak,' given below. The Prophet (pbuh) describes them as part of his Household ("Ahl Al-Bayt") when he said, "O God, these are the people of my house"

Aisha (may God be pleased with her) reported that God's Apostle (pbuh) went out one morning wearing a striped cloak of the black camel's hair, when Hassan ibn Ali (his grandson) came to him. The Prophet (pbuh) wrapped him inside his cloak; then Hussain (his other grandson) came to him and he (pbuh) also wrapped him inside it along with the other one (Hassan). Then Fatima came and he (pbuh) took her under it, then ᶜAli came and he (pbuh) also took him under it and recited this verse:

❖ *"God desires only to remove any impurity from you, O People of the Household, and purify you with a thorough purifying."* ❖ [Q 33:33]

Umm Salama (may God be pleased with her) narrated that she observed the Prophet (pbuh) put a garment around Hassan, Hussain, ᶜAli and Fatima, and then say: "O God, these are the family of my household (Ahl al-Bayti) and the close ones, so remove the impurity from them and purify them thoroughly." So Umm Salama said: 'And am I with them, O Messenger of God?' He (pbuh) said: 'You are upon good.'" [1]

During the time that the Prophet (pbuh) was in Medina, a delegation of Christians visited him to debate about the status of Jesus, whom they claimed was the son of God or God Himself. The Prophet (pbuh) spoke at length with them, and finally told them to bring their families and he would bring his family, and together they would ask God to curse those who are lying. So the Prophet (pbuh) brought Ali, Fatima, Hassan and Hussein, and the Christians looked at them and decided not to ask God to curse the liars. This incident is mentioned in the Holy Qur'an in Chapter 3, Verses 61 and 62, shown below.

❖*And to whomsoever disputes with you over it (the status of Jesus), after the knowledge that has come to you, say, "Come! Let us call upon our sons and your sons, our women and your women, ourselves and yourselves. Then let us pray earnestly, so as to place the curse of God upon those who lie." [61] This is indeed the true account; there is no god but God, and truly God is the Mighty, the Wise. [62]* ❖ [Q 3:61-62]

The Second Sphere includes the five mentioned in the first sphere, with the addition of other family members - some jurists added the wives of the Prophet (pbuh) and the tribe of Bani Hashim who were not allowed to accept charity (Sadaqah). God says in His Holy Qur'an:

---

(1) The speaker: Tirmidhi – Source: Sunan al-Tirmidhi – page or number: 3871. Conclusion of the speaker: fair and it is the best thing reported in this chapter.

❀O wives of the Prophet, you are not like other women. If you reverence God, then do not be overly soft in speech (to men), lest he in whose heart is a disease should be moved to desire, and speak in an honorable way. [32] And abide in your houses and do not display yourselves as (was) the practice during former times of ignorance. Perform the prayer, give charity, and obey God and His Messenger. God intends only to remove from you impurity (of sin), O people of the (Prophet's) Household, and to purify you completely. [33] And remember that which is recited to you in your houses from among the verses of God and His Wisdom. Truly God is the Ever-Subtle and Well-Acquainted (with all things).[34] ❀ [Q 33:32-34]

Abdul-Muttalib ibn Rabiah ibn al-Harith and al-Fadl ibn Abbas ibn Abdul-Muttalib (may God be pleased with them) were told to go to the Messenger of God (pbuh) and say to him, "O Messenger of God, appoint us to collect the 'Sadaqah' (money to be distributed as charity to the poor).' Ali ibn Abi Talib came along when we were like that, and he said to us: 'The Messenger of God (pbuh) will not appoint any of you to collect the Sadaqah.' Abdul-Muttalib said: 'So I went with Al-Fadl until we came to the Messenger of God (pbuh), and he (pbuh) said to us: 'This Sadaqah comes from the people who donate it to purify themselves of their sins; it is not permissible for Muhammad or for the family of Muhammad.' [1]

For anyone who was a blood relative of the Prophet (pbuh), but was not righteous, his blood relationship will be of no good to him on the Day of Judgement, as is shown in the following verse.

❀And when the trumpet is blown, there shall be no kinship between them that Day, nor will they question one another. [101] And as for those whose scales are heavy, it is they who shall prosper. [102] And as for those whose scales are light, it is they who shall lose their souls, abiding in Hell. [103] The Fire will smite their faces, and they shall grimace therein. [104] ❀ [Q 23:101-104]

We can conclude from the verse below that whoever betrayed one of God's prophets (peace be upon them), or refused to believe in God, even though they were a member of that prophet's immediate family

---

(1) The speaker: al-Albani / Source: Sahih al-Nasa'i Page or number: 2608 / Conclusion of the speaker: sound.

(such as Prophet Noah's wife and Prophet Lot's wife), did not escape punishment.

God sets forth as an example for those who disbelieve: the wife of Noah and the wife of Lot. They were wed to two of Our righteous servants but betrayed them, so those prophets did not avail them from God at all, and it was said to them, "Enter the Fire with those who enter." [Q 66:10]

One of Noah's sons chose to disbelieve, and thus God caused him to be among those left behind and who then drowned.

He (God) said, "O Noah! Truly he (your son) is not from your family; surely, his conduct was not righteous. So question Me not concerning that whereof you have no knowledge. Truly, I urge you, lest you be among the ignorant." [Q 11:46]

The Third Sphere, and the most common one, is for those who are connected to Prophet Muhammad (pbuh) because of their faith and belief in the One God, or their kinship in remaining conscious of the One God, being obedient to Him, and following the example of the Prophet (pbuh). This relationship existed even before the era of the Prophet (pbuh), as evidenced in Noah's prayer to God, shown in the verse below.

(Noah said) *"... My Lord, forgive me and my parents, whosoever enters my house as a believer, and the believing men and the believing women. And do not increase the wrongdoers in anything but ruin."* [Q 71:28]

This relationship is also shown between Prophet Abraham (pbuh) and his wife Sarah, in the verse shown below. Angels visited them to give the good news that they would soon have a son. The angels asked his wife why she was so surprised at this news.

They (the angels) said (to Abraham's wife), "Do you marvel at the Command of God? The Mercy of God and His Blessings be upon you, O Family of the House! Truly He is Ever-Praised, Glorious." [Q 11:73]

It is worth noting that the Messenger of God (pbuh) included Salman al-Farsi among the people of his Household (Ahl al-Bayt), even though Salman had no blood relationship to them.

There are seventy thousand believers who shall be admitted to Paradise without judgment, and these are the people of Taqwa (those who have a constant awareness of God's Presence) and Al-Salah (righteousness).

Imran ibn Hussain (may God be pleased with him) reported that he heard the Messenger of God (pbuh) say, "Seventy thousand of my 'community' (Umma) will enter Paradise without rendering account." They (the Companions of the Prophet) asked, 'Who will those be, Messenger of God?' He (the Prophet, pbuh) said: 'They will be those who neither practise charms (magic) and attribute negative outcomes to omens, nor lose hope; they instead place all their trust in their Lord." [1]

❧ *Whosoever obeys God and the Messenger, they are with those whom God has blessed, the prophets, the truthful ones, the witnesses, and the righteous. What beautiful companions they are!* ❧ *[Q 4:69]*

Amr ibn Ouf al-Mazni (may God be pleased with him) narrated that the Messenger (pbuh), in the year of the Confederates Battle, lined the trench with red clay, with one end at Bani Haretha up to Al-Madaheg, where he dedicated forty cubits for every ten people. The Mujahirun (Emigrants) and the Ansar (Helpers) argued over Salman al-Farsi, who was a strong man. The Emigrants said he was one of them, while the Helpers said he was one of them. The Messenger (pbuh) said "Salman is one of us, the family of the household (Ahl al-Bait)". [2]

For those who obey the commands of God and His Messenger, and decline from what God and His Messenger have forbidden them to do, God shall cause them to reside in houses of dignity in Paradise and join the company of the prophets, then to the following in rank: the believers, then the martyrs, and the faithful who are the righteous and whose deeds are from their hearts. Almighty God praised them when He said; "They have the best of company".

---

(1) The speaker: Muslim – Source: Sahih Muslim – page or number: 218. Conclusion of the speaker: sound.

(2) The speaker: al-Haythami – Source: Majma al-Zawa'id – page or number: 6/133. Conclusion of the speaker: includes Kathir ibn Abdallah al-Mazni and was weakened by the public. Tirmidhi made it fair. Other reporters are trusted (thequat).

The Prophet's Household were the first of the faithful to join the Prophet (pbuh) in the Hereafter. They are at a blessed lake in Paradise (known as 'The Hawd') with him (pbuh). And, as God has promised, the individual will be with whom he loves.

As a grace from God, the Most Merciful, for His servants who are true believers, He will cause their parents and progeny to join them in Paradise (the Gardens of Eden). We know that the Prophet (pbuh) will be in Paradise with his progeny and his Household, and – as mentioned in the hadith above – everyone will be joined with whom they love. By loving the Prophet (pbuh) and his Household, and being a righteous believer, one hopes to join them in Paradise, and God always fulfills His promises. In addition to the thought that every believer wishes to be with the Prophet (pbuh) and his Household, there are many hadiths which tell the believer to follow their example.

❧... who fulfill their pact with God and break not the covenant, [20] who join what God has commanded be joined, revere their Lord and dread an evil reckoning, [21] and who are patient, seeking the Face of their Lord, perform the prayer, and spend from that which We have provided them, secretly and openly, and who repel evil with good. For them there shall be the reward of the Abode – [22] Gardens of Eden that they shall enter along with those who were righteous from among their fathers, their spouses and their progeny; and angels shall enter upon them from every gate. [23] "Peace be upon you because you were patient." How excellent is the Ultimate Abode!" [24] ❧ [Q 13:20-24]

❧This is that whereof God gives glad tidings to His servants, those who believe and perform righteous deeds. Say, "I ask not of you any reward for this message, save affection among kinsfolk." And whosoever accomplishes a good deed, We shall increase him in goodness thereby. Truly God is Most Forgiving, Ever Appreciative. ❧ [Q 42:23]

❧And those who believe and whose progeny follow them in faith, We shall cause their progeny to join them, and will not deprive them of any of their deeds. Every person will be held in pledge for whatever they have earned. ❧ [Q 52:21]

For believers who are righteous, and their next of kin (family members) who are righteous, as a Grace from God, He will join them together, even if one of them does not have the same rank as the other in terms of good deeds. They will be blessed by the company of one another, and God will increase the rank of the one who is of lesser rank, while not lowering the rank of the one who is higher. He will then be with the ones he loves in the life to come. This is a great mercy from God towards the believers and their families. This Islamic concept shows that righteous families will be together in the Hereafter.

The concept of love is tied to fellowship, maintaining close and cordial ties with one's family and, by extension, to all believers, as brothers and sisters in faith. Almighty God says,

❖They are those whom God has guided, so follow their guidance. Say (O Muhammad), "I ask not of you any reward for it. It is nothing but a reminder for the worlds."❖ [Q 6:90]

Those who have been guided by God are the ones whom the Prophet (pbuh) commanded us to follow and love them. God has blessed His believers and those who are righteous of their parents and ancestors to follow them and enjoy the blessings of God. The Prophet's Household has joined the Prophet (pbuh) in the highest Paradise according to the Prophet's saying: "The person shall join those whom he loves". Therefore, whoever loves the Prophet (pbuh) and his Household, God has promised to have him join them in Paradise.

Ibn Hazem (may God be pleased with him) narrated that the Prophet (pbuh) said, "I leave among you two weighty matters: the Book of God and my household". [1]

Ibn Abbas (may God be pleased with him) narrated that the Messenger (pbuh) said, "Love God for what He sustains you with of His Blessings, love me due to your love of God, and love the family of my household due to your love of me." [2]

Ali ibn Abi Talib (may God be pleased with him) narrated that the Prophet (pbuh) took Hassan and Hussain by the hand and said: "Whoever loves me and loves these two, and their father and mother, he shall be with me at my level on the Day of Judgment." [3]

---

(1) The speaker: ibn Hazem – Source: Usul al-Ahkam – page or number: 2/27. Conclusion of the speaker: sound.

(2) The speaker: Tirmidhi – Source: Sunan al-Tirmidhi – page or number: 3789. Conclusion of the speaker: fair but strange.

(3) The speaker: Tirmidhi – Source: Sunan al-Tirmidhi – page or number: 3733. Conclusion of the speaker: fair but strange. We knew not from the saying of Jaafar ibn Mohamed except from this side.

Zaid ibn Arqam (may God be pleased with him) narrated that the Messenger (pbuh) said, "Indeed, I am leaving among you that which, if you hold fast to them, you shall not go astray after me. One of them is greater than the other: The Book of God, which is a rope extending from the sky to the earth, and my family - the family of my Household - they shall not split until they meet at a lake (known as 'The Hawd'), the water of which is clearer than milk, sweeter than honey (and whoever gets one drink of it shall never be thirsty). So look at how you deal with them after me." [1]

Ali ibn Abi Taleb (may God be pleased with him) narrated that, when the following verse was revealed:

❴ ... *those who believe and whose hearts are at peace in the remembrance of God. Are not hearts at peace in the remembrance of God?* ❵ *[Q 13:28],*

the Prophet (pbuh) said that this verse came down for those who sincerely love God, His prophet and his Household, and who also love their fellow believers, present and absent, who gather in the remembrance of God.

Ibn Umar (may God be pleased with him) narrated that Abu Bakr used to say, "Please Muhammad (pbuh) by doing good to his family." [2]

Abdullah ibn Hamid (may God be pleased with him) narrated that the Messenger (pbuh) said, "O people! I am a human being. God's Angel of Death is about to come, and I shall respond. I leave among you two weighty matters, the first of which is the Book of God wherein is Guidance and Light. He who holds fast to it shall be on right guidance, and he who fails to hold fast to it shall be astray. Take the Book of Almighty God and hold fast to it and to my Household. I remind you, by God, to care for my Household." [3]

---

(1) The Speaker: Tirmidhi – Source: Sunan al-Tirmidhi – page or number: 3788. Conclusion of the speaker: fair.

(2) The speaker: al-Bukhari – Source: Sahih al-Bukhari – page or number: 3751. Conclusion of the speaker: sound.

(3) The speaker: al-Suyuti – Source: al-Jaami' al-Kabîr – page or number: 1608. Conclusion of the speaker: sound

Therefore, believers should remember the Household of the Prophet (pbuh) with kindness and love, since to hate them would lead to Hellfire, as is stated in the following Hadith.

Abu Dhar al-Ghafari (may God be pleased with him) stood at the door and called out: "O people, do you know me? Those who know me, and those who do not, I am Jandab, companion of the Prophet (pbuh). I am Abu Dhar al-Ghafari. I heard the Messenger (pbuh) say, "My Household among you is like Noah's Ark. He who boards it survives and he who does not will drown. My Household among you is like the Heta Gate (the gate that leads to forgiveness)" [1]

All of us should 'board this Ark' by loving the Prophet (pbuh) and his Household. It is said that our duty is to give them preference over love of ourselves and our own households, as when Omar ibn Abdel-Aziz said to Fatima, daughter of Ali ibn Abi Talib, "O Ali's daughter! By God, there is no household in the universe whom I love more than yours. I love your Household more than my own."

2-3 Love for the sake of God

When believers extend their love to their fellow believers, for the sake of God, they will earn His love. It is very important in Islam that believers should love for others what they love for themselves. There are so many hadiths that talk about establishing a society where the relationship between one another is based on mutual love and respect, and that the strength of one's faith is a Grace from God.

And hold fast to the rope of God, altogether, and be not divided. Remember the Blessings of God upon you, when you were enemies and He joined your hearts, such that you became brothers by His Blessing. You were on the brink of a pit of fire and He delivered you from it. Thus does God make clear to you His signs, that perhaps you may be rightly guided. [Q 3:103]

Holding fast to God's guidance, staying together through love of one's fellow believers and their love of God and His prophet (pbuh), will strengthen believers' faith. Being distant from one another because of disunity will cause us to go astray.

---

(1) The speaker: al-Būsīrī – Source: Ithāf al-Khiayra al-Mahara – page or number: 7/229. Conclusion of the speaker: its chain of narrators is weak.

The sign of strong faith, where society is at peace and in harmony through mutual love and respect, and each one loves for their brother and sister what they love for themselves, is narrated in the following hadith.

Anas ibn Malik (may God be pleased with him) narrated that the Prophet (pbuh) said, "None of you (truly) believes until he loves for his brother that which he loves for himself." [1]

God Almighty, by His Mercy, joins hearts together, which shows that the Most Merciful wants believers to love one another and establish His religion based on love, peace and justice, which can only be attained through love of God and love of one another.

It is God's Will that joins people's hearts together. God tells His Prophet (pbuh) that if he had spent all the treasure on earth, he would never have joined the hearts of those around him, but God gathered them in faith and so they became loving brothers. He alone is the Almighty, the Wise. This is emphasized in the following three Quranic verses.

❈*... it was He who strengthened you with His help, and with the believers, [62] and brought their hearts together. Even if you had given away everything in the earth, you could not have done this, but God brought them together: God is Mighty and Wise. [63]* ❈ *[Q 8:62-63]*

❈*The believers are but brothers; so make peace between your brethren, and remain conscious of God that perhaps you may receive His Mercy.*❈ *[Q 49:10]*

❈*Muhammad is the Messenger of God. Those who are with him are firm and unyielding against the disbelievers, yet full of mercy to one another ...* ❈ *[Q 48:29]*

God reminds us that all believers are united in their faith, and that they should always remain conscious of Him in order to enjoy His Mercy. God also promises believers who love one another for God's sake, a great reward on the Day of Resurrection, as shown in the hadiths below.

---

(1) The speaker: al-Bukhari – Source: Sahih al-Bukhari – page or number: 13. Conclusion of the speaker: sound.

Abu Hurairah (may God be pleased with him) reported God's Messenger (pbuh) as saying, "Truly, God will ask, on the Day of Resurrection, 'Where are those who have mutual love for the sake of My Glory? Today I shall shelter them in My shade when there is no other shade but My shade.'" [1]

Mu'adh ibn Jabal (may God be pleased with him) reported, "The Messenger of God (pbuh) stated, 'God, the Ever-Exalted, has said: 'For those who love one another for the sake of My Glory, there will be seats of light (for them on the Day of Resurrection), and they will be greatly admired by the Prophets and martyrs.'" [2]

Abu Hurairah (may God be pleased with him) reported: "I heard the Messenger of God (pbuh) say, 'Whosoever visits an ailing person or a brother of his to seek the Pleasure of God, an (angelic) announcer will call out: 'May you be happy, may your coming and going be blessed, and may you be awarded a dignified position in Paradise.'" [3]

Abu al-Darda (may God be pleased with him) reported that the Messenger of God (pbuh) said: "On the Day of Resurrection, God will raise people with their faces radiant with light; they will be sitting in podiums made of pearls. People will marvel at them for they are neither prophets nor martyrs." Abu al-Darda said further that a Bedouin rose on his knees and addressed the Prophet (pbuh): 'O Messenger of God, describe to us their appearance so that we may recognize them.' The Messenger of God (pbuh) said: "Despite coming from different tribes and areas, these people love one another for the sake of God; they get together and remember God as one group." [4]

Abu Hurairah (may God be pleased with him) narrated, "The Prophet (pbuh) said, 'God will give shade to seven (types of people) on the Day when there will be no shade but His. These seven are: a just ruler; a youth who has been brought up in the worship of the One God (i.e. worships God sincerely from childhood); a man whose heart is

---

(1) The speaker: Muslim – Source: Sahih Muslim – page or number: 2566. Conclusion of the speaker: sound.

(2) The speaker: Tirmidhi – Source: Sunan al-Tirmidhi – page or number: 2390. Conclusion of the speaker: fair and sound.

(3) The Speaker: Tirmidhi – Source: Sunan al-Tirmidhi – page or number: 2008. Conclusion of the speaker: fair and strange.

(4) The Speaker: al-Albani – Source: Sahih al-Targhīb – page or number: 3025. Conclusion of the speaker: fair.

attached to the mosques; two people who love each other only for God's sake and they only meet and part in God's cause; a man who refuses the call of a beautiful woman of noble birth and says: 'I revere God'; a person who gives charity so secretly that his left hand does not know what his right hand has given (i.e. nobody knows how much he has given in charity); and a person who remembers God in seclusion to the point that their eyes are flooded with tears." [1]

al-Miqdam ibn Ma'dikarib (may God be pleased with him) narrated: "The Prophet (pbuh) said: 'When a man loves his brother, he should tell him that he loves him." [2]

Anas ibn Malik (may God be pleased with him) narrated: "A man was with the Prophet (pbuh) and another man passed by them and said, 'O Apostle of God! I love this man'. The Apostle of God (pbuh) then asked: 'Have you informed him?' He replied, 'No.' He (pbuh) said: 'Inform him.' He then went to him and said: I love you for God's sake. He replied: 'May He, for Whose sake you love me, love you!'" [3]

Nu'man ibn Bashir (may God be pleased with him) reported that the Prophet (pbuh) said, "Muslims are like the body of a person: if the eye is sore, the whole body is sore, and if the head aches, the whole body aches." [4]

Anas ibn Malik (may God be pleased with him) narrated: "God's Apostle (pbuh) said, 'Do not hate one another, do not be jealous of one another, do not desert one another and, O God's worshippers, be brothers! Indeed, it is impermissible for any Muslim to deliberately ignore his brother for more than three days.'" [5]

Abdullah ibn Umar (may God be pleased with him) narrated: "God's Apostle (pbuh) said, 'A Muslim is the brother of another Muslim, so

---

(1) The speaker: al-Bukhari – Source: Sahih al-Bukhari – page or number: 6806. Conclusion of the speaker: sound.

(2) The speaker: Abu Dawood – Source: Sunan Abu Dawood – page or number: 5124. Conclusion of the speaker: Did not. "comment. [He wrote in his letter to the people of Mecca that whenever he did not comment, it is accepted]".

(3) The speaker: Abu Dawood – Source: Sunan Abu Dawood – page or number: 5125. Conclusion of the speaker: Did not. "comment. [He wrote in his letter to the people of Mecca that whenever he did not comment, it is accepted]".

(4) The speaker: Muslim – Source: Sahih Muslim – page or number: 2586. Conclusion of the speaker: sound.

(5) The speaker: al-Bukhari – Source: Sahih al-Bukhari – page or number: 6065. Conclusion of the speaker: sound.

he should not oppress him, nor should he hand him over to an oppressor. Whoever fulfills the needs of his brother, God will fulfill his needs; whoever delivers his believing brother from hardship, God will deliver him from hardship on the Day of Resurrection, and whoever shields a Muslim, God will shield him on the Day of Resurrection.'" [1]

Abu Darda (may God be pleased with him) reported: "The Messenger of God (pbuh) said, 'One of Prophet David's supplications was: 'O God! I ask You for Your Love, the love of those who love You, and deeds which will cause me to attain Your Love. O God! Make Your Love dearer to me than myself, my family and cold water.'" [2]

2-4 God Loves Those Who are Conscious of Him

Hearts that are full of love for God, His prophet (pbuh), and all fellow believers are the hearts of those who remain conscious of Him at all times. This is the practice of 'Taqwa', and is a path to God's contentment, as mentioned in the Qur'anic verses below.

Yes! Whosoever fulfills their pact and remains conscious of Him - truly God loves those who are conscious of Him. [Q 3:76]

God, the Glorious, mentions in the Holy Qur'an the qualities of righteous people. He says that He commanded the believers, as well as all people, to be conscious of Him. He commanded our ancestors to be conscious of Him. Moreover, all the messengers advised their people to remain conscious of God. When consciousness of God touches the heart, the heart will be at peace and, when the heart is at peace, the whole body is peaceful, and our deeds will be good. The effect of always being conscious of God is that He will be pleased with us in this life and in the life to come. God, the Almighty says:

We enjoined those who were given the Book before you, and We enjoin you to remain conscious of God ... [Q 4:131]

God, the Infinite, emphasizes this concept in many verses and tells us that Prophet Noah (pbuh) commanded his people to be conscious of Him, as did Prophets Hud, Saleh, Lot and Shuaib – they all commanded their people to be ever-conscious of their Lord. Prophet Muhammad

---

(1) The speaker: al-Bukhari – Source: Sahih al-Bukhari – page or number: 2442. Conclusion of the speaker: sound.
(2) The speaker: Tirmidhi – Source: Sunan al-Tirmidhi – page or number: 1490. Conclusion of the speaker: fair and strange.

(pbuh), and all of God's prophets and messengers, commanded their people to be constantly aware of and conscious of Him.

Consciousness in the language

Consciousness is derived from the meaning of being 'conscious' or 'aware', which includes the meaning of being protected. It is what protects man from his lower self.

Definition of Consciousness

It is being aware of God's Presence and Power, Unseen, and being keenly aware that He is the All-Seeing, All-Hearing, All-Knowing, and Well-Acquainted with all things. In this way believers will want to do everything that keeps them close to God, the Almighty, seeking only to please Him out of their love for Him. This awareness should guide believers to be loving, sincere and honest in their obedience to God and His prophet (pbuh), and lead them to happiness and contentment on the Day of Judgment.

It is the greatest bounty and benevolence of God, the Gracious and Compassionate, that He made consciousness man's way out of every hardship. The wisdom and beauty of the two verses below rests in their brevity and generality.

❊... And whosoever remains conscious of God, He will appoint for them a way out (of unhappiness)... ❊ [Q 65:2]

❊ ... And whosoever remains conscious of God, He will make their path easy. ❊ [Q 65:4]

Those who remain conscious of God should not boast of their ability, strength and learning, but rather sincerely believe that whatever they achieve is by the Will of God and His Mercy and Bounty. God enables mankind to execute the duties He has assigned to them. Those who remain conscious of God and never exceed His limits, will find a way out from sin to righteousness, from hardship to ease, and from hell to heaven.

Throughout the Holy Quran, God urges believers to practise Taqwa - it is a central spiritual virtue in Islam. All who cultivate Taqwa are those with a good heart and who perform righteous deeds. Practising Taqwa results in a prosperous life in the here and the Hereafter. Taqwa is not new – it is the essence of all religions. In various places throughout the Qur'an, God instructed the prophets and messengers, such as Noah, Abraham, Lot, Moses, and Saleh and their followers, to practise Taqwa.

The meaning of Taqwa in the Arabic language comes from the word 'Tuqyah,' which refers to what the believer uses to protect himself from evil. A common understanding of Taqwa in Islam is loving obedience to God and His messenger (pbuh), remaining conscious of God, being righteous, and being keen to do whatever brings one closer to God. All these should lead one to a good life and entry to His Paradise. God makes Taqwa our way out of all difficulties, as mentioned in the two verses shown above.

The Holy Quran provides guidance through which believers can find ease from hardship when they put their whole trust in God and rely on Him to deliver them from difficulty, and reward them with contentment in the here and Hereafter. In so many cases, hardships can appear insurmountable, causing one to feel despair but, through practising Taqwa, these obstacles can be overcome. Believers can withstand hardships through patience and accepting God's Will, in the hope that He will replace their hardship with ease, which is succinctly stated in Verse 4 of Chapter 65, shown above.

Seeking God's protection is an important aspect of Taqwa, and is a key part of one's relationship with one's family, and every other type of relationship.

2-4-1 Examples of the meaning of 'Taqwa' in the Holy Qur'an

A brief explanation is given below about how the word 'Taqwa' is used in the Holy Quran. Firstly, it is used to indicate a kind of protection against any harm – whether physical or spiritual. Secondly, it includes the meaning of protecting oneself against provoking God's discontent – there is no refuge from God except with Him. Its meaning also encompasses all good deeds and righteous conduct. God will safeguard and protect the sincere believer from whatever is harmful.

2-4-1-1 Taqwa in the sense of being protected from evil and harm

Taqwa can be understood in the sense of protection and fortification against all evils, against whoever wants to harm you, and against those who may plot against you.

There are verses that give a sense of protection when believers are committed to what God, the All-Encompassing, has commanded, and when they avoid all those things which God prohibits. By this, God protects them from all evils and fears. This sense is clarified in the following verses.

❖*So God shielded him (a believer who dared to challenge Pharaoh) from the evils of that which they (Pharaoh and his supporters) had plotted, while a terrible punishment engulfed the House of Pharaoh ...* ❖ *[Q 40:45]*

❖*So God has shielded them (believers) from the evil of that Day, bestowed upon them radiance and joy ...* ❖ *[Q 76:11]*

❖*If good comes to you, it angers them (the disbelievers), and if misfortune befalls you, they rejoice in it. But if you are patient in adversity and remain conscious of God, their scheming will not harm you in the least. Truly God encompasses all that they do.* ❖ *[Q 3:120]*

God, the Almighty, will protect the believer who remains conscious of Him, against the harm of plotters and the enmity of those who are angered when you achieve victory and pleased when you are harmed by defeat or loss of money, property or children. If you are patient with what God has willed for you, are obedient in what He has commanded you to do and prohibited you from, then their evil will never harm you. God is Well-Acquainted with all that they do, and He will punish them for their corruption.

❖*Behold! Truly, those who are close to God, no fear shall come upon them, nor shall they grieve – [62] those who believe and remain conscious of Him. [63] For them are glad tidings in the life of this world and in the Hereafter. There is no altering the Words of God. That is the great triumph. [64]* ❖ *[Q 10:62-64]*

Those who are close to God do not fear His punishment, nor regret what they have missed in the present life. The qualities of those who are close to Him are that they believe in Him, follow His Messenger (pbuh), are grateful for what they have received in this life, are conscious of Him, obey His commands, and avoid His prohibitions.

2-4-1-2 Taqwa saves one from becoming distanced from God and causing His discontentment with you

Believers can protect themselves from God's discontent by following His guidance, orders and laws. Examples are given in the following three verses.

❖*O Children of Adam! Should there come to you messengers from among yourselves, recounting My signs to you, then whosoever is conscious of Me and makes amends, no fear will come upon them, nor will they grieve.* ❧ [Q 7:35]

❧Above them they (rejecters of faith) will have canopies of fire and below them canopies (of fire); with that does God strike fear into His servants. O My Servants! Remain conscious of Me! ❧ [Q 39:16]

❧And be mindful of the Fire that has been prepared for the disbelievers! ❧ [Q 3:131]

2-4-1-3 Virtues and Rewards of Taqwa

The Holy Qur'an, also known as 'The Criterion' (Al-Furqān), leads believers to peace, benefits them by its provisions, and guides them to the right path. The Qur'an is the beacon of guidance for righteous people.

❧This is the Book in which there is no doubt, a guidance for all who remain conscious of Him. ❧ [Q 2:2]

❧O you who believe! If you remain conscious of God, He will endow you with a standard by which to discern the true from the false, and will efface your bad deeds, and will forgive your sins, for God is possessed of Tremendous Bounty. ❧ [Q 8:29]

If you remain conscious of God by fulfilling His commands and avoiding His prohibitions, He will lead you to what is right, and forgive all your sins. God's blessings and bounty are limitless.

❧O you who believe! Remain conscious of God, and believe in His Messenger; He will give you a two-fold portion of His Mercy, make a light for you by which you may walk, and forgive you. God is Ever-Forgiving, Most Merciful … ❧ [Q 57:28]

God bestows His bountiful mercy and guidance upon the people who are conscious of Him and believe in His prophet (pbuh).

❧… Surely the most noble of you before God are the most deeply conscious of Him. Truly God is the All-Knowing, All-Aware. ❧ [Q 49:13]

Being conscious of God makes believers the most honourable among God's creation. In Islam, the most honoured people are those who are most conscious of God, and only He knows who are the most deeply conscious of Him.

... So deem not yourselves purified. He knows best who is conscious of Him. [Q 53:32]

Consciousness of God is the way to Paradise and achieving a high rank there. God will give those believers who are conscious of Him, high ranks in Heaven, above those who used to look down upon them in this world. And God gives His abundant sustenance to whomsoever He wills, without taking account. These believers, on the Day of Judgment, will acknowledge the goodness given to them in this life, and their reward in the Hereafter will be excellent indeed, where the God-conscious will reside.

The life of this world is made to seem fair to those who disbelieve, and they ridicule those who believe. But those who remain conscious of God shall be above them on the Day of Resurrection. And God provides for whomsoever He wills without reckoning. [Q 2:212]

And it will be said to those who remain conscious of God, "What has your Lord sent down?" They will say, "Goodness." For those who are virtuous in this world, there shall be good, and the Abode of the Hereafter is better. Excellent indeed is the abode of those who remain conscious of Him. [Q 16:30]

Whosoever obeys God and His Messenger, and who reveres God and remains conscious of Him, it is they who shall triumph. [Q 24:52]

Those who obey God and His prophet (pbuh) in every aspect of their lives will have the reward of a righteous life in this world and, in the Hereafter, they will have the highest ranks.

(Moses said) "... And prescribe good for us in the life of this world, and in the Hereafter; truly we have turned to You." He said, "I cause My punishment to smite whomsoever I will, though My Mercy encompasses all things. I shall prescribe it for those who remain conscious of Me, and give alms, and who believe in Our signs ..." [Q 7:156]

God's Mercy encompasses all of creation. He bestows it upon those who are conscious of Him in all their deeds, who do what is required of them, avoid what is forbidden, and put all their trust in Him. He will reward them for the best of their deeds, and the fruits of being conscious of Him are forgiveness of their bad deeds and a great reward. Those who seek a good and righteous life in this world and in the next, in the Gardens of Paradise, should remain ever-conscious of Him.

(Prophet Joseph said) ❀ *"... Truly, whosoever remains conscious of God and is patient – surely, God neglects not the reward of the virtuous."* ❀ *[Q 12:90]*

❀*That is the Command of God that He has sent down to you. Whosoever remains conscious of God, He will absolve him of his evil deeds and honor him with reward.* ❀ *[Q 65:5]*

❀*And God saves those who remain conscious of Him by their triumph; evil will not befall them; nor will they grieve.* ❀ *[Q 39:61]*

On the Day of Judgment God will save the believers who are conscious of Him. They demonstrate their consciousness of God by adhering to their obligations and avoiding what He has forbidden. They will have a great reward by having their hope of entering Paradise fulfilled. They will be saved from punishment and rewarded with joy and happiness.

Abdullah ibn Amr (may God be pleased with him) narrated: "It was said to the Messenger of God (pbuh), 'Which of the people is best?' He replied, 'Everyone who is pure of heart and sincere in speech.' They said: 'We know what 'sincere in speech' means, but what is 'pure of heart'?' He replied: 'It is (the heart) that is pure and always conscious of God, with no sin, injustice, hatred or envy in it.'" [1]

Abdullah ibn Masood (may God be pleased with him) reported that God's Messenger (pbuh) used to supplicate (in these words): "O God! I ask You for right guidance, being ever-conscious of You, chastity, and contentment." [2]

The way to become more deeply consciousness of God, in addition to regular prayer, supplication and reading the Qur'an, is to keep in mind that He is the Ever-Near, the Ever-Loving.

❀ *"... We are closer to him (mankind) than his jugular vein.'* ❀ *[Q 50:16]*

---

(1) The speaker: al-Albani – Source: Sahih ibn Majah – page or number: 3416. Conclusion of the speaker: sound.

(2) The speaker: Muslim – Source: Sahih Muslim – page or number: 2721. Conclusion of the speaker: sound.

2-5 Kindness to parents leads to God's contentment and love

Being kind to one's parents is one of the virtuous deeds that God rewards with His contentment and love. Both the Holy Quran and the Prophet's Tradition urge all believers to be kind to their parents, by such actions as listening to them, being polite with them, dealing with them in the best manner, and helping them whenever one can, materially and spiritually. This will bring God's contentment with you and increase His love for you. Being thankful for your parents and treating them in the best way is one of the deeds that will earn the highest rewards in the Hereafter, even if your parents are of a different faith than you.

❊Worship God (alone), and do not ascribe partners to Him. And be virtuous towards (your) parents ... ❊ [Q 4:36]

❊... your Lord decrees that you worship none but Him, and be virtuous to (your) parents. Whether one or both of them reaches old age, say not to them "Uff!" or chide them, but (always) speak to them a noble word. Lower to them the wing of humility out of mercy and say, "My Lord! Have mercy on them, as they raised me when I was a child." ❊ [Q 17:23-24]

❊And We have enjoined man concerning his parents - his mother bore him, weakness upon weakness, and his weaning was two years — give thanks to Me and to your parents. To Me is the journey's end. ❊ [Q 31:14]

The Prophetic Traditions shown below also urge believers to be good to their parents to acquire God's contentment.

Abdullah ibn Masood (may God be pleased with him) narrated that he asked the Messenger of God (pbuh), "Which deed is the best?" The Prophet (pbuh) replied: 'Prayer at its appointed time.' I (again) asked, "Then what?" The Prophet (pbuh) replied, 'Kindness to parents.' I (again) asked, "Then what?" The Prophet (pbuh) replied, "Earnest endeavour or striving in the cause of God." I would have not ceased asking more questions except out of regard (for his feelings).[1]

---

(1) The speaker: al-Bukhari – Source: Sahih al-Bukhari – page or number: 527. Conclusion of speaker: sound.

Abdullah ibn Amro ibn al-Aas (may God be pleased with him) narrated that he heard the Messenger of God (pbuh) say, "God's pleasure results from the parent's pleasure, and God's displeasure results from the parent's displeasure." [1]

Abdullah ibn Amr (may God be pleased with him) narrated that a man said to the Prophet, "Shall I participate in striving for the cause of God?" The Prophet (pbuh) replied, "Are your parents living?" The man said, "Yes." The Prophet (pbuh) said, "Taking (good) care of them is your striving for the cause of God." [2]

Abu Huraira (may God be pleased with him) reported that God's Apostle (pbuh) said: "Let him be humbled into dust; let him be humbled into dust." One of those with him asked, 'God's Messenger, who is he?' The Prophet (pbuh) replied, "He who is with either of his parents during their old age and does not enter Paradise (i.e. he did not take care of them or treat them well, thereby missing a golden opportunity to enter Paradise)." [3]

Abu Hurairah (may God be pleased with him) narrated that the Prophet (pbuh) said, "Three supplications are answered, there being no doubt about them: that of a father, that of a traveller, and that of one who has been wronged." [4]

Anas ibn Malik (may God be pleased with hm) narrated that he heard the Prophet (pbuh) say, "Whoever wishes for a long life and good sustenance should be good to his parents and keep in touch with his next of kin." [5]

---

(1) The speaker: al-Albani – Source: Sahih al-Tirmidhi – page or number: 1899. Conclusion of the speaker: sound.

(2) The speaker: al-Bukhari – Source: Sahih al-Bukhari – page or number: 3004. Conclusion of speaker: sound.

(3) The speaker: Muslim – Source: Sahih Muslim – page or number: 2551. Conclusion of the speaker: sound.

(4) The speaker: Abu Dawood – Source: Sunan Abu Dawood – page or number: 1536. Conclusion of the speaker: Did not. "comment. [He wrote in his letter to the people of Mecca that whenever he did not comment, it is accepted]".

(5) The speaker: Shuaib Al Arna'ut – Source: Musnad Ahmed – page or number: 13811. Conclusion of the speaker: sound.

Kindness to parents should also be extended to them even after they have passed away. This include praying that God will forgive them and increase their rank in the Hereafter, and by performing charitable deeds on their behalf, and keeping in touch with, and being good to, their relatives and friends.

O our Sustainer, grant Your forgiveness to me and my parents, and all believers on the Day when the (last) Reckoning will come to pass!" [Q 14:41]

(Prophet Noah said) "My Lord, forgive me and my parents and whoever enters my house a believer and the believing men and believing women. And do not increase the wrongdoers except in destruction." [Q 71:28]

Abu Dawood narrated, from Abu Aseed Malik ibn Rabiyah al-Saadi (may God be pleased with them), that as they were sitting with the Prophet (pbuh), a man from Bani Selma (the Selma Tribe) said, "O Prophet of God, can I still be kind to my parents after they have passed away?" The Prophet (pbuh) replied, 'Yes, pray for forgiveness for them, keep your promises to them, stay in contact with their next of kin to whom they were close, and be generous to their friends.' [1]

Abu Hurairah (may God be pleased with him) narrated that he heard God's Messenger (pbuh) say: "When a son of Adam (i.e. any human being) dies, his deeds are discontinued, with three exceptions: a continuing charity, or knowledge from which people continue to benefit, or a righteous child who prays for him." [Reported by Muslim] [2]

Saad ibn Ubada (may God be pleased with him) narrated that he said to the Prophet (pbuh), "O Messenger (pbuh)! My mother died in my absence; will it be of any benefit to her if I give charity on her behalf?" The Prophet (pbuh) said, "Yes." Saad said, "I make you a

---

(1) The speaker: Abu Dawood – Source: Sunan Abu Dawood – page or number: 5145. Conclusion of the speaker: weak

(2) The speaker: Muslim – Source: Sahih Muslim – page or number: 1631. Conclusion of the speaker: sound.

witness that I have given my garden, called al-Makhraf, in charity on her behalf) "[1]

2-6 Summary and Conclusions

Love is part of the foundations of Islam and a fundamental principle. Islam encourages love between God and His servants (the believers) and between believers and the Prophet (pbuh), whom God sent to the world as a mercy, bearing good news for believers and warnings for disbelievers.

O Prophet! Truly We have sent you as a witness (to the Truth), as a bearer of glad tidings, and as a warner … [Q 33:45]

God disseminates love among believers, awarding those who love each other the highest ranks in Paradise and encourages them to perform all those deeds that will earn them His love and contentment by remaining conscious of Him, being charitable, patient, reliant on Him, fair, honest and just. God promises a great reward for those who believe and do good deeds. The first means to the love of God is remaining conscious of Him at all times. Such consciousness yields great rewards as it leads believers to the highest ranks in His paradise. God promises righteous believers a light that will guide them and distinguish them among people.

Behold! Truly, those who are close to God, no fear shall come upon them, nor shall they grieve – [62] those who believe and remain conscious of Him. [63] For them are glad tidings in the life of this world and in the Hereafter. There is no altering the Words of God. That is the great triumph. [64] [Q 10:62-64]

Our love for God leads to His contentment with us, by such means as remaining conscious of Him, loving His Messenger (pbuh), being committed to His guidance and loving one another, which makes one's heart pure. The faith in one's heart is the unshakeable belief in God, His Messengers, and acceptance of His Will, as is clarified in the next chapter.

---

(1) The speaker: al-Bukhari – Source: Sahih al-Bukhari – page or number: 2756 Hadith number: 3209. Conclusion of speaker: sound.

Chapter 3

Achieving Contentment by Accepting God's Will (Qader and Qaddaa)

❀ *"Indeed, everything have We created in due measure and proportion"* ❀ *[Q 54:49]*

❀ *The Originator is He of the heavens and the earth: and when He wills a thing to be, He but says to it, "Be" – and it is.* ❀ *[Q 2:117]*

❀ *God annuls or confirms whatever He wills (of His earlier messages) – for with Him is the source of all revelation.* ❀ *[Q 13:39]*

❀ *We test you (all) through the bad and the good (things in life) by way of trial: and to Us you will all be returned.* ❀ *[Q 21:35]*

بِسْمِ اللَّهِ الرَّحْمَنِ الرَّحِيمِ

﴿ إِنَّا كُلَّ شَيْءٍ خَلَقْنَاهُ بِقَدَرٍ وَمَا أَمْرُنَا إِلَّا وَاحِدَةٌ كَلَمْحٍ بِالْبَصَرِ ﴾

عَلَى الْأَرْضِ زِينَةً لَهَا لِنَبْلُوَهُمْ ... مِنْ مَعْقِرٍ وَلَا يُنْقَصُ مِنْ عُمُرِهِ

قل لن يصيبنا
إلا ما كتب الله لنا

صَدَقَ اللَّهُ الْعَظِيمُ

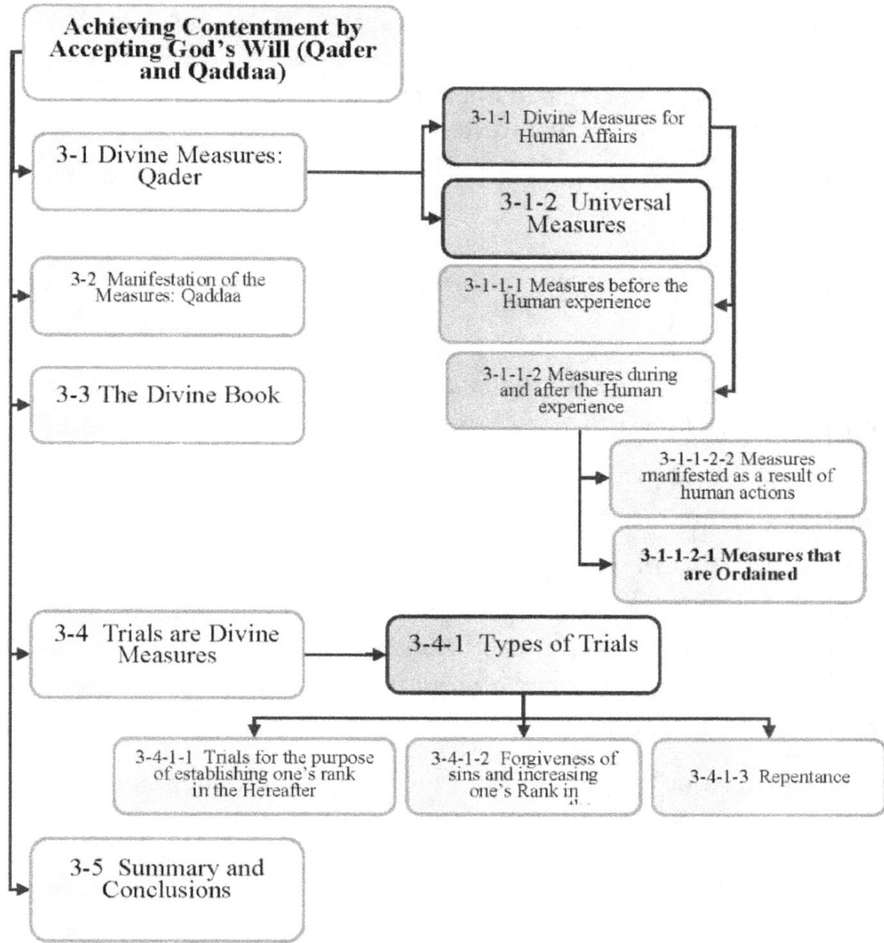

Fig. 1: Structure of Chapter 3

3-0 Introduction

Before God creates anything, He sets the necessary measures with His absolute Wisdom and Mercy, and He then manifests these measures according to His Will. These measures are known in Arabic as 'Aqdar' and, before anything is created, there are measures set for it. Whenever He wills a measure to be manifested, He only says to it 'be' and it is.

Behold, everything have We created in due measure and proportion. [Q 54:49]

… it is He Who creates everything, then measured it out with due measure. [Q 25:2]

The Originator is He of the heavens and the earth: and when He decrees a thing to be, He only says to it, "Be!" and it is. [Q 2:117]

In His absolute Wisdom and Mercy, all His measures and their manifestation are recorded in a book.

For, with Him are the keys to the things that are beyond the reach of a created being's perception: none knows them but He. And He knows all that is on land and in the sea; and not a leaf falls but He knows it, and neither is there a grain in the earth's deep darkness, nor anything living or dead, but is recorded in (His) clear decree. [Q 6:59]

And He alone can confirm or remove what is written in the book.

God annuls or confirms whatever He wills (of His earlier messages) – for with Him is the source of all revelation. [Q 13:39]

In this chapter we discuss at length these measures and how they are manifested. Their manifestation can be a trial for the believer in his life. A key element of contentment is to accept, and be thankful for, God's Will so that we can go through these trials successfully. In this way we can be contented with such divine measures and their manifestation and believe that they are for our own good in the here and the Hereafter.

3-1 Divine Measures: Qader

Before anything comes into existence and is manifested, it is preceded by divine measures (means, methods and ways) to achieve this. These divine measures ensure the achievement of God's Will and that they meet the function He intends in terms of establishing the resources, systems, processes and procedures to ensure everything is done according to His Command, Order and Plan, in His utmost Wisdom.

When God created, He brought into being the Universe according to measures, with His limitless Knowledge, Mercy and Perfection. These measures cover the time before we as humans existed on this Earth, during our presence on this Earth, and after we leave the Earth. This is reflected in Verse 49 of Chapter 54:

"Indeed, everything have We created in due measure and proportion" [Q 54:49]

God's measures are known in Arabic as 'Qader'. In God's Wisdom and Mercy, He can change or manifest these measures at any time, in the here or the Hereafter. His measures and their manifestation are recorded in the Mother of the Book (in Arabic: 'Um Al-Kitāb').

He to Whom the dominion over the heavens and the earth belongs, and Who begets no offspring, and has no partner in His dominion: for it is He Who creates everything with perfect measures and proportions and determines its nature in accordance with (His Own) design. [Q 25:2]

In the following section we will explain the types of measures (Qader), the different forms of their manifestation (Qaddaa), and how everything is recorded in the Mother of the Book (The Book). Relevant Quranic verses and Hadiths of the Prophet (pbuh) are included to show how these elements are an essential part of Islamic beliefs. Accepting them as God's Will is the foundation of Contentment (in Arabic: 'Rida').

The following verses confirm what is stated above. God modifies or confirms these measures, in His infinite Wisdom, before they are manifested.

He is the Originator of the heavens and the earth: and when He manifests a measure, He but says to it, "Be" – and it is. [Q 2:117]

(This is) the established and measured way of God which has ever obtained in the past – and never will you find any change in God's measures. [Q 48:23]

Thus, have We set the measure (the nature of man's creation), and excellent indeed is Our power to manifest those measures (what is to be). [Q 77:23]

❧ God eliminates what He wills or confirms, and with Him is the Mother of the Book. ❧ [Q 13:39]

Ali (may God be pleased with him) narrated, "While the Prophet (pbuh) was in a funeral procession, he picked up something and started scraping the ground with it, and said, 'There is none among you but has his place written for him either in the Hell Fire or in Paradise.' They said, 'O God's Messenger! Shall we not depend upon what has been written for us and give up deeds?' He said, 'Carry on doing (good) deeds, for everybody will find easy to do such deeds as will lead him to his destined place for which he has been created. So he who is destined to be among the happy (in the Hereafter), will find it easy to do the deeds characteristic of such people, while he who is destined to be among the miserable ones, will find it easy to do the deeds characteristic of such people.' Then he recited, 'As for him who gives (to others), reverences God, and believes in the Truth of the ultimate good – for him shall We make easy the path towards [ultimate] ease. But as for him who is miserly, and thinks that he is self-sufficient, and calls the ultimate good a lie – for him shall We make easy the path towards hardship.' [Q 92:5-10). [1]

Abdullah ibn 'Amr ibn al-'Aas (may God be pleased with him) reported, "I heard God's Messenger (pbuh) say: 'God ordained the measures of the creation fifty thousand years before He created the heavens and the earth, as His Throne was upon water.'" [2]

Abdullah ibn Mas'ud (may God be pleased with him) reported that God's Messenger (pbuh), who is the most truthful and his being truthful is a fact, said, "Truly your creation is as given here: the constituents of one of you are collected for forty days in his mother's womb in the form of blood, after which it becomes a clot of blood in another period of forty days. Then it becomes a lump of flesh and, forty days later, God sends His angel to it with instructions concerning four things, so the angel writes down his livelihood, his death, his deeds, his fortune and misfortune. By Him, besides Whom there is no god, that one amongst you acts like the people deserving

---

(1) The speaker: al-Bukhari – Source: Sahih al-Bukhari – page or number: 4949. Conclusion of the speaker: sound.

(2) The speaker: Muslim – Source: Sahih Muslim – page or number: 2653. Conclusion of the speaker: sound.

Paradise until between him and Paradise there remains but the distance of a cubit, when suddenly the writing of destiny overcomes him and he begins to act like the denizens of Hell and thus enters Hell, and another one acts in the way of the denizens of Hell, until there remains between him and Hell a distance of a cubit that the writing of destiny overcomes him and then he begins to act like the people of Paradise and enters Paradise. [1]

Ubada ibn al-Samit said to his son, "Son! You will not get a taste of the reality of faith until you know that what has come to you could not miss you, and that what has missed you could not come to you. I heard the Messenger of God (pbuh) say, 'The first thing God created was the pen. He said to it, 'Write.' It asked, 'What should I write, my Lord?' He said, 'Write what has been decreed about everything until the Last Hour comes.' "Son, I heard the Messenger of God (pbuh) say, 'He who dies on something other than this does not belong to me.' " [2]

Abu Huraira (may God be pleased with him) reported God's Messenger (pbuh) as saying, 'A strong believer is better and more lovable to God than a weak believer, and there is good in everyone, (but) cherish that which gives you benefit (in the Hereafter), seek help from God, and do not lose heart; if anything (in the form of trouble) comes to you, don't say: If I had not done that, so and so would not have happened, but instead say, 'God did that which He had ordained to do.' Your "if" opens the gate for Satan to enter. [3]

Divine measures were established by God as His Laws and systems that direct the Universe (His Kingdom). These measures are written in The Book, and only God can confirm or delete these measures.

When God wills any of these measures to be manifested, He orders it to 'Be' and it 'Is.' This is the manifestation of the measure, according to His Will, and is known in Arabic as 'Qaddaa'. When God established Qaddaa, He also established when it will be implemented, and in what form; in effect, we can think of it as God's Grand Master Plan and what

(1) The speaker: Muslim – Source: Sahih Muslim – page or number: 2643. Conclusion of the speaker: sound.
(2) The speaker: Abu Dawood – Source: Sunan Abu Dawood – page or number: 4703. Conclusion of the speaker: No comment [He wrote a letter to the people of Mecca: Whenever I do not comment, it is accepted].
(3) The speaker: Muslim – Source: Sahih Muslim – page or number: 2664. Conclusion of the speaker: sound.

will be manifested from it is decided by His Will, based on His Mercy and Wisdom, and the Laws He has set. He can apply it as He Wills.

In the following section we will discuss the different types of divine measures, and then the measures related to human life.

3-1-1 Divine Measures for Human Life

The measures for human life can be divided into two types – one that relates to the time before becoming human, and the other to the time when we become human.

3-1-1-1 Measures before the Human Experience

There are three types of measures that happened (came into existence) in this creational phase, as outlined in the following Qur'anic verses.

And whenever your Sustainer brings forth their offspring from the loins of the children of Adam, He (thus) calls upon them to bear witness about themselves: "Am I not your Sustainer?" – to which they answer: "Yes, indeed, we do bear witness thereto. (Of this We remind you,) lest you say on the Day of Resurrection, "Truly, we were unaware of this." [Q 7:172]

And, lo, God accepted, through the prophets, this solemn pledge (from the followers of earlier revelation): "If, after all the revelation and the wisdom which I have vouchsafed to you, there comes to you an apostle confirming the truth already in your possession, you must believe in him and help him. Do you" – said He – "acknowledge and accept My bond on this condition?" They answered: "We do acknowledge it." Said He: "Then bear witness (to this), and I shall be your Witness. [Q 3:81]

Hence, proclaim to all people the (duty of) pilgrimage: they will come to you on foot and on every (kind of) fast mount, coming from every far away point (on earth) ... [Q 22:27]

Three covenants were taken before the human experience. The first covenant stated that God is our Lord and Sustainer, the second one was taken with the Prophets to support God's final messenger, Prophet Muhammad (pbuh), based on the knowledge that was given to them, and the third concerned answering the call for pilgrimage (in Arabic: Hajj).

God took the first covenant with all souls in recognition of His Oneness and that He is their only Lord and Creator, and they acknowledged it. This was done so that they will not, on the Day of Resurrection, deny that this covenant existed (see Q 7:172 above).

God took the second covenant with the prophets, based on the wisdom and knowledge He had given them, that when a messenger would come confirming the knowledge they already had, they would believe in him and support him. They confirmed this pledge, and God was their Witness (see Q 3:81 above).

The third was about calling people for pilgrimage (see Q 22:27 above).

3-1-1-2 Measures during and after the Human Experience

There are two types of these measures, the first of which are ordained, while the second type concerns our actions and their outcomes. We will begin with the first type.

3-1-1-2-1 Measures that are Ordained

There are several examples given in the Holy Quran of this type of measure. The first example is the story of Mary (mother of Jesus) and the Angel Gabriel when he appeared before her to give her the news that she would bear a child and that she would name him Jesus. This was a very big trial for her and she prayed to God that she would not have to go through it. But because this was an ordained matter, nothing could change it because it had already been ordained by God.

The other example is that of Prophet Joseph (pbuh) who was in the presence of two other men in a prison, and they asked him to interpret their dreams. Joseph gave them his interpretation and stated that the events shown in their dreams were ordained matters and could not be changed.

In general, believers should believe and accept ordained matters as God's divine Will based on His Mercy, Wisdom, and Knowledge. We should pray to Him that the outcome will be good, and blessed by Him. Believers will not be held responsible, on the Day of Judgement, for these ordained events since they are purely God's Will and the believer had no choice in the matter.

❦ *(The angel) said, "Thus shall it be. Your Lord says, 'It is easy for Me.' " And (it is thus) that We might make him (Jesus) a sign to mankind, and a Mercy from Us. And it is a matter (already) decreed."* ❧ *[Q 19:21]*

❧*And the pains of childbirth drove her (Mary) to the trunk of a palm tree. She said, "Oh, I wish I had died before this and was in oblivion, forgotten."*❧ [Q 19:23]

❧ *(Joseph said to his two fellow prisoners) "…The matter about which you inquired has been decreed (by God)."* ❧ [Q 12:41]

3-1-1-2-2 Measures manifested as a result of human actions

A. Sustenance

What God provides for you in this life is ordained, and can be seen in the following verses. Even though our sustenance is set by measures, some of it can be changed. As we will explain later, it can increase with being thankful, doing good deeds and performing prayers, but sins will decrease it or even eliminate it.

❧*From a sperm-drop He created him and set the measures for him.* ❧ [Q 80:19]

❧*Behold, your Sustainer grants abundant sustenance, or gives it in scant measure, to whomever He wills: truly, fully aware is He of (the needs of) His creatures, and sees them all.* ❧ [Q 17:30]

❧*His are the keys of the heavens and the earth: He grants abundant sustenance, or gives it in scant measure, to whomever He wills: for, behold, He has full knowledge of everything.* ❧ [Q 12:42]

❧ *For if God were to grant (in this world) abundant sustenance to (all of) His servants, they would behave on earth with wanton insolence: but as it is, He bestows (His grace) from on high in due measure, as He wills: for, truly, He is fully aware of (the needs of) His creatures, and sees them all.* ❧ [Q 42:27]

❧*… and provides for him in a manner beyond all expectation; and for everyone who places his trust in God, He (alone) is enough. Truly, God always attains to His purpose: (and) indeed, to everything has God appointed its term and measure.* ❧ [Q 65:3]

❧*And there is not a thing but that with Us are its depositories, and We do not send it down except according to a known measure.* ❧ [Q 15:21]

Anas ibn Malik, may God be pleased with him, narrated that the Prophet (pbuh) said, "Whoever will be pleased if He increases his sustenance, he should keep in close touch with his next of kin." [1]

B. Measures as a consequence of our actions

The verses shown below are examples of how God's measures can be manifested as a consequence of people's actions. Such manifestations are the response to our actions. The first verse shows that if you wish to be rewarded in this life, God will give you that, and if you wish to receive your reward in the Hereafter, that is what God will give you. God will reward you according to what your intention is.

The other verses are self-explanatory, with measures set by the consequences of human actions. We will be judged in this life and in the Hereafter, based on the laws set by God. They show clearly that it is only God Who can benefit you or harm you, and that our good deeds will be rewarded ten times the like thereof, while for our bad deeds we will be punished once for the like thereof.

❈*And no human being can die save by God's leave, at a term pre-ordained. And if one desires the rewards of this world, We shall grant him thereof; and if one desires the rewards of the life to come, We shall grant him thereof; and We shall requite those who are grateful (to Us).*❈ *[Q 3:145]*

❈*Whoever shall come (before God) with a good deed will gain ten times the like thereof; but whoever shall come with an evil deed will be requited with no more than the like thereof; and none shall be wronged.*❈ *[Q 6:160]*

❈*That is because God would not change a favor which He had bestowed upon a people until they change what is within themselves. And indeed, God is Hearing and Knowing.*❈ *[Q 8:53]*

❈*Truly, they who are close to God – no fear need they have, and neither shall they grieve. [62] They who have attained to faith and have always been conscious of Him. [63] For them there is the glad tiding (of contentment) in the life of this world and in the life to come;*

---

(1) The speaker: al-Bukhari – Source: Sahih al-Bukhari – page or number: 2067. Conclusion of the speaker: sound.

(and since) nothing could ever alter (the outcome of) God's promises, this, this is the triumph supreme! [64] ❀ *[Q 10:62-64]*

❀*And (know that) if God should touch you with misfortune, there is none who could remove it save Him; and if He intends good for you, there is none who could turn away His bounty: He causes it to alight upon whomsoever He wills of His servants. And He alone is truly Forgiving, truly a dispenser of Grace. [107] Say (O Prophet), "O mankind! The truth from your Sustainer has now come to you. Whoever, therefore, chooses to follow the right path, follows it but for his own good; and whoever chooses to go astray, goes but astray to his own hurt. And I am not responsible for your conduct." [108]* ❀ *[Q 10:107-108]*

❀*And yet, among men there is many a one who argues about God without having any knowledge (of Him), and follows every rebellious satanic [3] force about which it has been decreed that whoever entrusts himself to it, him will it lead astray and guide towards the suffering of the blazing flame! [4]* ❀ *[Q 22:3-4]*

❀*God has promised those of you who believe and do righteous deeds that, of a certainty, He will cause them to accede to power on earth, even as He caused (some of) those who lived before them to accede to it; and that, of a certainty, He will firmly establish for them the religion which He has been pleased to bestow on them; and that, of a certainty, He will cause their erstwhile state of fear to be replaced by a sense of security — (seeing that) they worship Me (alone), not ascribing divine powers to aught beside Me. But all who, after (having understood) this, choose to deny the Truth — it is they, they who are truly iniquitous! [55] Hence, (O believers,) be constant in prayer, and render the purifying dues, and pay heed to the Apostle, so that you might be graced with God's Mercy. [56]*❀ *[Q 24:55-56]*

❀*... except for those who repent, believe and do righteous deeds. For them God will replace their evil deeds with good. And God is ever Forgiving and Merciful.* ❀ *[Q 25:70]*

❖Say, "What are you to my Lord without your supplication?" But since you (disbelievers) have denied the Truth, the inevitable will happen. ❖ [Q 25:77]

❖These it is who shall receive a twofold reward for having been patient in adversity, and having repelled evil with good, and having spent on others out of what We provided for them as sustenance. ❖ [Q 28:54]

❖But as for those who strive hard in Our cause – We shall most certainly guide them to paths that lead to Us: for, behold, God is indeed with the doers of good. ❖ [Q 29:69]

❖And no bearer of burdens shall be made to bear another's burden; and if one weighed down by his load calls on (another) to help him carry it, nothing thereof may be carried (by that other), even if it is one's near of kin. Hence, you can (truly) warn only those who stand in awe of their Lord although He is beyond the reach of their perception, and are constant in prayer, and (know that) whoever grows in purity, attains to purity but for the good of his own self, and (that) with God is all journeys' end. ❖ [Q 35:18]

❖O you who believe! If you help (the cause of) God, He will help you, and will make firm your steps. [7] As for those who are bent on denying the Truth, ill-fortune awaits them, since He will let all their (good) deeds go to waste. [8] It is because they hate (the very thought of) what God has bestowed from on high – and thus He causes all their deeds to come to naught! [9] ❖ [Q 47:7-9]

❖And those who believed and whose descendants followed them in faith - We will join with them their descendants, and We will not deprive them of anything of their deeds. Every person, for what he earned, is retained.❖ [Q 52:21]

❖… no soul shall be made to bear another's burden, [38] and man will only have what he has worked towards. [39] ❖ [Q 53:38-39]

❖Now when Moses spoke to his people, [it was this same truth that he had in mind:] "O my people! Why do you cause me grief, the while you know that I am an apostle of God sent to you?" And so, when they swerved from the right way, God let their hearts swerve from the

Truth: for God does not bestow His guidance upon iniquitous folk. [Q 61:5]

These are examples of so many verses in the Holy Quran that establish the measures by which the consequences of our deeds will be established and impact our destiny. As mentioned earlier, these are in The Book and God can modify or confirm them as He Wills.

3-1-2 Universal Measures

These types of measures establish the systems by which God orders the Universe, such as night and day, the phases of the Moon, the seasons of the year, weather patterns, etc..

He it is Who has made the sun a [source of] radiant light and the moon a light (reflected), and has determined for it phases so that you might know how to compute the years and to measure (time). None of this has God created without (an inner) Truth. Clearly does He spell out these messages to people of (innate) knowledge: [Q 10:5]

And the moon - We have set the measure for its phases, until it returns (appearing) like an old date stalk. [Q 36:39]

... and We caused the earth to burst forth with springs, such that the waters met for a matter already set by measures. [Q 54:12]

And God set (the extent of) the measures of the night and the day. [Q 73:20]

3-2 Manifestation of the Measures: Qaddaa

The following three verses show that when God Wills to manifest any measure, He commands it to 'Be' and it is. This is Qaddaa, or the measure made manifest. Once it is manifested, it is God's Will. How it is manifested, and in what form, depends upon His infinite Wisdom and Mercy.

He it is Who gives life and causes death; and when He decrees a matter, He but says to it, "Be," and it is. [Q 40:68]

His Command (His Being alone is such) when He Wills a thing to be, is that He says only to it, "Be," and it is. [82] Exalted is He in Whose Hand is the dominion over all things, and to Him you all will be returned! [83] [Q 36:82-83]

God's divine Mercy is limitless, and even after a measure is decreed, our supplications and prayers will help to prevent bad results from coming out of it, as shown in the Hadith below.

Thawban (may God be pleased with him) narrated that the Messenger of God (pbuh) said, "Nothing increases one's life-span except righteousness and nothing repels the Divine Decree except supplication, and a man may be deprived of sustenance by a sin that he commits."[1]

Abdullah ibn `Umar (may God be pleased with him) narrated that the Messenger of God (pbuh) said: "The supplication benefits against that which has been pre-determined, but not yet realized, so hold fast, O worshippers of God, to supplication." [2]

3-3 The Divine Book

God rules the Universe with His infinite Wisdom and utmost Perfection, and every aspect of every event is recorded. In The Book in which the measures are set, our actions are also recorded. God will confirm or eliminate whatever is in The Book, and the following verses show how vastly comprehensive this book is.

❖*God eliminates what He Wills or confirms, and with Him is the Mother of the Book.* ❖ *[Q 13:39]*

❖*And the Book (of deeds) will be placed (open), and you will see the criminals fearful of that within it, and they will say, "Oh, woe to us! What is this book that leaves nothing small or great except that it has enumerated it?" And they will find what they did present (before them). And your Lord does injustice to no one.* ❖ *[Q 18:49]*

❖*This, Our Book, speaks of you in all Truth: for, truly, We have caused to be recorded all that you ever did!"* ❖ *[Q 45:29]*

❖*And (O Muhammad), you are not (engaged) in any matter or recite any of the Qur'an, and you (people) do not do any deed except that We are Witness over you when you are involved in it. And not absent from*

---

(1) The speaker: al-Suyuti – Source: al-Jaami' al-Kabîr – page or number: 4262. Conclusion of the speaker: sound

(2) The speaker: Tirmidhi – Source: Sunan al-Tirmidhi – page or number: 3548. Conclusion of the speaker: Weird, do not know, only from the hadith of 'Abd al-Rahman ibn Abu Bakr, a weak hadith

your Lord is any (part) of an atom's weight within the earth or within the heaven or (anything) smaller than that or greater but that it is in a clear Book. ✾ [Q 10:61]

✾And God created you from dust, then from a sperm-drop; then He made you mates. And no female conceives nor does she give birth except with His knowledge. And no aged person is granted (additional) life nor is his lifespan lessened but that it is in a Book. Indeed, that for God is easy. ✾ [Q 35:11]

✾And there is no creature on earth but that from God is its provision, and He knows its place of dwelling and its final resting place. All is in a clear Book. ✾ [Q 11:6]

✾No disaster strikes the earth or among yourselves except that it is (recorded) in a Book before We bring it into being - indeed that, for God, is easy [22] In order that you not despair over what has passed you by, and not exult (in pride) over what He has given you. And God does not love those who are self-deluded and boastful. [23] ✾ [Q 57:22-23]

✾And with Him are the keys of the Unseen; none knows them except Him. And He knows what is on the land and in the sea. Not a leaf falls but that He knows it. And no grain is there within the darknesses of the earth and no moist or dry (thing) but that it is (written) in a clear Book.✾ [Q 6:59]

✾ (It will be said), "Read your Book. Sufficient are you against yourself this Day as accountant."✾ [Q 17:14]

✾But those who disbelieve say, "The Hour will not come to us." Say, "Yes, by my Lord, it will surely come to you. (God is) the Knower of the Unseen." Not absent from Him is an atom's weight within the heavens or within the earth or (what is) smaller than that or greater, except that it is in a clear Book. ✾ [Q 34:3]

✾Ha. Meem. [1] By the clear Book, [2] Indeed, We have made it an Arabic Quran that you might understand. [3] And indeed it is, in the Mother of the Book with Us, exalted and full of wisdom[4]✾ [Q43:1-4]

3-4 Trials are Divine Measures

We have explained the measures, manifestation of the measures, and how everything is recorded in The Book. This gives us the background to understand why we go through tests in life and why it is so important to accept God's Will and understand these tests in the right context. We are put on earth to be tested by God, and our life is a series of tests, great and small, good and bad.

We test you (all) through the bad and the good (things in life) by way of trial: and to Us you will all be returned. [Q 21:35]

Truly, it is We Who have created man from a drop of sperm intermingled, so that We might try him; and therefore We made him a being endowed with hearing and sight. [Q 76:2]

But as for man, whenever his Lord tries him by His generosity and by letting him enjoy a life of ease, he says, "My Lord has been (justly) generous towards me." [15] But whenever He tries him by straitening his means of livelihood, he says, "My Lord has disgraced me!" [16] But no (O men)! Consider all that you do and fail to do: you are not generous towards the orphan, [17] and you do not urge one another to feed the needy, [18] and you devour the inheritance (of others) with devouring greed, [19] and you love wealth with boundless love! [20] [Q 89:15-20]

God the Almighty, in His system of divine justice, represented by what He has decreed and manifested, sets us trials of poverty and wealth, sickness and health, fear and security, lack and abundance, and in that which we love and hate, all of these are trials, through which we are tested throughout our lives.

God may try you with misfortune, or with His blessings, and with wealth or poverty. God created mankind to test him.

3-4-1 Types of Trials

3-4-1-1 Trials for the purpose of establishing one's rank in the Hereafter

The verses below show that the tests or trials we go through in this life will be the basis for our rank on the Day of Judgement.

❝... *Did you think that you could enter Paradise (the Garden) without God knowing those among you who strived (in His cause) and without knowing those who were patient in adversity?* ❞ [Q 3:142]

❝*And it is He Who has entrusted you as vicegerents upon the earth and raised some of you above others in degrees (of rank), so that He might try you by means of what He has bestowed upon you. Truly your Lord is Swift in retribution, and truly He is Forgiving, Merciful.* ❞ [Q 6:165]

❝*Indeed, We have willed that all beauty on the earth be a means by which We put men to a test, (showing) which of them are best in conduct. [7] And truly, (in time) We shall reduce all that is on it (the earth) to a barren plain. [8]* ❞ [Q 18:7-8]

❝*Do men think that on their (mere) saying, "We have attained to faith", they will be left to themselves and will not be put to a test? [2] Yes, indeed, We tested those who lived before them, and so (too) will God certainly mark out those who prove themselves true from those who are liars. [3]* ❞ [Q 29:2-3]

These verses show that those who are believers, being patient and persevering during the trials God has set, are worthy of going to His Paradise.

The second aspect of testing is to strengthen our faith, forgive our sins and raise our rank in the Hereafter.

Muhammad ibn Khalid as-Sulami, on his father's authority (may God be pleased with them) said his grandfather reported that a Companion of the Prophet of God (Pbuh) said: "I heard the Prophet of God (Pbuh) say: "When God has previously decreed for one of His servants a rank which he has not been able to attain by his deeds alone, He afflicts him in his body, or his property or his children. God will then give him the patience to endure the affliction, until he attains the rank previously decreed for him by God." [1]

❝*We called out to him, "O Abraham! [104] You have been true to the vision." Thus indeed do We recompense the virtuous. [105] Truly this was the manifest trial. [106]* ❞ [Q 37:104-106]

---

(1) The speaker: al-Albani – Source: Sahih Abu Dawood – page or number: 3090. Conclusion of the speaker: sound.

❀ *... and most certainly We shall try you all, so that We might mark out those of you who strive (in Our cause) and are patient in adversity: for We shall test (the truth of) all your assertions.* ❀ *[Q 47:31]*

3-4-1-2 Forgiveness of sins and increasing one's rank in the Hereafter

❀ *And most certainly shall We try you by means of fear, hunger, loss of worldly goods, of lives and of the fruits of your labour. But give glad tidings to those who are patient in adversity [155] who, when disaster strikes them, say, "Indeed we belong to God, and indeed to Him we will return." [156]* ❀ *[Q 2:155-156]*

❀ *(But) do you think that you could enter Paradise without having suffered like those (believers) who passed away before you? Misfortune and hardship befell them, and so shaken were they that the apostle, and the believers with him, exclaimed, "When will God's help come?" Unquestionably, God's help is ever near!* ❀ *[Q 2:214]*

❀ *If a wound should afflict you, (know that) a similar wound has afflicted the (opposing) people as well; for it is by turns that We apportion to men such days (of fortune and misfortune) so that God may mark out those who believe and choose from among you such as (with their lives) bear witness to the Truth, since God does not love wrongdoers.* ❀ *[Q 3:140]*

❀ *You shall most certainly be tried in your possessions and in yourselves. And indeed you will surely hear much hurt from those who were given the Scripture before you and from those who associate others with God. But if you are patient and remain conscious of God, then this indeed is something to set one's heart upon.* ❀ *[Q 3:186]*

❀ *(Solomon said) ... "This is by the grace of my Lord, to test me as to whether I am grateful or ungrateful! And if any is grateful (to God), truly his gratitude is (again) for his own soul; and he who is ungrateful (should know that), truly my Lord is Self-Sufficient, Most Generous!"* ❀ *[Q 27:40]*

The above group of verses clearly show that tests and trials are the means by which God gives us ample opportunities to strengthen our patience and faith and make us stronger believers.

Sa'ad ibn Abu Waqqas (may God be pleased with him) narrated that he had asked the Prophet (pbuh): 'O Messenger of God, which people are most severely tried?' He (pbuh) replied: 'The Prophets, then the next best, and the next best. A person is tried according to his religious commitment. If he is steadfast in his religious commitment, he will be tried more severely, and if he is frail in his religious commitment, his trial will be according to his commitment. Trials will continue to afflict a person until he is left walking on the earth with no sin on him.'" [1]

Anas ibn Malik (may God be pleased with him) narrated that the Messenger of God (pbuh) said: "The greatest reward comes with the greatest trial. When God loves a people, He tries them. Whoever accepts this wins His contentment, but whoever is discontent with this earns His discontent." [2]

Muawiya ibn Qurrah (may God be pleased with him) narrated that his father said: "When the Prophet of God (pbuh) sat down, some of his Companions would sit with him. Among them was a man who had a young son who used to approach him from behind, and he would make him sit in front of him. The child died, and the father stopped attending the circle because it reminded him of his son and made him feel sad. The Prophet (pbuh) missed the father and said: 'Why do I not see so-and-so?' They said: 'O Messenger of God, his son whom you saw has died.' The Prophet (pbuh) met the father and asked him about his son, and he told him (pbuh) that he had died. He (pbuh) offered his condolences and said: 'O so-and-so, which would you like better, to enjoy his company all your life, or to come to any of the gates of Paradise on the Day of Resurrection, and find that he has arrived there before you, and he is opening the gate for you?' The father replied: 'O Prophet of God! For him to get to the gate of Paradise before me and open it for me is dearer to me.' He (pbuh) said: 'You will have that.'" [3]

---

(1) The speaker: Tirmidhi – Source: Sunan al-Tirmidhi – page or number: 2398. Conclusion of the speaker: fair and sound.

(2) The speaker: al-Albani – Source: Sahih ibn Majah – page or number: 2396. Conclusion of the speaker: sound.

(3) The narrator: Qurrah ibn Ayas al-Mazni – the speaker: al-Albani – Source: Sahih al-Nasa'i – page or number: 2087. Conclusion of the speaker: sound.

Abu Musa al-Ash'ari (may God be pleased with him) reported: "The Messenger of God (pbuh) said, "When a man's child dies, God the Exalted asks His angels, 'Have you taken the life of the child of My servant?' and they reply in the affirmative. He (all praise is due to Him alone) then asks, 'Have you taken the dearest thing to his heart?' and they reply in the affirmative. Thereupon He asks, 'What did my servant say?' They reply: 'He praised You and said, 'We belong to God and to Him we shall return.' God says: 'Build a house for my servant in Paradise and name it The House of Praise." [1]

Suhaib (may God be pleased with him) reported that God's Messenger (pbuh) said: "The ways of believers are a wonder, for there is good in every affair of theirs, but this is not the case with anyone else except in the case of believers, for if they have an occasion to feel delight, they thank God, thus there is good in it for them, and if they get into trouble and show resignation (and endure it patiently), there is good in it for them." [2]

Anas ibn Malik (may God be pleased with him) narrated that he heard God's Messenger (pbuh) say, "God said, 'If I deprive my servant of his eyesight and he remains patient, I will let him enter Paradise in compensation for it.'" [3]

Anas ibn Malik (may God be pleased with him) reported: "We went with God's Messenger (pbuh) to the blacksmith, Abu Saif, whose wife was the wet-nurse of Ibrahim, son of the Prophet (pbuh). God's Messenger (pbuh) took Ibrahim and kissed him and smelled him; later we entered Abu Saif's house and, at that time, Ibrahim was dying, and the eyes of God's Messenger (pbuh) started shedding tears. `Abd al-Rahman ibn `Auf said, 'O Apostle of God, even you are weeping!' He (pbuh) said, 'O ibn `Auf, this is mercy.' Then he (pbuh) wept more and said, "The eyes shed tears and the heart grieves,

---

(1) The speaker: Tirmidhi – Source: Sunan al-Tirmidhi – page or number: 1021. Conclusion of the speaker: fair but strange.
(2) The speaker: Muslim – Source: Sahih Muslim – page or number: 2999. Conclusion of the speaker: sound.
(3) The speaker: al-Bukhari – Source: Sahih al-Bukhari – page or number: 5653. Conclusion of the speaker: sound.

and we will say only what pleases our Lord. O Ibrahim! Indeed we are grieved by your separation." [1]

3-4-1-3 Repentance

God tries us so that the ones who go astray can repent, mend their ways and come closer to Him in faith.

❖And We dispersed them throughout the earth as (separate) communities. Some of them were righteous, and some of them less than that. And the latter We tried with blessings as well as with afflictions so that they might mend their ways (return to obedience).❖ [Q 7:168]

❖If God had so willed, He could surely have made you all one single community (united in religion), but (He willed it otherwise) in order to try you by means of what He has given you. Compete, then, with one another in doing good works! To God you all will return, and then He will make you truly understand all that on which you used to differ.❖ [Q 5:48]

❖Corruption has appeared throughout the land and sea by (reason of) what men's hands have done. So He may let them taste part of (the consequences of) what they have done that perhaps they will return (to righteousness).❖ [Q 30:41]

❖And know that your property and your children are a test, and that with God is an immense reward.❖ [Q 8:28]

Tests and trials have four basic functions: firstly to see if you are worthy of being accepted into Paradise. Secondly, to strengthen your faith so that you can succeed in the various tests. Thirdly, so that God can forgive your sins and increase your rank in the Hereafter, and fourthly, so that you might repent and mend your ways.

Anas ibn Malik (may God be pleased with him) reported that the Messenger of God (pbuh) said, "When God intends good for His servant, He tests him in this world, but when He does not intend good

---

(1) The speaker: al-Bukhari – Source: Sahih al-Bukhari – page or number: 1303. Conclusion of the speaker: sound.

for His servant, He delays taking him to task, calling him to account on the Day of Resurrection." [1]

3-5 Summary and Conclusions

Believing in God's Mercy and Wisdom, and that He sets His measures before anything is manifested, is a source of contentment for the believer, and that God's measures are set for his own good, coming from the Most Merciful and Wise. He should maintain his prayer that these measures will be manifested for his highest good, and that God can modify or confirm these measures as a response to our actions. All the trials we go through in life are part of these measures, manifested as part of God's Will to strengthen our faith, reward us in the Hereafter, or increase our rank by proving our patience and perseverance. We should always keep in mind, and reflect on the truth that, in the final judgment, everything will be counted; we need to do our best to be victorious on that Day.

… in order that you not despair over what has eluded you and not exult (in pride) over what He has given you. And God does not love those who are proud and boastful. [Q 57:23]

Once believers know that all they are going through in this life is a series of tests, and what counts is their rank in the Hereafter, they will be able to deal with all the trials in their lives, be content with the outcome, and focus on doing only those deeds that bring the best for them in the here and the Hereafter.

For our deeds to produce the desired outcome, they should be done with sincerity, and only for the cause of God, while placing our whole trust in God's Compassion, Mercy and Wisdom. This leads us to the topic of the next chapter, which is sincerity and trusting in God.

… And it is God (alone) Who manifests and implements all His measures perfectly. [Q 18:45]

---

(1) The speaker: Tirmidhi – He said: fair but strange – Refer to: Sunan al-Tirmidhi – Hadith number: 2507.

Chapter 4

Sincerity and
Putting Our Trust in God

❝So call upon Him, devoting religion entirely to Him.❞
[Q 40:65]

*❝... not recompensing any for a favor thereby; [19] save
for seeking the Face of his Lord, the Most High, [20] and
surely he shall be content. [21] ❞ [Q 92:19-21]*

*❝... consult them in affairs. And when you are resolved,
trust in God; truly God loves those who trust. [159] If
God helps you, none shall overcome you ...[160] ❞
[Q 3:159-160]*

بِسْمِ اللَّهِ الرَّحْمَنِ الرَّحِيمِ

﴿ وَمَا لِأَحَدٍ عِنْدَهُ مِنْ نِعْمَةٍ تُجْزَى إِلَّا ابْتِغَاءَ وَجْهِ رَبِّهِ الْأَعْلَى وَلَسَوْفَ يَرْضَى ﴾

فمن أمري إلى الله إن الله بصير بالعباد

فادعوه مخلصين له الدين

ومن يتوكل على الله فهو حسبه

صدق الله العظيم

Fig. 1: The Structure of Chapter 4

4-0 Introduction

All believers should be dedicated to God alone and not set up any partner(s) with Him in their deeds. Their work should be sincerely for Him only. God has promised that such deeds will be rewarded with contentment, as mentioned in so many places in the Holy Quran, such as Verses 19 to 21 in Chapter 92 shown below. Moreover, many hadith included in this chapter show the same. The deeds that are accepted by God are those done sincerely for Him. This is the sign of believers who put all their trust in God and rely completely on Him; He will then give them His unlimited support, as He has promised.

Sincerity lies in the heart, and every deed the believer performs should be dedicated only to God. This is what is meant by 'Tawhid' or purity of faith, when you do not set up any partner with God, that He is the One God, and you perform all your deeds for Him alone. Those who have purity of faith will be among the 70,000 who will enter Paradise without being questioned. God has set a condition for accepting our deeds, earning His contentment, and putting our trust in Him. Sincerity of deeds and the rewards for this are peace of mind, tranquility of heart, and becoming closer to God.

Sincerity in worship includes prayers, fasting, charity, performing the major pilgrimage (hajj), striving against one's worldly desires, repentance, praying for forgiveness, reading the Holy Quran – whatever deeds you do to be closer to God – as well as adhering to the highest moral values – practising modesty, and putting your complete trust in God. All these deeds should be done to please God, earn His reward, and gain His contentment.

4-1 Sincerity in the Holy Quran

❦*So call upon Him, devoting religion entirely to Him.*❧ *[Q 40:65]*

❦*... not recompensing any for a favour thereby; [19] save for seeking the Face of his Lord, the Most High, [20] and surely he shall be content. [21]*❧ *[Q 92:19-21]*

4-1-1 Quranic Verses Calling for Sincerity

❦*And who is better in religion than the one who submits his whole being to God, and is virtuous,* ❧ *[Q 4:125]*

This means that you should always be sincere in your intentions and actions, and follow the traditions of the Prophet (pbuh). For those who do these things for the sake of God, He gives them glad tiding of a great reward in the Hereafter.

Say, ❀ "Truly my prayer and my sacrifice, my living and my dying are for God (alone), Lord of all the worlds. [162] He has no partner. This I am commanded, and I am the first of those who submit (to Him)." [163] ❀ [Q 6:162-163]

❀ Make your soul patient with those who call upon their Lord morning and evening, seeking His Face ... ❀ [Q 18:28]

❀ ... whoever hopes for the meeting with his Lord, let him perform righteous deeds and make no one a partner to his Lord in worship. ❀ [Q 18:110]

❀ Hence, give to the near of kin their right, and to the needy and the traveller; this is best for all who seek the Face of God. It is they who shall prosper. ❀ [Q 30:38]

For those who dedicate their deeds to God, and do good, they are the ones who will achieve the supreme triumph in the Hereafter and be safe from any punishment.

*❀ Indeed, We have sent down to you the Book in truth; so worship God, devoting religion entirely to Him. * Behold! To God belongs the pure religion, ❀ [Q 39:2-3]*

Say [O Muhammad], "Indeed, I have been commanded to worship God, [being] sincere to Him in religion. ❀ [Q 39:11]

Because of the importance of the virtue of sincerity, it has been mentioned so many times in the Holy Qur'an, and some of these verses are given below.

Say, ❀ "God do I worship, devoting my religion entirely to Him (alone). ❀ [Q 39:14]

❀ So call upon God, devoting religion entirely to Him, though the disbelievers oppose it. ❀ [Q 40:14]

❖*... and be rewarded only according to your deeds. [39] For God's sincere servants [40] shall have a known provision – [41] fruits of various kinds; and they shall be honoured, [42] in the Gardens of Bliss ... [43]* ❖ [Q 37:39-43]

❖*They were not commanded but to worship God, devoting religion entirely to Him.* ❖ [Q 98:5]

Sincerity is the foundation of true religion – where one does everything in the name of God, and this sincerity includes everything in Islam, from sacrificial offerings to prayers, giving charity, going for pilgrimage, and all other deeds. In Islam, if one intends to do a good deed, but is unable to carry it out for a reason beyond his control, God will reward him the same as if he had carried it out. The basis for these deeds being accepted by God is one's sincerity and good intention. There are several Hadith in the Prophet's Tradition that emphasize this, saying that God accepts only those deeds that are dedicated to Him.

4-2 Sincerity in the Prophetic Traditions (Hadith)

Umar ibn al-Khattab (may God be pleased with him) narrated that he heard the Prophet (pbuh) say, "The reward for deeds depends on one's intentions, and every person will get their reward according to what they intend. So whoever emigrated for worldly benefits or to marry a woman, his emigration was for what he emigrated for." [1]

Abu Hurairah (may God be pleased with him) reported that God's Messenger (pbuh) said: "Truly, God does not look at your face and how you look, but He looks into your heart and your deeds." [2]

Abu Hurairah (may God be pleased with him) narrated that the Messenger of God (pbuh) said: "No worshipper has ever said, 'There is no deity but God' with sincere devotion, but that the gates of Heaven are opened for it, until it reaches the Throne, so long as he avoids the major sins." [3]

---

(1) The speaker: al-Bukhari – Source: Sahih al-Bukhari – page or number: 1. Conclusion of the speaker: sound.

(2) The speaker: Muslim – Source: Sahih Muslim – page or number: 4651. Conclusion of the speaker: sound.

(3) The speaker: Tirmidhi – Source: Sunan al-Tirmidhi – page or number: 3590. Conclusion of the speaker: fair but strange from this side.

Abu Hurairah (may God be pleased with him) narrated that he asked the Prophet (pbuh): "O God's Apostle! Who will be the luckiest person to gain your intercession on the Day of Resurrection?" God's Apostle (pbuh) answered, 'O Abu Huraira! I have thought that none will ask me about it before you, as I know your longing for the (learning of) Hadith. The luckiest person who will have my intercession on the Day of Resurrection will be the one who says with sincere devotion, from the bottom of his heart, 'There is no deity but God.'" [1]

As can be seen from these verses and hadith, performing good deeds with sincerity and with the intention of pleasing God, will be a source of great reward.

Sa'ad ibn Abu Waqqas (may God be pleased with him) narrated that he heard God's Messenger (pbuh) say, "You will be rewarded for whatever you spend for God's sake, even if it is a morsel of food which you put in your wife's mouth." [2]

Abu Hurairah (may God be pleased with him) reported that he heard the Prophet (pbuh) say: "When you pray over the dead, make a sincere supplication for them." [3]

4-3 Putting our Trust in God

Putting one's trust in God comes from being sincere in whatever you do, so that everything is done for the sake of God, and with God in mind. When you put your trust in God, you trust Him with all your affairs and believe that His choices are the best for you in terms of what is good for you and what is bad for you. This includes what you obtain as sustenance, recovering from sickness, easing of hardships, and whatever He bestows on you from His Bounty.

We put our trust in Him so that He will guide us to a virtuous life, full of good deeds and wise decisions, useful knowledge, contentment, and whatever is good for us in the here and the Hereafter. Placing our trust in God encompasses all our intentions and actions. The signs of putting our trust in God are that we know He will have the final say in

---

(1) The speaker: al-Bukhari – Source: Sahih al-Bukhari – page or number: 99. Conclusion of the speaker: sound.

(2) The speaker: al-Bukhari – Source: Sahih al-Bukhari – page or number: 56. Conclusion of the speaker: sound.

(3) The speaker: Ibn Hibban – Source: Bulugh al-Maram – page or number: 159. Conclusion of the speaker: sound.

everything, and whatever He has ordained and decreed will be for our own good. This is the way to earn God's contentment, as shown in the verses given below.

And take counsel with them in all matters of public concern; then, when you have decided upon a course of action, place your trust in God: for, truly, God loves those who place their trust in Him. [Q 3:159]

The fruit of sincerity and its signs are that you put all your trust in God, assign all your affairs to Him, and believe that only He can bring good and prevent misfortune from coming to you, including providing you with sustenance, support, healing if you are sick, easing of any difficulties, and all affairs of worldly benefit, including being guided in the world, acquiring useful knowledge, doing good deeds and being content.

Putting your complete trust in God is the best evidence of one's faith, and the form of worship which will be the source of all your good deeds. Imam Ahmed said, "Putting your trust and reliance in God is the work of the heart." Ibn El-Quim said, "Putting your trust and faith in God is the base and sum of all good deeds, from faith and every virtue in Islam. And the sign for it is that you think about God in a positive, trusting way." As Al-Hassan said, "The sign of putting your trust in God is that you rely only on Him." So trust in God and be sure that He is the foundation for trusting your affairs to Him, believing that no one can overrule it. Whenever God gives a share of His sustenance, knowledge, or any other Grace, that person will get it.

4-3-1 Trusting in God as mentioned in the Holy Quran

The Muslim prayer always starts by acknowledging that one puts one's trust in God, and seeks His help. Muslims have been ordered to consult with one another before deciding to do anything. Then they put their trust in God. People should therefore consult with one another, and with others who have knowledge and information, so they can fully understand the issue at hand, and the action that needs to be taken, while taking into consideration all relevant factors to understand the consequences of what they are about to do. After that, they leave the final outcome to God, and trust in His Mercy and Wisdom.

God loves those who put their trust in Him. Placing our full trust in Him is a characteristic of those with solid, pure faith, which will bring

God's Bounty and Grace, and God always keeps His promise. Trust only in God and no one else.

❖ It is You we worship and from You we seek help. ❖ [Q 1:5]

❖... to whom the people said, "Truly the people (the disbelievers) have gathered against you, so fear them." But it increased them (the believers) in faith, and they said, "God suffices us, an excellent Guardian is He!" [173] So they returned (from the battle) with Blessing and Bounty from God, untouched by evil. And they pursued the Contentment of God, and God is Possessed of Tremendous Bounty. [174] ❖ [Q 3:173-174]

❖... and trust in God. God suffices as a Guardian.❖ [Q 4:81]

❖... "Enter upon them by the gate (the 'hittah' gate), for once you have entered it, you will be victors. And trust in God, if you are believers." ❖ [Q 5:23]

❖(Prophet Shuaib said to his people) "... It is not for us to revert thereto unless God, our Lord, should will. Our Lord encompasses all things in (His infinite) Knowledge. In God do we trust ...❖ [Q 7:89]

Putting your trust in God has to be supported by your actions, and by deep faith in your heart. This is emphasized in the following Quranic verses.

❖Only they are believers whose hearts tremble with awe whenever God is mentioned, and when His signs are recited to them, they increase them in faith, and they trust in their Lord ... ❖ [Q 8:2]

❖And if they incline toward peace, you incline to it as well, and trust in God. Truly He is the All-Hearing, the All-Knowing. ❖ [Q 8:61]

❖Say (O Prophet), "Never can anything befall us save that which God has decreed for us! He is our Lord Supreme, and in God let the believers place their trust." ❖ [Q 9:51]

The intention to put your trust in God is considered to be a good deed and will be rewarded.

(Prophet Shuʿayb said to his people), ❖"I desire no more than to set matters aright so far as I am able; but my success lies with God Alone. In Him do I trust, and to Him do I always turn." ❖ [Q 11:88]

❖ *... And it is not for us (God's prophets) to bring you an authority, save by God's leave; so in God let the believers place their trust.* ❖ [Q 14:11]

❖ *... those who are patient and trust in their Lord.* ❖ [Q 16:42]

The virtue of putting one's complete trust in God is mentioned in so many places in the Quran, and God reminds the Prophet (pbuh) of this many times.

❖ *And trust in the Ever-Living, Who dies not ...* ❖ [Q 25:58]

The reward is that you gain a place in Paradise.

❖ *And those who believe and perform righteous deeds, We shall surely settle them in lofty dwellings of the Garden, with rivers running below, therein to abide. Excellent indeed is the reward for the workers (of righteousness), [58] those who are patient and trust in their Lord. [59]* ❖ [Q 29:58-59]

The following two verses mention part of the story of the believer who lived among the People of Pharaoh.

❖ *"... You will soon remember what I have said to you. I entrust my affair to God. Truly God sees (all) His servants." [44] So God shielded him (the believer) from the evils of that which they (Pharaoh and his followers) had plotted ... [45]* ❖ [Q 40:44-45]

❖ *And whosoever trusts in God, He suffices him.* ❖ [Q 65:3]

One will never attain a full comprehension of the Oneness of God unless one understands the critical importance of putting one's full and complete trust in God Alone, and no one else.

❖ *(He is the) Lord of the East and the West, there is no god but He, so take Him as your guardian.* ❖ [Q 73:9]

4-3-2 Trusting in God as mentioned in the Prophetic Traditions

Umar ibn al-Khattab (may God be pleased with him) narrated that the Messenger of God (pbuh) said: "If you trust in God as He should be trusted, then He will provide for you just as a bird is provided for; it goes out in the morning empty, and returns full." [1]

---

(1) The speaker: Tirmidhi – Source: Sunan al-Tirmidhi – page or number: 2344. Conclusion of the speaker: fair and sound. We know it only from this side.

Abdullah ibn Abbas (may God be pleased with him) reported that the Messenger of God (pbuh) said, "I was shown the past nations. I saw a prophet who had a very small group (less than ten in total) with him, another prophet who was accompanied by only one or two men and some did not have even one. Suddenly I was shown a huge crowd and I thought that they were my Ummah, but I was told: 'This is Moses and his people, but look towards the other side.' I looked and beheld a great assemblage. I was told: 'These are your people and amongst them there are seventy thousand who shall enter Paradise without being taken to account or tormented.' " Then the Prophet (pbuh) stood up and went into his dwelling, and the Companions began to guess who those people might be that would enter Paradise without any accounting or torment. Some said, 'Probably they are the ones who kept company with the Messenger of God (pbuh).' Others said, 'Probably they are the ones who have been born as Muslims and have never associated anyone with God in worship.' Then the Messenger of God (pbuh) came out and asked, "What are you discussing?" So they told him. He then said, "They are those who do not make 'Ruqyah' (blowing over themselves after reciting the Quran or some prayers and supplications the Prophet (pbuh) used to say, nor seek or perceive omens, i.e., they are not pessimistic) but place their trust in God." Upon hearing this, Ukashah ibn Mihsan stood up and said, 'Pray to God to make me one of them.' The Prophet (pbuh) said, "You are one of them." Then another man stood up and said the same thing. The Prophet (pbuh) answered, "Ukashah has surpassed you." [1]

Abdullah ibn Abbas (may God be pleased with him) narrated the following: "God is Sufficient for us and He suffices us" was said by (Prophet) Abraham (pbuh) when he was surrounded by the fire; and it was said by Muhammad (pbuh) when they (the hypocrites) said, *"Truly the people have gathered against you; therefore, fear them." But it increased them (Muhammad and his followers) in faith, and they said: "God suffices us, an excellent Guardian is He!" [Q 3:173]* [2]

---

(1) The speaker: al-Albani – Source: Sahih al-Jaami'– page or number: 3999. Conclusion of the speaker: sound.

(2) The speaker: al-Bukhari – Source: Sahih al-Bukhari – page or number: 4563. Conclusion of the speaker: sound.

Umm Salama, also known as Umm Al-Mu'minīn (may God be pleased with her) narrated the following: "The Apostle of God (pbuh) never went out of my house without raising his eyes to the sky and saying: 'In the name of God, I place my trust in God. O God! I seek refuge in You lest I stray or be led astray, or slip or be made to slip, or cause injustice, or suffer injustice, or do wrong, or have wrong done to me.'" [1]

Abdullah ibn Abbas (may God be pleased with him) reported that God's Messenger (pbuh) used to say: "O God, it is to You that I surrender myself. I affirm my faith in You, and repose my trust in You, and turn to You in repentance, and with Your help fight my adversaries. O God, I seek refuge in You with Your Power; there is no deity but You, lest You lead me astray. You are the Ever-Living and die not, while the jinn and mankind die." [2]

As an example of putting your trust in God, He advises believers what to do when they intend to travel to a place where there is disease or illness. If you are already in that place, you should not leave, so as not to spread the disease, but if you have not yet reached that place, do not enter it. This is the same as the present-day rules of quarantine.

A'isha, also known as Umm Al-Mu'minīn (may God be pleased with her) narrated that the Messenger of God (pbuh) said, "Whoever seeks God's contentment while the people are discontent, God will suffice him from the people. And whoever seeks the people's contentment by doing something with which God would be discontent, God will leave him to the people." [3]

Jabir ibn `Abdullah (may God be pleased with him) reported that God's Messenger (pbuh) used to teach them the way of doing 'Istikhara' (Istikhara means to ask God to guide one to the right sort of action concerning any job or deed), in all matters, as he taught us the Suras of the Qur'an. He (pbuh) said, "If anyone of you thinks of making an important decision, he should offer a two-rak'at prayer

---

(1) The speaker: Abu Dawood – Source: Sunan Abu Dawood – page or number: 5094. Conclusion of the speaker: No comment [He wrote a letter to the people of Mecca: Whenever I do not comment, it is accepted].

(2) The speaker: Muslim – Source: Sahih Muslim – page or number: 2717. Conclusion of the speaker: sound

(3) The speaker: al-Albani – Source: Sahih al-Jaami'– page or number: 6097. Conclusion of the speaker: sound.

other than the compulsory ones, and say (after the prayer): O God! I ask guidance from Your knowledge, and Power from Your Might, and I ask for Your great blessings. You are capable and I am not. You know and I do not, and You know the Unseen. O God! If You know that this decision is good for my religion and my subsistence and in my life in the Hereafter--(or said: If it is better for my present and later needs)--Then ordain it for me and make it easy for me to make (this decision), and then bless me in it, and if You know that this decision is harmful to me In my religion and subsistence and in the Hereafter--(or said: If it is worse for my present and later needs)--Then keep it away from me and let me be away from it. And ordain for me whatever is good for me, and make me satisfied with it. The Prophet (pbuh) added that then the person should name (mention) his need. [1]

Abu Hurairah (may God be pleased with him) narrated that God's Messenger (pbuh) said, "People will enter Paradise whose hearts are like the hearts of birds." [2]

Al-Bara ibn Azib (may God be pleased with him) reported, "The Messenger of God (pbuh) asked me to recite, whenever I go to bed: 'O God! I submit myself to You, I turn my face to You, and entrust my affairs to You; I seek Your support out of desire for You and fear of You, expecting Your reward and fearing Your punishment. There is no refuge and no place of safety from You but with You. I believe in the Book You have revealed and in the Prophet You have sent.' The Messenger of God (pbuh) then said that if anyone recites these words and dies that night, he will die in the true religion. In case he remains alive until the morning, he will be rewarded." [3]

4-4 Associating partners with God Nullifies one's Deeds

A very important concept in Islam is that if your action or deed is not sincere, there will be no reward for it. More importantly, if you set up a partner with God for what you do, you will get no reward for it. On the Day of Judgement, God will tell you to go and get your reward

---

(1) The speaker: al-Bukhari – Source: Sahih al-Bukhari – page or number: 1162. Conclusion of the speaker: sound.

(2) The speaker: Muslim – Source: Sahih Muslim – page or number: 2840. Conclusion of the speaker: sound.

(3) The speaker: al-Bukhari – Source: Sahih al-Bukhari – page or number: 7488. Conclusion of the speaker: sound.

from the partner you set up beside Him. If you put your trust in a partner with God, and he becomes your trustee, God will let it be between you and your trustee, and that will always end in great disappointment.

God emphasized this fact to the Prophet (pbuh), and safeguarded him from setting up any partner with Him.

Surely it has been revealed to you and to those before you that if you ascribe partners [to God], your work will surely become worthless, and you will be among the losers. [Q 39:65]

They were commanded only to worship God, devoting religion entirely to Him ... [Q 98:5]

The punishment for lack of sincerity in seeking knowledge for the sake of God is shown in the following Hadith.

Abu Hurairah (may God be pleased with him) narrated that the Prophet (pbuh) said: "If anyone acquires knowledge that should be sought seeking the Face of God, but acquires it only to get some worldly advantage, he will not experience the fragrance of Paradise." (1)

Abu Hurairah (may God be pleased with him) reported that he heard the Messenger of God (pbuh) say: "The first person against whom judgment will be pronounced on the Day of Resurrection will be a man who died as a martyr. He will be brought before God Who will make known to him His favours and he will recognize them. He (the Almighty) will say: 'And what did you do about them?' The man will say: I fought for You until I died a martyr.' He (the Almighty) will say: 'You have lied - you fought only that it might be said (of you): He is courageous. And so it was said.' Then he will be ordered to be dragged along on his face until he is cast into Hell-fire. (Another) will be a man who had studied (religious) knowledge and had taught it and who used to recite the Quran. He will be brought before God Who will make known to him His favours and he will recognize them. He (the Almighty) will then say: And what did you do about them? The man will say: I studied (religious) knowledge and taught it and recited the Quran for Your sake.' He (the Almighty) will say: 'You have lied - you did but study (religious)

---

(1) The speaker: Ibn Hibban – Source: Sahih Ibn Hibban – page or number: 3186. Conclusion of the speaker: he included it in Sahih Ibn Hibban.

knowledge that it might be said (of you): 'He is learned.' And you recited the Quran that it might be said (of you): 'He is a reciter.' And so it was said.' Then he will be ordered to be dragged along on his face until he is cast into Hell-fire. (Another) will be a man whom God had made rich and to whom He had given all kinds of wealth. He will be brought before God, Who will make known to him His favours and he will recognize them. He (the Almighty) will say: And what did you do about them? The man will say: 'I left no path (untrodden) in which You like money to be spent for Your sake.' He (the Almighty) will say: 'You have lied - you did but do so that it might be said (of you): 'He is open-handed.' And so it was said. Then he will be ordered to be dragged along on his face until he is cast into Hell-fire. (This was also related by Muslim, al-Tirmidhi and al-Nasa'i). [1]

During his reporting of this Hadith, Abu Hurairah was about to faint, so he took a drink of water frequently so that he could finish narrating the Hadith.

Abdullah ibn ʿUmar (may God be pleased with him) narrated that he heard the Messenger of God (pbuh) say, "Whoever seeks knowledge in order to argue with the foolish, or to show off before the scholars, or to attract people's attention, will end up in Hell." [2]

Sincerity purifies the heart from evil, jealousy and anger, and will cause one's deeds to be accepted by God. Through sincerity you purify your soul and free it from negative and harmful thoughts, and consequently you will not set up partners with God in any of your deeds. Therefore, seek all your reward from God alone.

Abu 'Umamah al-Bahili (may God be pleased with him) reported: "A man came to the Prophet (pbuh) and asked, 'What do you think of a man who fights seeking reward and fame - what will he have?' The Prophet (pbuh) replied: 'He will not have anything.' He (pbuh) repeated it three times, and said again to him, 'He will not have anything.' Then he added: 'God does not accept any deed, except that which is devoted purely for Him, and seeking His Face.' " [3]

---

(1) The speaker: Muslim – Source: Sahih Muslim – page or number: 1905. Conclusion of the speaker: sound.

(2) The speaker: al-Albani – Source: Sahih al-Jaami'– page or number: 6382. Conclusion of the speaker: fair.

(3) The speaker: al-Albani – Source: Ahkam Janaza, "Funeral Rulings" – page or number: 70. Conclusion of the speaker: the chain of narrators is good.

Those who set up partners in their deeds, their deeds will be in vain, they will not be rewarded or recognized by God, and they will be counted against them. By setting up partners in your deeds, God will make such deeds of no benefit to you and one will gain nothing from them. The only deeds you will have counted to your credit on the Day of Judgement will be those that were done for the sake of God and done under His Guidance.

Mahmoud ibn Labīd al-Ansari (may God be pleased with him) reported that the Messenger of God (pbuh) said: "Truly, what I fear most for you is the minor idolatry." They asked: "What is the minor idolatry, O Messenger of God?" He answered: "It is hypocrisy. When God the Exalted rewards people according to their deeds on the Day of Resurrection, He says to them: Go to those with whom you have practised hypocrisy for their sake during your lifetime and look at them. Do you find any reward with them?" [1]

Abu Saeed ibn Abu Fadalah al-Ansari, one of the Companions (may God be pleased with him), reported, "I heard the Messenger of God (pbuh) say: 'When God gathers [all] people on the Day of Judgment - a Day in which there is no doubt - a caller will announce: 'Whoever set up partners with God in any of the deeds he did for God - let him seek his reward from those partners. Truly, God is not in need of any partners." [2]

For those who are not sincere in their worship and do not do as they are supposed to do, their deeds will be nullified and they will gain nothing from them in the Hereafter.

Abu Hurairah (may God be pleased with him) reported that the Messenger of God (pbuh) said, "God, Glorious and Exalted is He, says: 'I am the Self-Sufficient and have no need for a partner. Thus he who does an action for that partner's sake as well as Mine, will have that action renounced by Me to him whom he associated with Me.' " It was also related by Muslim and Ibn Majah. [3]

---

(1) The speaker: al-Mundhiree – Source: al-Targhib Wat-Tarhib – page or number: 1/52. Conclusion of the speaker: the chain of narrators is good.

(2) The speaker: Tirmidhi – Source: Sunan al- Tirmidhi – page or number: 3154. Conclusion of the speaker: fair but strange. We only knew it from the saying of Muhammad ibn Bakr.

(3) The speaker: Muslim – Source: Sahih Muslim – page or number: 2985. Conclusion of the speaker: sound.

4-5 Summary and Conclusions

Sincerity is one of the most important virtues to reside in the heart and is a sign of those who worship the One God. Sincerity is also a condition for your deeds being accepted. Sincerity and trust in God are intertwined: putting your trust in God is a sign of sincerity and that you worship Him alone. It is also a sign that you trust in Him alone. This will result in your contentment with God and your striving to do more and more good deeds to attain a deeper level of faith and a higher rank in the Hereafter.

Abu Hurairah (may God be pleased with him) reported that the Messenger of God (pbuh) said, "Adhere to that which is beneficial for you. Keep seeking God's help and do not refrain from it." [1]

❖ *Truly he (Satan) has no authority over those who believe and trust in their Lord.* ❖ *[Q 16:99]*

❖ *... And whosoever trusts in God, He suffices him ...* ❖ *[Q 65:3]*

This chapter has focused on those Quranic verses and Prophetic Traditions (Hadith) which establish that all one's deeds should be dedicated to God alone, so that they will be accepted by Him and will cause Him to be contented with you. Consequently we will be content with Him. Trust will increase our faith and cause us to perform more good deeds, the most important of which is continuous remembrance of God, and this is the subject of the next chapter.

---

(1) The speaker: Muslim – Source: Sahih Muslim – page or number: 2664. Conclusion of the speaker: sound.

Chapter 5

Remembrance of God is Key to Contentment

❖Those who believe, and whose hearts find contentment in the remembrance of God – truly, it is in the remembrance of God that hearts find contentment.❖   [Q 13:28]

بِسْمِ اللَّهِ الرَّحْمَنِ الرَّحِيمِ

﴿فَاصْبِرْ عَلَى مَا يَقُولُونَ وَسَبِّحْ بِحَمْدِ رَبِّكَ قَبْلَ طُلُوعِ الشَّمْسِ وَقَبْلَ غُرُوبِهَا وَمِنْ آنَاءِ اللَّيْلِ فَسَبِّحْ وَأَطْرَافَ النَّهَارِ لَعَلَّكَ تَرْضَى﴾

يَا أَيُّهَا الَّذِينَ آمَنُوا صَلُّوا عَلَيْهِ وَسَلِّمُوا تَسْلِيمًا

أَلَا بِذِكْرِ اللَّهِ
تَطْمَئِنُّ الْقُلُوبُ

صَدَقَ اللَّهُ الْعَظِيمُ

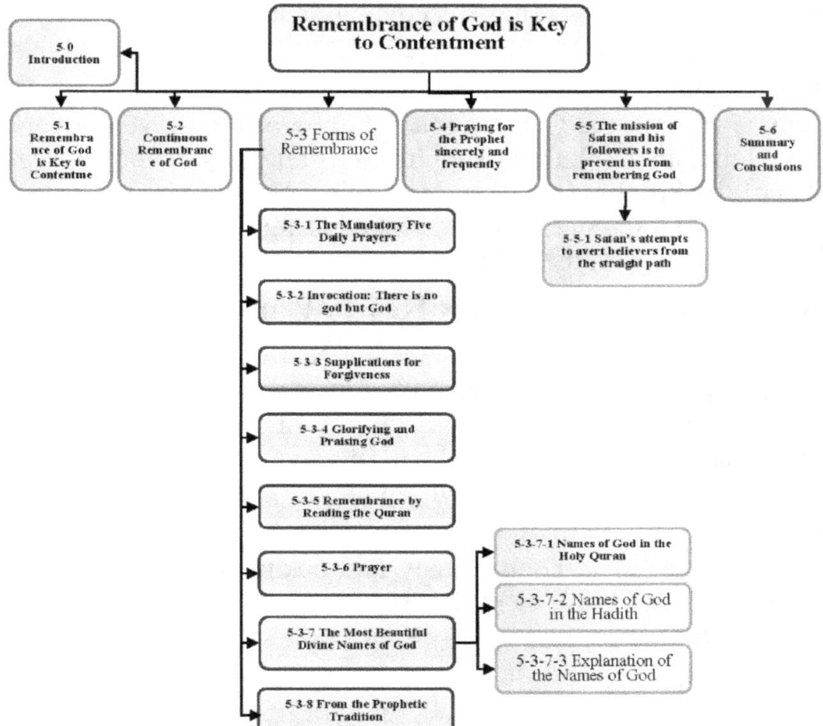

Fig. 1: The Structure of Chapter 5

5-0 Introduction

Remembrance (in Arabic: 'Dhikr') in Islam includes all the thoughts, words spoken, and good deeds done by the believer while remembering God and seeking His contentment.

This remembrance can be unspoken in the heart, or spoken aloud, and include good deeds done solely for the sake of pleasing God. They can include reading the Quran, reciting some of the prayers given by Prophet Muhammad (pbuh) or supplications reported by the household (family) of the Prophet (pbuh) or Muslim scholars. There are so many avenues to follow in continuously remembering God, and this chapter will outline them, with the goal of always being close to Him.

5-1 Remembrance of God is Key to Contentment

The nearer you are to God and His Mercy, the better a life of contentment you will be rewarded with. The closer to God you become, by practicing continuous remembrance, the further away you will be from Satan and his followers. God will bless you and protect you from evil, as outlined in the following Quranic verses and Prophetic Traditions.

Remembering God continuously and acknowledging His Grace, Mercy and Bounty will increase His blessings upon you and His contentment with you.

"... those who believe, and whose hearts find contentment in the remembrance of God, for truly it is in the remembrance of God that hearts find contentment. [28] Those who believe and perform righteous deeds, theirs is blessedness and a beautiful return. [29]" [Q 13:28-29]

And remember the Name of your Lord and devote yourself to Him with complete devotion. [Q 73:8]

... so remember Me, and I shall remember you; give thanks to Me, and do not deny Me. [Q 2:152]

... and all men and women who remember God unceasingly: for (all of) them has God readied forgiveness of sins and a mighty reward. [Q 33:35]

And when you have completed your (religious) rites, remember God as you remember your fathers or with (much) greater remembrance. [Q 2:200]

Abu Hurairah (may God be pleased with him) reported that Prophet Muhammad (pbuh) said that God, the Exalted and Glorious, stated, "I am near to the thought of My servant as he thinks about Me, and I am with him as he remembers Me. And if he remembers Me in his heart, I also remember him in My Mercy, and if he remembers Me in assembly I remember him in assembly, better than his (remembrance), and if he draws near Me by the span of an arm, I draw near him by a cubit, and if he draws near Me by a cubit I draw near him by the space of two hands. And if he walks towards Me, I run towards him."

[Note: A cubit is the span from one's elbow to the tip of one's outstretched fingers, approximately 17 to 20 inches.] [1]

A'isha, known as Umm Al-Mu'minīn [Mother of the Believers] (may God be pleased with her) narrated that Prophet Muhammad (pbuh) said, "Going around the House (the Ka'bah), running between Al-Safa and Al-Marwa (two small hills in Mecca) and stoning of the pillars, are meant for the remembrance of God." [2]

Abu Hurairah (may God be pleased with him) narrated that Prophet Muhammad (pbuh) stated that God the Exalted said, "O son of Adam! So long as you mention Me and are thankful to Me, you believe in Me; but if you forget about Me, then you disbelieve in Me." [3]

Abu Hurairah (may God be pleased with him) narrated that Prophet Muhammad (pbuh) said, "Whenever a group of people sit in a gathering remembering God, the angels surround them, mercy covers them, tranquillity descends upon them, and God remembers them among those who are with Him." [4]

Moez ibn Jabal (may God be pleased with him) narrated that Prophet Muhammad (pbuh) said, "For those people who are destined for

---

(1) The speaker: Muslim – Source: Sahih Muslim – page or number: 2675. Conclusion of the speaker: sound.

(2) The speaker: Abu Dawood – Source: Sunan Abu Dawood – page or number: 1888. Conclusion of the speaker: Did not comment [He wrote in his letter to the people of Mecca that whenever he did not comment, it is accepted].

(3) The speaker: al-Albani / Source: Silsalat al-Hadith ad-Da'ifah Page or number: 4041

(4) The speaker: ibn Hibban – Source: Sahih ibn Hibban – page or number: 855. Conclusion of the speaker: He included it in his Sahih Ibn Hibban.

Paradise, the only thing they will regret shall be one hour during their lifetime when they did not spend it in remembrance of God the Exalted." [1]

Abu Musa al-Ashari (may God be pleased with him) narrated that Prophet Muhammad (pbuh) said, "The example of one who remembers his Lord compared to one who does not remember Him, is that of a living creature compared to a dead one." [2]

5-2 Continuous Remembrance of God

Like any good deed the believer does, or intends to do, he should seek God's support to enable him to carry it out and keep doing more, as the Hadith given below shows. It was narrated by Abu Hurairah, who heard Prophet Muhammad (pbuh) say that the believer should pray to God to help him maintain his daily prayers. To continuously remember God requires patience, persistence, and discipline. This remembrance should be continuous throughout the day and night, as emphasized by the Quran in so many verses, some of which are given below. Remembrance as a continuous practice in the believer's heart and mind will bring him nearer to God, and further away from bad thoughts and deeds.

Abu Hurairah (may God be pleased with him), narrated that Prophet Muhammad (pbuh) said, "Do you like people to strive in the prayer and remembrance?" Say, 'O God, help us and enable us to thank You, remember You, and worship You in the best manner.' [3]

Hence, bear patiently that which they (who deny the truth) say, and extol your Lord's limitless glory and praise Him before the rising of the sun, and before its setting; and extol His glory in the hours of the night, and at the ends of the day, so that you may be content. [Q 20:130]

Hence, bear patiently that which they (deniers of the truth) say, and extol your Lord's limitless glory and praise before the rising of the sun

---

(1) The speaker: al-Suyuti – Source: al-Jaami' al-Saghir – page or number: 7682. Conclusion of the speaker: fair.

(2) The speaker: al-Bukhari – Source: Sahih al-Bukhari – page or number: 6407. Conclusion of the speaker: sound.

(3) The speaker: al-Albani / Source: Sahih al-Jami' Page or number: 18 / Conclusion of the speaker: sound.

and before its setting. [39] And at night extol His glory, and after prostrations (prayers). [40] ❧ *[Q 50:39-40]*

Praising God before sunrise refers to the dawn (Fajr) prayer, and before sunset refers to the afternoon (Asr) prayer.

Jarīr Abdullah (may God be pleased with him) narrated, "We were with Prophet Muhammad (pbuh) on a full moon night. He looked at the moon and said, 'You will certainly see your Lord as you see this moon, and there will be no trouble in seeing Him. So, if you can avoid missing (through sleep, business, etc.) the prayer before the rising of the sun (Fajr) and before its setting (Asr) you must do so. He (pbuh) then recited the following verse: 'And extol your Lord's limitless glory and praise before the rising of the sun and before its setting.'" (see Q 50:39) [1]

❧*And make your soul patient with those who call on their Lord morning and evening, seeking His countenance. And turn not your eyes away from them, desiring the adornments of the life of this world; nor obeying one whose heart We have made heedless of the remembrance of Us and who follows his own desires, and whose affair exceeds the limits.* ❧ *[Q 18:28]*

❧*... hence, be patient – for, truly, God's Promise is true – and ask forgiveness for your sins, and praise your Lord at sunset and at dawn.*❧ *[Q 40:55]*

❧*O mankind! There has now come to you an exhortation from your Lord, and a healing for that which lies within hearts, and a guidance and a mercy for the believers.* ❧ *[Q 10:57]*

The remembrance of God keeps you close to Him, and brings the grace of His protection and guidance. Turning thoughtlessly away from His remembrance will cause you to go astray and become vulnerable to Satan's temptations. God warns us against this lack of remembrance of Him and its consequences in the Quranic verse shown below. Believers should be very aware of this and do their utmost to remain in continuous remembrance of God, which will keep them on the straight path.

---

(1) The speaker: Muslim / Source: Sahih Muslim – page or number: 633 / Conclusion of the speaker: sound.

❀Whoever turns blindly away from the remembrance of the Compassionate, to him We assign a satan who is then a companion to him. ❀ [Q 43:36]

5-3 Forms of Remembrance

5-3-1 The Mandatory Five Daily Prayers

All Muslims should maintain their five daily prayers: at dawn, at mid-day, in the afternoon, at sunset, and at night (before bedtime). These mandatory five daily prayers are one of the five pillars of Islam. All Muslim scholars are agreed that they are an essential part of Islamic life that should be maintained all through their lives, just as Prophet Muhammad (pbuh) did, as mentioned in the verse shown below.

The prayers protect us from committing bad deeds and keep us in regular remembrance of God.

❀And when you have finished your prayer, remember God – standing and sitting and lying down; and when you are once again secure, observe your prayers (fully). Truly, for all believers, prayer is indeed a sacred duty linked to particular times (of day). ❀ [Q 4:103]

❀Recite that which has been revealed to you of the Book, and perform the prayer. Truly, prayer prevents against indecency and loathsome deeds, but the remembrance of God is surely greater. And God knows all that you do. ❀ [Q 29:45]

The importance of keeping the five daily prayers is also emphasized in various Prophetic Traditions (Hadith), as shown below.

Abdullah ibn Masood (may God be pleased with him) narrated that he asked Prophet Muhammad (pbuh), 'Which deeds are liked by God?' The Prophet (pbuh) answered: 'Prayer at its proper time.' I enquired further: "What next?" He (pbuh) replied, 'Then goodness to your parents.' I again asked: "What then?" He (pbuh) replied: 'Then striving (jihad) in the cause of God.' Abdullah added: "This is what I was told by the Prophet (pbuh). Had I questioned further, he (pbuh) would have told me more."[1]

---

(1) The speaker: Muslim – Source: Sahih Muslim – page or number: 85 Conclusion of the speaker: sound.

Performing the daily prayers is the second pillar of Islam, as detailed in the Hadith of Prophet Muhammad (pbuh), when he spoke about the five pillars of Islam. This Hadith is shown below.

Abdullah ibn Umar (may God be pleased with him) narrated that Prophet Muhammad (pbuh) said, "Islam is based on (the following) five (principles):

1. Testifying that none has the right to be worshipped but God, and that Muhammad is God's Messenger (pbuh).
2. Offering the prayers dutifully and perfectly.
3. Paying zakat (i.e. obligatory charity).
4. Fasting during the month of Ramadan.
5. Performing Hajj (i.e. pilgrimage to Mecca) [1]

Abu Hurairah (may God be pleased with him) narrated that Prophet Muhammad (pbuh) said, "Whoever keeps the five mandatory prayers is not one of the heedless, and one who reads, at night, one hundred verses, is not of the heedless, but is sincere, devoted and obedient to his Lord. Whoever prays with a hundred verses in his prayers, he is not from the heedless, and the one who prays with two hundred verses is sincere, devoted and obedient to his Lord." [2]

The importance of the daily prayers is not only limited to the Islamic nations, but also to the previous nations. One of the Ten Commandments given to Moses was to keep up prayer. Also, as shown in the Quran, one of the prayers of Prophet Abraham (pbuh) was to ask God to help him maintain his prayers and those of his children, as shown below.

❁ *(Prophet Abraham said), "My Lord, make me a performer of prayer, and my offspring. Our Lord! Accept my supplication."* ❁ *[Q 14:40]*

❁ *"Truly I am God; there is no deity but Me. So worship Me, and perform the prayer for the remembrance of Me.* ❁ *[Q 20:14]*

---

(1) The speaker: al-Bukhari – Source: Sahih al-Bukhari – page or number: 8. Conclusion of the speaker: sound.
(2) The speaker: al-Albani – Source: Sahih al-Targhib– page or number: 640. Conclusion of the speaker: sound.

5-3-2 Invocation: There is no god but God (La ilaha il Allah)

The words 'There is no god but God' (لا إله إلا الله) confirms the belief of Muslims and their submission to God, acknowledging that this is the way to Paradise and affirming their commitment to follow God's path, as outlined in the following Quranic verses and Hadith. They explain the rewards and blessings of affirming this fact continuously.

God is He other than Whom there is no deity: Knower of the Unseen and the seen. And He is the Compassionate, the Merciful. [Q 59:22]

Say, "He is the One God, [1] God the Eternal, the Uncaused Cause of All That Exists. [2] He begets not, and neither is He begotten; [3] and there is nothing that can be compared with Him." [4] [Q 112:1-4]

You alone do we worship; and from You do we seek help. [Q 1:5]

Abu Hurairah (may God be pleased with him) reported that he heard Prophet Muhammad (pbuh) say, "If one says, one hundred times in a day, 'None has the right to be worshipped but God, The Alone, Who has no partners; to Him belongs the Dominion, and to Him belongs all Praise, and He has power over all things (i.e. is Omnipotent),' one will get the reward of freeing ten slaves, and one hundred good deeds will be written in his account, and one hundred bad deeds will be erased from his account, and on that day he will be protected from the morning until the evening from Satan, and nobody will be superior to him except one who has done more than that which he has done."[1]

Ubada ibn al-Samit (may God be pleased with him) narrated that he heard Prophet Muhammad (pbuh) say, "Whoever gets up at night and recites: 'None has the right to be worshipped but God. He is the Only One and has no partners. For Him is the Kingdom and all praise. He is Omnipotent. All praise is for God alone. All glory is for God alone. God is the Greatest, and there is neither might nor power except with God' and then says, 'O God! Forgive me', or invokes God,

---

(1) The speaker: al-Bukhari – Source: Sahih al-Bukhari – page or number: 6403. Conclusion of the speaker: sound.

he will be responded to and if he performs ablution and prays, his prayer will be accepted."(1)

5-3-3 Supplications for Forgiveness

When believers pray for forgiveness, requesting from God that their sins be forgiven, they should have the sincere intention of repenting, and trying to avoid any shortcomings on their part towards God. It is a prayer for forgiveness of such things as actions they took that they should not have taken, or actions they neglected to do, but should have done. This requires humility to acknowledge one's shortcomings and wrong-doing, with the intention of not repeating actions one regrets having taken.

There are many examples of prayers for forgiveness, and the following verses show some of them.

Supplications for Forgiveness in the Quran

❖*They (Adam and his wife) replied, "Our Lord, we have wronged ourselves. If You do not forgive us and have mercy on us, we shall most certainly be among the losers."* ❖ *[Q 7:23]*

❖*And (remember) Dhu'l-Nūn (Prophet Jonah) when he departed in anger; he imagined that We had no power over him. But then he cried out in the darkness, "There is no deity but You! Glory be to You! Truly I have been among the wrongdoers."* ❖ *[Q 21:87]*

❖*... and who, when they commit an indecency or wrong themselves, remember God and then seek forgiveness for their sins – and who forgives sins but God? - and who do not knowingly persist in what they have done.* ❖ *[Q 3:135]*

❖*Whoever does evil or wrongs himself, and thereafter seeks forgiveness of God, he shall find God Oft-Forgiving, Most Merciful.* ❖ *[Q 4:110]*

Another important aspect of praying for forgiveness, and being sincerely repentant, is that God has promised mankind rewards in various forms, such as increased sustenance, children, or rain as part of his Mercy and Kindness, especially for those who pray for forgiveness as shown in the following Quranic verses:

---

(1) The speaker: al-Bukhari – Source: Sahih al-Bukhari – page or number: 1154. Conclusion of the speaker: sound.

❧ *"I (Prophet Noah) said, 'Seek forgiveness from your Lord! Truly, He is Oft-Forgiving! [10] He will send the sky upon you with abundant rains, [11] support you with wealth and children, and make for you gardens and rivers.' " [12]* ❧ *[Q 71:10-12]*

❧ *Know, then, (O man,) that there is no deity save God, and (while there is yet time,) ask forgiveness for your sins and for (the sins of) all other believing men and women: for God knows all your comings and goings as well as your abiding (at rest).* ❧ *[Q 47:19]*

❧ *Little of the night did they sleep, [17] and before dawn they would seek forgiveness. [18]* ❧ *[Q 51:17-18]*

Examples of Prophet Muhammad's Prayers for Forgiveness

Abu Ayyub al-Ansari (may God be pleased with him) reported that Prophet Muhammad (pbuh) said, "If you were not to commit sins, God would have swept you out of existence and replaced you by another people who commit sins and then ask for forgiveness from God, and He would grant them pardon."[1]

Abu Hurairah (may God be pleased with him) narrated that Prophet Muhammad (pbuh) said, "Whoever sits in a gathering and engages in much empty, meaningless talk and then says, before getting up, 'Glory be to You, O God, and praise; I bear witness that there is none worthy of worship except You; I seek Your forgiveness, and I repent to You' - whatever occurred in that gathering would then be forgiven for him."[2]

Abu Hurairah (may God be pleased with him) reported that Prophet Muhammad (pbuh) said, "Our Lord, the Blessed and Exalted, descends every night to the lowest heaven when one-third of the latter part of the night still remains, and says, 'Who supplicates to Me so that I may answer him? Who asks Me so that I may give to him? Who asks Me for forgiveness so that I may forgive him?'"[3]

---

(1) The speaker: Muslim – Source: Sahih Muslim – page or number: 2748. Conclusion of the speaker: sound.
(2) The speaker: Tirmidhi – Source: Sunan al-Tirmidhi – page or number: 3433. Conclusion of the speaker: strange but sound from this side.
(3) The speaker: al-Albani – Source: Sahih al-Tirmidhi – page or number: 3498. Conclusion of the speaker: sound.

Shaddad ibn 'Aus (may God be pleased with him) narrated that he heard Prophet Muhammad (pbuh) say, "The most superior way of asking for forgiveness from God is to recite, 'O my Lord, there is no deity but You. You created me and I am Your servant. I will keep my covenant with You as much as I can. I acknowledge all Your Grace and Bounty, and also acknowledge all my sins. I seek refuge in You from all the evil I have done." If anyone recites this prayer during the night, and if he should then die, he will go to Paradise (or he will be from the people of Paradise). And if he recites it in the morning, and then dies on the same day, he will have the same fate."[1]

Abu Hurairah (may God be pleased with him) reported that Prophet Muhammad (pbuh) said, "I seek God's forgiveness and repent to Him one hundred times each day."[2]

Abada ibn al-Samit (may God be pleased with him) narrated that Prophet Muhammad (pbuh) said, 'Whoever prays for forgiveness of the believing men and believing women, God will reward him with a good deed for every one of whom he prayed for forgiveness. [3]

Abu Musa al-Ashari (may God be pleased with him) narrated that Prophet Muhammad (pbuh) said, "God sent down two guarantees of safety for the benefit of my Community (Ummah). And God will not punish them while you (the Prophet) are among them, nor will He punish them while they seek forgiveness (see Q 8:33). So when I (the Prophet) pass away, I leave seeking forgiveness among them until the Day of Resurrection."[4]

Abu Sa'eed al-Khudri (may God be pleased with him) narrated that the Prophet (pbuh) said, "Whoever says, when he goes to bed: 'I seek forgiveness from God, the Magnificent, the One other than Whom there is none worthy of worship except Him, the Ever-Living, the Ever-Sustaining, and I repent to Him' three times, God will forgive him

(1) The speaker: al-Bukhari – Source: Sahih al-Bukhari – page or number: 6323. Conclusion of the speaker: sound.
(2) The speaker: al-Bukhari – Source: Sahih al-Bukhari – page or number: 6307. Conclusion of the speaker: sound.
(3) The speaker: al-Albani / Source: Sahih al jami' Page or number: 6026 / Conclusion of the speaker: fair.
(5) The speaker: Tirmidhi – Source: Sunan al-Tirmidhi – page or number: 3082. Conclusion of the speaker: strange and Gharib bin Mohajer weakens the hadith.

his sins even if they are like the foam of the sea, even if they are as numerous as the leaves on the trees, even if they are as numerous as the sand particles of Alij (a huge extended valley of sand near Medina), even if they are as numerous as the days of the world."[1]

5-3-4 Glorifying and Praising God

- ♥ Glory be to God

- ♥ Praise be to God

- ♥ God is Great

- ♥ All knowledge and power belong to God

The seven heavens, and the earth, and all that they contain glorify Him and there is not a single thing but extols His limitless glory and praise: but you (O men) fail to grasp the manner of their glorifying Him! Truly, He is Oft-Forbearing, Ever-Forgiving! [Q 17:44]

And had he (Prophet Jonah) not been among those who glorify (God), [143] he would have remained inside its (the fish's) belly until the Day of Resurrection. [144] [Q 37:143-144]

Hence, (O believer), glorify your Lord's limitless Grace before the rising of the sun and before its setting. [39] And at night, glorify Him, and after prostrations (prayer). [40] [Q 50:39- 40]

... their supplication there (in Paradise) shall be, "Glory be to You, O God!" And therein their greeting shall be, "Peace!" And the conclusion of their supplication shall be, "Praise be to God, the Lord of all the worlds!" [Q 10:10]

So glory be to God when you enter upon the evening and when you rise in the morning. [17] His is the praise in the heavens and on the earth – when the sun declines and when you reach noon-time. [18] [Q 30:17-18]

O you who believe! Remember God with frequent remembrance, [41] and glorify Him morning and evening. [42] [Q 33:41-42]

---

(1) The speaker: Tirmidhi – Source: Sunan al-Tirmidhi – page or number: 3397. Conclusion of the speaker: fair.

❧*So be patient. Surely God's Promise is true. And ask forgiveness for your sins, and glorify your Lord in the evening and at dawn.* ❧ *[Q 40:55]*

❧*Be patient with the judgment of your Lord: for truly you are before Our eyes. And glorify your Lord when you rise, [48] and at night glorify Him, and at the receding of the stars. [49]* ❧ *[Q 52:48-49]*

❧*And say, "Praise be to God, Who has no child. He has no partner in sovereignty; nor has He any protector out of lowliness." And glorify His limitless Greatness.* ❧ *[Q 17:111]*

❧*Praise be to God, Who sent down the Book to His servant, and placed no crookedness therein ...* ❧ *[Q 18:1]*

Supplications in the Hadith Literature

Samurah ibn Jundub (may God be pleased with him) narrated that Prophet Muhammad (pbuh) said, "The words dearer to God are four: 'Glory be to God'; and 'All praise is for God'; and 'There is no deity but God'; and God is Great'. It does not matter which you say first." (1)

Abu Hurairah (may God be pleased with him) narrated that he heard Prophet Muhammad (pbuh) say, "There are two expressions which are very easy for the tongue to say, but very heavy in the balance and are very dear to the Most Compassionate, and they are: 'Glory be to God the Magnificent' and 'Glory be to God and all praise is due to Him (alone)." (2)

Sa'ad ibn Abu Waqqas (may God be pleased with him) narrated that he heard Prophet Muhammad (pbuh) say, "Is one amongst you powerless to get one thousand virtues every day?" Amongst those who were sitting there, one asked, 'How can one amongst us get one thousand virtues every day?' The Prophet (pbuh) answered: "Recite 'Glory be to God' one hundred times, for (by reciting them) one thousand virtues are recorded (to your credit) and one thousand of

---

(1) The speaker: al-Albani – Source: Sahih al-Jaami'– page or number: 173. Conclusion of the speaker: sound.

(2) The speaker: al-Bukhari – Source: Sahih al-Bukhari – page or number: 6682. Conclusion of the speaker: sound.

your vices are blotted out."[1]

Abu Sa'eed al-Khudri (may God be pleased with him) reported that Prophet Muhammad (pbuh) said, "Perform the enduring good deeds more frequently." His companions asked, 'What are these enduring good deeds?' The Prophet (pbuh) replied: "saying 'God is Great'; There is no deity but God; Glory be to God; All praise belongs to God alone; and There is no ability nor power except from God.'"[2]

Juwairiya (one of the Prophet's wives, and may God be pleased with her) reported that Prophet Muhammad (pbuh) came out (from her dwelling) in the morning as she was observing her dawn prayer in her place of worship. He came back in the forenoon and she was still sitting there. He (pbuh) asked her: "Have you been in the same position since I left you?" She said: 'Yes'. Thereupon he (pbuh) said: "I recited four phrases three times after I left you, and if these were to be weighed against what you have recited since the morning, these would outweigh them and they (these phrases) are: "Glory be to God, and All praise is due to Him (alone), according to the number of His creation, to the contentment of His Self, to the weight of His Throne, and to the ink used (in recording the words) for His Praise."[3]

Abu Malik al-Ashari (may God be pleased with him) reported that Prophet Muhammad (pbuh) said, 'Cleanliness is half of faith' and 'Praise be to God' fills the scale, and 'Glory be to God' and 'Praise be to God' fill up what is between the heavens and the earth. Prayer is a light, charity is proof of one's faith, patience is a brightness, and the Holy Quran is a proof on your behalf or against you. All men go out in the morning and barter themselves, thereby setting themselves free or enslaving themselves."[4]

---

(1) The speaker: Muslim – Source: Sahih Muslim – page or number: 2698. Conclusion of the speaker: sound.

(2) The speaker: Abdel Haqq al-Ashbili – Source: al-Ahkam al-Sughra – page or number: 891. Conclusion of the speaker: He referred in the introduction that the chain of speakers is sound.

(3) The speaker: Muslim – Source: Sahih Muslim – page or number: 2726. Conclusion of the speaker: sound.

(4) The speaker: Muslim – Source: Sahih Muslim – page or number: 223. Conclusion of the speaker: sound.

5-3-5 Remembrance by Reading the Quran

Reciting the Quran and enjoying the spiritual experience of reading the final words of God to humanity, revealed to His final messenger, Prophet Muhammad (pbuh) will always bring peace of mind, tranquility and guidance to those who believe, and a great blessing and reward. Every believer should make sure he keeps in constant contact with the Quran, reading or reciting it, seeking guidance in it, and peace of mind.

The Quran is a great Mercy sent to mankind, and we should take advantage of such a wonderful gift by living our lives according to its wise teachings, and continuously remember God and His infinite Greatness, and thank Him for all the blessings He has sent down to us.

Shown below are a selection of verses from the Quran that shed light on its blessings for believers.

O Mankind! There has now come to you an admonition from your Lord, and a healing for all (the ills) that may be in men's hearts, and guidance and grace to all who believe (in Him). [Q 10:57]

And We send down of the Quran that which is a healing and a mercy for the believers, the while it increases the wrongdoers in nothing but loss. [Q 17:82]

... and recite the Quran at a measured pace. [Q 73:4]

Truly it is a Noble Quran [77] in a Book concealed. [78] None touch it, save those made pure, [79] a revelation from the Lord of all the worlds.[80] [Q 56:77-80]

... whenever you recite the Quran, seek refuge with God from Satan, the outcast. [Q 16:98]

And when the Quran is recited, pay attention and listen, so that you may receive (His) Mercy." [Q 7:204]

Recite, then, as much of the Quran as you may do with ease. [Q 73:20]

Truly, this Quran guides towards that which is most upright, and gives glad tidings to the believers who perform righteous deeds that theirs will be a great reward. [Q 17:9]

But (thus it is) whenever you recite the Quran, We place an invisible barrier between you and those who will not believe in the life to come. [Q 17:45]

Thus, indeed, have We propounded to men all kinds of parables in this Quran, so that perhaps they might remember (that We have revealed it). [Q 39:27]

Do they not contemplate the Quran? Or are there locks upon their hearts? [Q 47:24]

Prophet Muhammad (pbuh) pointed out, many times, that there are particular verses in the Quran that have certain blessings. The Hadith below also show that there are special blessings connected with the recitation of certain Quranic verses, and believers should take note of these and avail themselves of these special blessings by reciting these verses often.

Ali ibn Abi Talib (may God be pleased with him) narrated that Prophet Muhammad (pbuh) said, "The best of you is he who learns the Quran and teaches it."[1]

Abdullah ibn Masood (may God be pleased with him) reported that Prophet Muhammad (pbuh) said, 'Whoever recites [a letter] from God's Book, he receives the reward for it, and the reward of ten like it. I do not say that Alif Lam Mim is a letter, but Alif is a letter, Lam is a letter and Mim is a letter."[2]

Abu Hurairah (may God be pleased with him) reported that Prophet Muhammad (pbuh) said, "Whenever people get together in one of the houses of God (i.e. a mosque), reciting the Holy Quran, and learning it together among themselves, calmness comes down to them, (Divine) Mercy covers them (from above), the angels surround them, and God makes mention of them among those who are with Him."[3]

---

(1) The speaker: Tirmidhi – Source: Sunan al-Tirmidhi – page or number: 2909. Conclusion of the speaker: We do not know this Hadith except from Abd ar-Rahman ibn Ishaq.

(2) The speaker: Tirmidhi – Source: Sunan al-Tirmidhi – page or number: 2910. Conclusion of the speaker: fair, sound but strange from this side.

(3) The speaker: Abu Dawood – Source: Sunan Abu Dawood – page or number: 1455. Conclusion of the speaker: Did not comment [He wrote in his letter to the people of Mecca that whenever he did not comment, it is accepted].

Abu Saeed al-Khudri (may God be pleased with him) narrated that Prophet Muhammad (pbuh) said, "It will be said to the companions of the Quran, when they enter Paradise, 'Recite and rise one degree for every verse,' until they recite the last thing that they know." [1]

Reciting Chapter 1, 'The Opening' (al-Fatihah) and the last two verses of Chapter 2, 'The Cow' (al-Baqarah)

Abdullah ibn Abbas (may God be pleased with him) narrated that he was near the Sacred House (the Kaaba in Mecca) and said to Abu Masood al-Ansari: "A hadith has been conveyed to me on your authority about the last two verses of Surah Al-Baqarah [Q 2:285-286]." He replied: 'Yes, Prophet Muhammad (pbuh) actually said, 'Anyone who recites, at night, these two verses at the end of Chapter 2, they will suffice (be enough to protect) him.'" [2]

Abu Masood al-Ansari (may God be pleased with him) narrated that Prophet Muhammad (pbuh) said, "If one recites the last two verses of Chapter 2 (al-Baqarah) [Q 2:285-286] at night, it is sufficient for him (for that night). [3]

Abu Umama (may God be pleased with him) reported that he heard Prophet Muhammad (pbuh) say, "Recite the Quran, for on the Day of Resurrection it will come as an intercessor for those who recited it. Recite the two bright chapters, Al-Baqarah and Al-Imran (Chapters 2 and 3), for on the Day of Resurrection they will come as two clouds or two shades, or two flocks of birds in ranks, pleading for those who recited them. Recite Chapter Al-Baqarah, for to take recourse to it is a blessing and to give it up is a cause of grief, and the ones who practise magic cannot confront it. [4]

al-Muslim (may God be pleased with him) reported that he heard Prophet Muhammad (pbuh) say, "Whoever memorizes the first ten

(1) The speaker: al-Albani – Source: Sahih Ibn Majah – page or number: 3062. Conclusion of the speaker: sound.
(2) The speaker: Muslim – Source: Sahih Muslim – page or number: 806. Conclusion of the speaker: sound.
(3) The speaker: al-Bukhari – Source: Sahih al-Bukhari – page or number: 5040. Conclusion of the speaker: sound.
(4) The speaker: Muslim – Source: Sahih Muslim – page or number: 804. Conclusion of the speaker: sound.

verses of Chapter 18, The Cave (Surah al-Kahf) *[Q 18:1-10]* will be protected from the Anti-Christ (al-Dajjal)."

This hadith was transmitted by Qatada with the same chain of transmitters, but Shu'ba (one of the narrators) said, "At the end of Surah al-Kahf (Chapter 18: The Cave)," but Hammam said, "At the beginning of Surah Al-Kahf." [1]

Anas ibn Malik (may God be pleased with him) narrated that Prophet Muhammad (pbuh) said, "Indeed, for everything there is a heart, and the heart of the Quran is Ya Seen (Chapter 36). Whoever recites Ya Seen, God writes for him that he recited the Quran ten times." [2]

Abu Umama al-Bahia (may God be pleased with him) narrated that he heard Prophet Muhammad (pbuh) say, "Whoever reads the last ten verses of Chapter 59 (Surah al-Hashr (Q 59:15-24) and then dies that day or night, he will enter Paradise." [3]

Ibn Omar (may God be pleased with him) narrated that the Prophet (pbuh) said, "Whoever wishes to see the Day of Judgment as if he is seeing it with his own eyes, should read Chapter 81 (The Enfolding) which begins with 'When the sun is enfolded' and Chapter 82 (The Cleaving Asunder) which begins with 'When the sky is cleft asunder', and Chapter 84 (The Splitting Asunder) which begins with 'When the sky is split asunder.' [4]

Abdullah ibn Abbas (may God be pleased with him) narrated that the Prophet (pbuh) said that he had been shown what his nation will have, and he could see treasure after treasure, and he was happy with that. God then revealed Chapter 93 (The Morning Brightness), verse 5: 'And surely your Lord shall give to you, and you shall be content.' Then he is given, in Paradise, thousands and thousands of palaces,

---

(1) The speaker: Muslim – Source: Sahih Muslim – page or number: 809. Conclusion of the speaker: sound.

(2) The speaker: Tirmidhi – Source: Sunan al-Tirmidhi – page or number: 2887. Conclusion of the speaker: strange (it includes) Haroun Abu Mohamed – anonymous sheikh.

(3) The speaker: al-Bayhaqi – Source: Shu`ab al-Iman (The branches of faith) – page or number: 2/977. Conclusion of the speaker: only told by Salim bin Othman.

(4) The speaker: Tirmidhi – Source: Sunan al-Tirmidhi – page or number: 3333. Conclusion of the speaker: fair but strange.

and within the palaces, there are palaces, and then spouses and servants. [1]

Abdullah ibn Omar (may God be pleased with him) narrated that the Prophet (pbuh) said, "Can one of you read a thousand verses every day?" They said, 'No one can read a thousand verses every day. The Prophet replied, "He can if he recites Chapter 102 (Vying for Increase) which begins with: 'Vying for increase (in worldly gains) distracts you.' [2]

Abdullah ibn Abbas (may God be pleased with him) narrated that Prophet Muhammad (pbuh) said, (The reward for reading) "The Earthquake (Chapter 99, verses 1-8) is equal (in reward) to (reading) half of the Quran, 'Qul hu Allah hu Ahad' (Chapter 112, verses 1-4) is equal (in reward) to a third of the Quran, and 'Qul Ya Ayyu hal-Kafirun' (Chapter 109, verses 1-6) is equal to a quarter of the Quran."[3]

Uqba ibn Amir (may God be pleased with him) reported that Prophet Muhammad (pbuh) said to him, "There have been sent down to me verses the like of which have never been seen before. They are the two Chapters of 'Refuge': The Dawn [Q 113:1-5] and Mankind [Q 114:1-6].[4]

5-3-6 Prayer

It is a grace from God that He asks His servants to call on Him and pray for whatever they need, and He promises to answer according to His infinite Wisdom and Mercy. Nothing is more useful to believers than calling on God throughout their lives, during the ups and downs of life, to ask for His Guidance, Protection and Help. In our prayers and supplications for forgiveness and support, or for specific needs and situations - whatever they may be - we should call upon God for His Mercy and put our complete trust in Him, firmly believing that He will answer us.

---

(1) The speaker: Ibn Kathir – Source: Tafseer al-Qur'ān al-'Aẓeem – page or number: 447/8. Conclusion of the speaker: its chain of narrators is sound.

(2) The speaker: al-Albani – Source: Takhrij Mishkat al-Masabih – page or number: 2125. Conclusion of the speaker: Al-Haqim narrated it, but did not verify its authenticity.

(3) The speaker: Tirmidhi – Source: Sunan al-Tirmidhi – page or number: 2894. Conclusion of the speaker: strange and is only known from the saying of Yamman bin Mogheira.

(4) The speaker: Muslim – Source: Sahih Muslim – page or number: 814. Conclusion of the speaker: sound.

❖When My servants ask you about Me, truly I am near; I answer the call of the caller, whenever he calls to Me: so let them respond to Me, and believe in Me, that they may be led the right way. ❖ [Q 2:186]

The Quran includes many different prayers that believers can use as a guide. Examples of these prayers are given below, starting with its second chapter.

Chapter 2:

❖(Moses) said, "I seek refuge in God from being among the ignorant!"❖ [Q 2:67]

❖… Abraham said, "My Lord, make this a land secure, and provide its people with fruits: those among them who believe in God and the Last Day." ❖ [Q 2:126]

❖(Abraham and Ishmael prayed), "Our Lord, accept this from us. Truly, You alone are the All-Hearing, the All-Knowing! ❖ [Q 2:127]

❖"And, our Lord, make us submit to You, and from our offspring a community submitting to You, and show us our rites (ways of worship), and relent to us. Truly You alone are the Relenting, the Merciful. ❖[Q 2:128]

❖But among them (mankind) are those who say, "Our Lord, give us good in this world and good in the Hereafter, and shield us from the punishment of the Fire." ❖ [Q 2:201]

❖… they (King Saul and his soldiers) said, "Our Lord, pour patience upon us, make firm our steps, and help us against the disbelieving people." ❖ [Q 2:250]

❖ "(We, the believers, seek) Your forgiveness, our Lord! And to You is the journey's end." ❖ [Q 2: 285]

❖God tasks no soul beyond its capacity. It shall have what it has earned and be subject to what it has perpetrated. "Our Lord, take us not to task if we forget or err! Our Lord, lay not upon us a burden like You laid upon those before us. Our Lord, impose not upon us that which we have not the strength to bear. And pardon us, forgive us, and have mercy upon us! You are our Master, so help us against the disbelieving people." ❖ [Q 2:286]

Chapter 3:

❋... who say, "Our Lord, make not our hearts swerve after having guided us, and bestow on us mercy from Your Presence. Truly, You are the Ever-Endowing." ❋ *[Q 3:8]*

❋... who say, "Our Lord, truly we believe, so forgive us our sins and shield us from the punishment of the Fire." ❋ *[Q 3:16]*

❋In that self-same place (where Mary lived), Zachariah prayed to his Lord, saying: "My Lord, bestow on me (too), out of Your grace, the gift of goodly offspring; for You, indeed, hear all prayer." ❋ *[Q 3:38]*

❋"... Our Lord, we believe in what You have sent down, and we follow the messenger, so inscribe us among the witnesses." ❋ *[Q 3:53]*

❋... and all that they said was this: "Our Lord, forgive us our sins and the lack of moderation in our deeds. And make firm our steps, and help us against people who deny the truth." ❋ *[Q 3:147]*

❋"Our Lord, give us what You have promised us through Your messengers, and do not disgrace us on the Day of Resurrection. Truly You will not fail the tryst." ❋ *[Q 3:194]*

Chapter 4:

❋"Our Lord, bring us forth from this town, whose people (the disbelievers) are oppressors, and appoint for us from Yourself a protector, and appoint for us from Yourself a helper!" ❋ *[Q 4:75]*

Chapter 5:

❋... say: "Our Lord, we do believe; make us one, then, with all who bear witness to the Truth. ❋ *[Q 5:83]*

Chapter 7:

❋They (Adam and Eve) said, "Our Lord, we have wronged ourselves. If You do not forgive us and have mercy upon us, we will surely be among the losers." ❋ *[Q 7:23]*

❋... they will say, "Our Lord, do not place us among the wrongdoing people!" ❋ *[Q 7:47]*

❦… (Prophet Shu'ayb said) "In God do we trust. Our Lord, decide between us and our people in truth, and You are the best of deciders."❧ [Q 7:89]

❦(Pharaoh's sorcerers said) … "Our Lord, shower us with patience and let us die as submitters." ❧ [Q 7:126]

❦(Moses said) "Glory be to You! I turn to You in repentance, and I am the first of the believers." ❧ [Q 7:143]

❦He (Moses) said, "My Lord, forgive me and my brother and bring us into Your Mercy, for You are the most Merciful of the merciful." ❧ [Q 7:151]

❦(Moses said) "You are our Protector, so forgive us and have mercy upon us; and You are the best of forgivers."❧ [Q 7:155]

Chapter 10:

❦And they said, "In God do we trust. Our Lord, make us not a temptation for the wrongdoing people."❧ [Q 10:85]

❦"… and save us, by Your grace, from people who deny the Truth!" ❧ [Q 10:86]

Chapter 11:

❦(Prophet Noah said) "My Lord, truly I seek refuge in You from asking You concerning that of which I have no knowledge. If You do not forgive me and have mercy upon me, I shall be among the losers."❧ [Q 11:47]

Chapter 12:

❦(Prophet Joseph said) "My Lord, You have given me (something) of sovereignty and taught me of the interpretation of dreams. Creator of the heavens and the earth, You are my Protector in this world and in the Hereafter. Cause me to die as a Muslim and join me with the righteous."❧ [Q 12:101]

Chapter 14:

❦And (remember the time) when (Prophet) Abraham spoke (thus): "O my Lord, make this land secure, and preserve me and my children from ever worshipping idols." ❧ [Q 14:35]

❧ (Prophet Abraham said) "Praise be to God, Who bestowed upon me Ishmael and Isaac in my old age. Truly my Lord is the Hearer of supplications. [39] My Lord, make me a performer of prayer and my offspring. Our Lord! Accept my supplication.[40] ❧ [Q 14:39-40]

❧ (Prophet Abraham said) "Our Lord! Forgive me and my parents and the believers on the Day when the Reckoning is established." ❧ [Q 14:41]

Chapter 17:

❧ Say (O Muhammad): "O my Lord! Let my entry be by the Gate of Truth and Honour, and likewise my exit by the Gate of Truth and Honour, and grant me, from Your Presence, an authority to aid (me)." ❧ [Q 17:80]

Chapter 18:

❧ (The youths in the cave said) "Our Lord! Bestow on us mercy from Yourself, and dispose of our affair for us in the right way." ❧ [Q 18:10]

Chapter 20:

❧ (Moses) said, "My Lord, expand for me my heart (with assurance) [25] and ease for me my task. [26] And untie the knot from my tongue. [27]" ❧ [Q 20:25-27]

❧ "... and say, "My Lord, increase me in knowledge." ❧ [Q 20:114]

Chapter 21:

❧ (Prophet Job said) "Truly affliction has touched me. And You are the Most Merciful of the merciful." [83] So We answered him and removed the affliction that was upon him ... [84] ❧ [Q 21:83-84]

❧ (Prophet Jonah said) "There is no god but You! Glory be to You. Truly I have been among the wrongdoers." [87] So We answered him, and saved him from grief. [88] ❧ [Q 21:87-88]

❧ (Prophet Zachariah said) "My Lord, leave me not childless, though You are the best of inheritors." [89] So We answered him, and bestowed John upon him ... [90] ❧ [Q 21:89-90]

Chapter 23:

❧ (Noah said) "O my Lord! Help me, for they accuse me of falsehood!" ❧ [Q 23:26]

❖"And say: 'O my Sustainer! Cause me to reach a destination blessed (by You) - for You are the best to show man how to reach his (true) destination!"❖ [Q 23:29]

❖... do not, O my Sustainer, let me be one of those evildoing folk!"❖ [Q 23:94]

❖And say: "O my Sustainer! I seek refuge with You from the promptings of all evil impulses; ❖ [Q 23:97]

❖... and I seek refuge with You, O my Sustainer, lest they come near to me!"❖ [Q 23:98]

❖We have come to believe (in You); forgive, then, our sins and bestow Your mercy on us: for You are the truest bestower of mercy!' ❖ [Q 23:109]

❖Hence, (O believer,) say: "O my Lord, grant (me) forgiveness and bestow Your mercy (upon me): for You are the truest bestower of mercy!"❖ [Q 23:118]

Chapter 25:

❖Say (to those who believe): "No weight or value would my Sustainer attach to you were it not for your faith (in Him)!" (And say to those who deny the Truth) "You have indeed given the lie (to God's message), and in time this (sin) will cleave to you!"❖ [Q 25:77]

❖... and who pray: "O our Sustainer, avert from us the suffering of Hell — for, truly, the suffering caused by it is bound to be a torment dire.❖ [Q 25:65]

❖... and who pray: "O our Sustainer! Grant that our spouses and our offspring be a joy to our eyes, and cause us to be foremost among those who are conscious of You!"❖ [Q 25:74]

Chapter 26:

❖(And Prophet Abraham said), "My Lord! Grant me (sound) judgment, and join me with the righteous."❖ [Q 26:83]

❖"And (Abraham said) grant me the power to convey the Truth to those who will come after me, [84] and place me among those who shall inherit the Garden of bliss.[85]"❖ [Q 26:84-85]

❈ "And (Abraham said) forgive my father – for, truly, he is among those who have gone astray [86] and do not put me to shame on the Day when all shall be raised from the dead.[87]" ❈ [Q 26:86-87]

❈ ... and then he (Prophet Lot) prayed: "O my Sustainer! Save me and my household (family) from all that they (the disbelievers) are doing!"❈ [Q 26:169]

Chapter 27:

❈ (King Solomon said, after overhearing the speech of an ant) "O my Lord, so order me that I may be grateful for Your favours which You have bestowed on me and on my parents, and that I may work the righteousness that will please You; and admit me, by Your Grace, to the ranks of Your righteous servants." ❈ [Q 27:19]

Chapter 28:

❈ (Moses said, after he had struck and killed a man) "My Lord! Truly I have wronged my own soul! Forgive me." So He forgave him. Truly He is the Forgiving, the Merciful. ❈ [Q 28:16]

❈ He (Moses) said, "My Lord! Save me from the wrongdoing people!"❈ [Q 28:21]

Chapter 29:

❈ He (Prophet Lot) said, "My Lord, help me against the people who spread corruption!"❈ [Q 29:30]

Chapter 37:

❈ And he (Prophet Abraham) said, "Truly I am going to my Lord. He will guide me. [99] My Lord! Grant me (a child) from among the righteous." [100] So We gave him glad tidings of a gentle son. [101] ❈ [Q 37:99-101]

Chapter 40:

❈ Those who bear the Throne (of God) and those who dwell near to it praise the Lord and believe in Him and seek forgiveness for those who believe: "Our Lord, You encompass all things in (Your) mercy and Knowledge. Forgive those who repent and follow Your ways, and shield them from the punishment of Hellfire. [7] Our Lord, make them enter Gardens of Eden that You have promised them and those among their fathers, their spouses, and their progeny who were righteous. Truly You are the Mighty, the Wise. [8] And protect them from evil deeds. Whosoever You shield from evil deeds on that Day, on him have You had mercy. And that indeed is the great triumph. [9]" ﴾ [Q 40:7-9]

﴾(Moses said) "Truly, I have sought refuge in my Lord and your Lord from every arrogant one who does not believe in the Day of Account."﴿ [Q 40:27]

﴾But your Sustainer says: "Call to Me, (and) I shall respond to you! Truly, they who are too proud to worship Me will enter hell, contemptible!"﴿ [Q 40:60]

﴾(the believer among Pharaoh's people said) "I entrust my affair to God. Truly, God is All-Seeing of (His) servants."﴿ [Q 40:44]

Chapter 44:

﴾(The dwellers in the Fire will say) "Our Lord, remove from us the punishment; truly, we (now) believe (in You)!"﴿ [Q 44:12]

Chapter 46:

﴾... he (the believer) says, "My Lord, inspire me to give thanks for Your blessing with which You have blessed me and my parents, and that I may work righteousness such that it pleases You; and make righteous for me my offspring. Truly I turn in repentance to You, and truly, I am among those who submit (to You)."﴿ [Q 46:15]

Chapter 59:

﴾And so, they who come after them pray: "Our Lord, forgive us our sins, as well as those of our brethren who preceded us in faith, and let not our hearts entertain any unworthy thoughts or feelings against (any of) those who have attained to faith. Our Lord, truly, You are the Most Compassionate, the Most Gracious!"﴿ [Q 59:10]

Chapter 60:

﴾"Our Lord, upon You we have relied, and to You we have returned, and to You is the (final) destination."﴿ [Q 60:4]

❝ *"Our Lord, make us not (objects of) torment for the disbelievers and forgive us, our Lord. Truly it is You Who are the Exalted in Might, the Wise."* ❞ *[Q 60:5]*

Chapter 66:

❝ *"Our Lord, perfect for us our light and forgive us. Indeed, You have power over all things."* ❞ *[Q 66:8]*

❝ *(Pharaoh's wife prayed) "My Lord, build for me, in nearness to You, a house in Paradise and save me from Pharaoh and his deeds and save me from the wrongdoing people."* ❞ *[Q 66:11]*

Chapter 71:

❝ *(Noah prayed) "My Lord, forgive me and my parents and whoever enters my house as a believer and (all) the believing men and believing women. And do not increase the wrongdoers except in destruction."* ❞ *[Q 71:28]*

Chapter 113:

❝ *Say: "I seek refuge with the Lord of the rising dawn, [1] from the evil of what He has created, [2] from the evil of darkness when it descends, [3] from the evil of those who practise black magic, [4] and from the evil of the envier when he envies. [5]"* ❞ *[Q 113:1-5]*

Chapter 114:

❝ *Say: "I seek refuge with the Lord of mankind, [1] the Sovereign of mankind, [2] the God of mankind, [3] from the evil of the stealthy (elusive) whisperer (Satan), [4] who whispers into the hearts of mankind —[5] from (all temptation to evil by) jinn (invisible forces) and mankind." [6]* ❞ *[Q 114:1-6]*

Prophet Muhammad (pbuh) was also very keen to gather believers together for prayer and explain to them how important it is to call upon God in any and all situations. Here are some examples of his advice in this regard.

Al-Numan ibn Bashir (may God be pleased with him) narrated that Prophet Muhammad (pbuh) said, "Supplication is the worship." Then he recited: 'And your Lord says, Call upon Me, I will answer you.

Truly, those who scorn My worship will surely enter Hell in humiliation.'" [see Q 43:72].[1]

Anas ibn Malik (may God be pleased with him) narrated that he heard Prophet Muhammad (pbuh) say, "Let one of you ask his Lord for his every need, even until he asks Him for the strap of his sandal when it breaks."[2]

Salman al-Farsi (may God be pleased with him) narrated that Prophet Muhammad (pbuh) said, "Truly, God is the Ever-Living, the Generous. When a believer raises his hands to Him, He feels too shy to return them to him empty and rejected."[3]

Abu Hurairah (may God be pleased with him) narrated that Prophet Muhammad (pbuh) said, "Call upon God with certainty of being answered, for God does not respond to the supplication of one who is half-hearted and unfocused."[4]

Abu Hurairah (may God be pleased with him) narrated that Prophet Muhammad (pbuh) said, "There is not a believer who calls upon God with a supplication, except that he is answered. Either it shall be granted to him in this world, or reserved for him in the Hereafter, or his sins shall be expiated for it according to the extent that he supplicated - as long as he does not supplicate for some sin, or for the severing of ties of kinship, and he does not become impatient." They (his companions) said: "O Messenger of God! How would he be impatient?" He (pbuh) said: "If he says, 'I called upon my Lord, but He did not answer me.' "[5]

Abu Hurairah (may God be pleased with him) narrated that Prophet Muhammad (pbuh) said, "Whoever wishes that God will respond to him during hardship and grief, then let him supplicate plentifully when he is in prosperous times."[6]

---

(1) The speaker: Tirmidhi – Source: Sunan al-Tirmidhi – page or number: 3372. Conclusion of the speaker: sound.
(2) The speaker: al-Suyuti – Source: al-Jaami' al-Saghîr – page or number: 7562. Conclusion of the speaker: sound
(3) The speaker: al-Albani – Source: Sahih al-Tirmidhi – page or number: 3556. Conclusion of the speaker: sound.
(4) The speaker: al-Albani – Source: Sahih al-Tirmidhi – page or number: 3479. Conclusion of the speaker: fair.
(5) The speaker: al-Albani – Source: Sahih al-Jaami' – page or number: 5714. Conclusion of the speaker: sound.
(6) The speaker: al-Suyuti – Source: al-Jaami' al-Saghîr – page or number: 8743. Conclusion of the speaker: fair

Abu Hurairah (may God be pleased with him) narrated that Prophet Muhammad (pbuh) said, "There is nothing dearer and more noble to God, the Ever-Glorified, than supplication."[1]

Abu Hurairah (may God be pleased with him) reported that Prophet Muhammad (pbuh) said, "The nearest a servant comes to his Lord is when he is prostrating himself (in prayer), so make supplication (in this position)."[2]

Abu Huraira (may God be pleased with him) narrated that Prophet Muhammad (pbuh) said, "God will always answer the prayer of these three: one who remembers God much, one who is oppressed or suffers injustice, and a just ruler."[3]

Abdullah ibn Umar (may God be pleased with him) reported that Prophet Muhammad (pbuh) supplicated in these words, "O God! I seek refuge in You from the withdrawal of Your blessing or Your protection (from me), from Your sudden anger, and from every displeasure of Yours."[4]

5-3-7 The Most Beautiful Divine Names of God

5-3-7-1 Names of God in the Holy Quran

The following verses refer to the Most Beautiful Names of God.

To God belong the Most Beautiful Names; so call Him by them, and leave those who deviate with regard to His Names. Soon they shall be recompensed for that which they used to do. [Q 7:180]

Say, "Call upon God, or call upon the Compassionate. Whichever you call upon, to Him belong the Most Beautiful Names." And be not loud in your prayer, nor too quiet therein, but seek a way between." [Q 17:110]

---

(1) The speaker: ibn Hibban – Source: Boulough al-Maram – page or number: 454. Conclusion of the speaker: sound

(2) The speaker: Muslim – Source: Sahih Muslim – page or number: 482. Conclusion of the speaker: sound.

(3) The speaker: al-Albani – Source: Silsalat al-Hadith al-Sahiha – page or number: 1211. Conclusion of the speaker: fair.

(4) The speaker: Muslim – Source: Sahih Muslim – page or number: 2739. Conclusion of the speaker: sound.

❧*God, there is no god but He. To Him belong the Most Beautiful Names.* ❧ [Q 20:8]

❧*He is God, other than Whom there is no god, Knower of the Unseen and the seen. And He is the Compassionate, the Merciful.* ❧ [Q 59:22]

❧*He is God, other than Whom there is no god, the Sovereign, the Holy, Peace, the Faithful, the Protector, the Mighty, the Compeller, the Proud. Glory be to Him above the partners they ascribe.* ❧ [Q 59:23]

❧*He is God, the Creator, the Maker, the Fashioner; to Him belong the Most Beautiful Names. Whatsoever is in the heavens and on the earth glorifies Him, and He is the Mighty, the Wise.* ❧ [Q 59:24]

5-3-7-2 Names of God in the Hadith

The following Hadith also refer to the Most Beautiful Names of God.

Abu Hurairah (may God be pleased with him) narrated that he heard Prophet Muhammad (pbuh) say, "God has ninety-nine names, i.e. one hundred minus one, and whoever knows them will go to Paradise." (Please see Hadith No. 419 Vol. 8) [1]

Many of these Divine Names are mentioned in numerous verses of the Quran, and some of these verses are given below. Other names have been extracted from Hadith, and religious scholars over the centuries have proposed additional names to complete the list of 99. These scholars relied on the following hadith, where the Prophet (pbuh) stated that God would inform some of His servants of His Divine Names.

Abdullah ibn Masood (may God be pleased with him) reported that one of the prayers of Prophet Muhammad (pbuh) was, "O God, I am your servant, the son of your servants (my father and mother). My destiny is in Your Hand. What you have ordained for me has been made manifest, and Your judgment is fair. I ask You, with all the Names You have given Yourself, or that You have revealed in Your Book, or that You have taught one of Your creation, or that You have kept for Yourself in the world of the Unseen. Make the Quran the joy of my heart, the light of my chest, and the remover of my sadness and fear." [2]

---

(1) The speaker: Abū Hurairah – the speaker: al-Bukhari – Source: Sahih Bukhari – page or number: 7392. Conclusion of the speaker: sound.

(2) The speaker: Ibn Hibban – Source: Sahih Ibn Hibban – page or number: 972. Conclusion of the speaker: He included it in his Sahih Ibn Hibban.

These names must be beautiful, and should glorify God; they should describe His Majesty, Mercy and beautiful attributes, as mentioned in the following two verses.

❂... His is the essence of all that is most sublime in the heavens and on earth, and He Alone is the Mighty, the Wise. ❂ [Q 30:27]

❂Blessed is the Name of your Lord, Possessor of Majesty and Bounty❂ [Q 55:78]

We will start with the Names that are mentioned in the Quran, then the names mentioned in the Prophetic Traditions (Hadith), and then the names used most commonly in the Islamic literature.

#	Arabic Name Transliterated	Arabic Name	Other Translators	Dr. Abdelaziz Hamdy
1	Ar-Raḥmān	الرَّحْمَنُ	The All-Merciful	The Rahman
2	Ar-Raḥīm	الرحيمُ	The Ever-Merciful	The Merciful
3	Al-Malik	الملكُ	The King	The King
4	Al-Quddūs	القدُّوسُ	The Holy	The Holy
5	As-Salām	السَّلامُ	The Peace	The Peace
6	Al-Mu'min	المؤمنُ	The Faithful, The Believer	The Faithful
7	Al-Muhaymin	المُهَيْمنُ	The Overseer, The Guardian	The Dominator
8	Al-'Azīz	العزيزُ	The Exalted	The Mighty
9	Al-Jabbār	الجَبَّارُ	The All-Compelling, The Compeller, The Invincible	The Ever-Compeller
10	Al-Mutakabbir	المتَكَبِّرُ	The Proud	The Lofty
11	Al-Khāliq	الخالقُ	The Creator	The Creator
12	Al-Bari'	البارىُ	The Maker	The Maker
13	Al-Musawwir	المصوِّرُ	The Form-Giver, The Shaper	The Fashioner
14	Al-Ghaffār	الغفَّارُ	The All-Forgiving	The Ever-Forgiving
15	Al-Qahhār	القَهَّارُ	The Severe, The Paramount	The Ever-Subduing

#	Arabic Name Transliterated	Arabic Name	Other Translators	Dr. Abdelaziz Hamdy
16	Al-Wahhāb	الوَهَّابُ	The Bestower	The Ever-Endowing
17	Ar-Razzāq	الرَّزَّاقُ	The Provider, The Sustainer	The Ever-Sustaining
18	Al-Fattāh	الفتَّاحُ	The All-Opening, The Opener	The Ever-Opening
19	Al-'Alīm	العليمُ	The Knower, The Knowing	The Omniscient
20	As-Sami'	السَّميعُ	The Hearing	The All-Hearing
21	Al-Basir	البصيرُ	The Seeing	The All-Seeing
22	Al-Latīf	اللَّطيفُ	The Gentle, The Subtle	The Gracious
23	Al-Khabīr	الخبيرُ	The Aware	The Knower
24	Al-Halīm	الحَليمُ	The Forbearing	The Forbearer
25	Al-'Azīm	العظيمُ	The Tremendous	The Great
26	Al-Ghafūr	الغَفورُ	The Forgiving	The All-Forgiving
27	Ash-Shakūr	الشَّكورُ	The Grateful, The Appreciative	The All-Thankful
28	Al-'Alī	العليُّ	The High, The Most High	The High One
29	Al-Kabīr	الكبيرُ	The Great	The Grand
30	Al-Hafīz	الحفيظُ	The Guardian	The All-Preserving
31	Al-Muqīt	المقيتُ	The Nourisher	The All-Providing
32	Al-Hasīb	الحسيبُ	The Reckoner, The Sufficer	The All-Reckoning
33	Al-Karīm	الكريمُ	The Generous	The Munificent
34	Ar-Raqīb	الرَّقيبُ	The Watcher	The Watchful
35	Al-Mujīb	المُجيبُ	The Responder	The Answerer
36	Al-Wāsiᶜ	الواسعُ	The Embracing, The Expansive, The Vast	The Broad
37	Al-Hakīm	الحَكيمُ	The Wise	The Wise
38	Al-Wadud	الودودُ	The Loving, The Beloved, The Ever-Loving	The Affectionate

#	Arabic Name Transliterated	Arabic Name	Other Translators	Dr. Abdelaziz Hamdy
39	Al-Majeed	المجيدُ	The Splendorous	The Glorious
40	Ash-Shahīd	الشَّهيدُ	The Witness	The All-Witness
41	Al-Haqq	الحقُّ	The Real	The Truth
42	Al-Wakīl	الوَكيلُ	The Trustee	The Advocate
43	Al-Qawī	القويُّ	The Strong, The Powerful	The Almighty
44	Al-Matīn	المتينُ	The Firm	The Firm
45	Al-Walī	الوليُّ	The Friend	The Patron
46	Al-Hamīd	الحميدُ	The Praiser, The Praised	The Praiseworthy
47	Al-Ḥayy	الحيُّ	The Alive, The Ever-Living	The Living
48	Al-Qayyūm	القيُّومُ	The Self-Standing	The Ever-Rising
49	Al-Wāḥid	الواحدُ	The One	The One
50	Al-Aḥad	الأَحَدُ	The Unique, The Indivisible	
51	As-Ṣamad	الصَّمَدُ	The Self-Sufficient, The Transcendent	The Steadfast
52	Al-Qādir	القادِرُ	The Powerful, The All-Powerful	The Powerful
53	Al-Muqtadir	المقتَدرُ	The Potent	The Omnipotent
54	Al-Awwal	الأَوَّلُ	The First	The First
55	Al-Ākhir	الآخرُ	The Last	The Last
56	Az-Ẓāhir	الظَّاهرُ	The Outward	The Manifest
57	Al-Bāṭin	الباطنُ	The Inward, The Hidden	The Unmanifest
58	Al-Muta'ali	المتَعالِ	The Transcendent, The Supreme	The Transcendent
59	Al-Barr	البَرُّ	The Kind	The Beneficent
60	Al-Tawwāb	التَّوَّابُ	The Ever Turning	The Ever Accepting of Repentance
61	Al-ᶜAfū	العفوُّ	The Pardoner	The Pardoner

#	Arabic Name Transliterated	Arabic Name	Other Translators	Dr. Abdelaziz Hamdy
62	Ar-Ra'ūf	الرَّءُوفُ	The Clement	The Compassionate
63	Al-Ghanī	الغَنِيُّ	The Unneedy	The Rich
64	Al-Wārith	الوَارثُ	The Inheritor	The Inheritor
65	Al-Qābid	القابضُ	The Contractor	The Constrictor
66	Al-Bāsit	الباسِطُ	The Expander	The Expander
67	Al-Hakam	الحَكَمُ	The Ruler	The Judge
68	Al-Muqaddim	المقدِّمُ	The Forward-Setter	The Advancer
69	Al-Mu'akhkhir	المؤخِّرُ	The Behind-Keeper	The Delayer
70	Al-Khāfid	الخافضُ	The Downletter, The Debaser	The Demoter
71	Ar-Rāfi	الرَّافعُ	The Uplifter	The Promoter
72	Al-Mu'izz	المعزُّ	The Exalter, The Exalted	The Exalting
73	Al-Mudhill	المذلُّ	The Abaser	The Humiliator
74	Al-'Adl	العَدلُ	The Just	The Just
75	Al-Jalīl	الجَليلُ	The Majestic	The Majestic
76	Al-Bā'ith	الباعثُ	The Upraiser	The Resurrector
77	Al-Muhṣī	المُحصي	The Enumerator, The Accounter	The Reckoner
78	Al-Mubdi'	المبدئُ	The Originator	The Initiator
79	Al-Mu'īd	المعيدُ	The Returner	The Restorer
80	Al-Muhyi	المُحيي	The Life-Giver	The Life-Giver
81	Al-Mumīt	المميتُ	The Death-Giver	The Life-Taker
82	Al-Wājid	الواجِدُ	The Finder, The Founder	The Author
83	Al-Mājid	الماجِدُ	The Glorious	The Glory-Giver
84	Al-Wali	الوالي	The Protector	The Ordainer
85	Al-Muntaqim	المنتقِمُ	The Avenger	The Avenger

#	Arabic Name Transliterated	Arabic Name	Other Translators	Dr. Abdelaziz Hamdy
86	Mālik al-Mulk	مالك المالِكُ	The Owner of the Kingdom	The Owner of Dominion
87	Dhu'l Jalāl wa'l-Ikrām	ذُوالجلالِ والإكْرامِ	The Possessor of Majesty and Generous Giving	The Majestic and Bounteous One
88	Al-Muqsiṭ	المقسِطُ	The Impartial	The Equitable
89	Al-Jāmi'	الجامِعُ	The Gathering	The Gatherer
90	Al-Mughnī	المُغني	The Need-Lifter	The Enricher
91	Al-Māni'	المانِعُ		The Preventer
92	Al-Nāfiᶜ	النَّافِعُ	The Benefiter	The Propitious
93	Al-Ḍārr	الضَّارُّ	The Harmer	The Distresser
94	Al-Nūr	النُّورُ	The Light	The Light
95	Al-Hādī	الهادي	The Guide	The Guide
96	Al-Badīᶜ	البَديعُ	The Innovating	The Originator
97	Al-Bāqī	الباقي	The Subsistent, The Everlasting	The Ever-Lasting
98	Ar-Rashīd	الرَّشيدُ	The Director, The Guide to Good Judgment	The All-Guiding
99	As-Ṣabūr	الصَّبورُ	The Patient, The Most Patient	The All-Patient

5-3-7-3 Explanation of the Names of God

1. The Rahman – Ar-Rahman (الرّحْمَنُ ﷻ)

The Compassionate – meaning His Compassion and Mercy extend to His whole creation. This name is mentioned fifty-seven times in the Quran and is included in the 'Bismillah' (In the name of God) which Muslims say whenever they begin any action.

❀Say: "Call upon God, or call upon the Compassionate. Whichever you call upon, to Him belong the Most Beautiful Names. ❀ [Q 17:110]

﴾*The Compassionate [1] taught the Qur'ān; [2] created man; [3] taught him articulate speech. [4] (At His behest) the sun and the moon run their appointed courses; [5]*﴿ [Q 55:1-5]

Abd al-Rahman ibn Awf (may God be pleased with him) narrated that he heard Prophet Muhammad (pbuh) say, "God, the Mighty and Exalted, said, 'I am the Compassionate (Ar-Rahman). I have created ties of kinship and derived a name (rahm) for it from My Name. If anyone maintains ties of kinship, I maintain connection with him, and I shall cut off anyone who cuts them off.'"[1]

2. The Merciful – Ar-Rahim (الرحيم ﷻ)

The Merciful – His Mercy includes all His creatures and this name is mentioned in the Quran over one hundred times; it is part of the 'Bismillah' ('In the name of God').

﴾*God is He save whom there is no god: the One Who knows all that is beyond the reach of a created being's perception, as well as all that can be witnessed by a creature's senses or mind: He is the Most Gracious and Merciful, the Dispenser of Grace and Mercy.*﴿ [Q 59:22]

﴾*... and place your trust in The Mighty, The Merciful ...*﴿ [Q 26:217]

3. The King - Al-Malik (الملك ﷻ)

The King – He is the One Who sets all the measures to direct His kingdom, and He is the Absolute King. Anything that happens in His kingdom is decided with His infinite Wisdom and Knowledge.

﴾*(Know) then, (that) God is sublimely exalted, the King, the Ultimate Truth: there is no god save Him, Lord of the Munificent Throne!*﴿ [Q 23:116]

Abu Hurairah (may God be pleased with him) narrated that he heard Prophet Muhammad (pbuh) say, "On the Day of Resurrection, God will hold the whole earth and fold the heavens with His right hand

---

(1) The speaker: Tirmidhi – Source: Sunan al-Tirmidhi – page or number: 1907. Conclusion of the speaker: fair.

and say, 'I am the King! Where are the kings of the earth?'"[1]

4. The Holy - Al-Quddus (القدوس ﷻ)

The Holy – this name includes His immaculate virtues, His perfection, and His Majesty.

God is He save whom there is no god: The King, the Holy, Peace, the Faithful, the Dominator, the Mighty, the Ever-Compelling, the One, the Lofty. Utterly remote is God, in His limitless glory, from anything to which men may ascribe a share in His Divinity! [Q 59:23]

All that is in the heavens and all that is on the earth extol the limitless glory of God, The King, the Holy, the Mighty, the Wise! [Q 62:1]

'A'isha (may God be pleased with her) reported that Prophet Muhammad (pbuh) used to recite, while bowing and prostrating himself, "All Glorious, All Holy, Lord of the Angels and the Spirit." [2]

5. Peace - As-Salam (السلام ﷻ)

Peace – He is the giver of peace to His servants and His Guidance will lead to peace in the Hereafter. He sustains peace and, with His guidance, His servants will live in peace. See the Quranic verse above [59:23].

"Peace!" a word from a Lord Most Merciful. [Q 36:58]

Abu Hurairah (may God be pleased with him) reported that Prophet Muhammad (pbuh) observed, "You shall not enter Paradise as long as you do not affirm belief (in all those things which are the Articles of Faith). And you do not believe as long as you do not love one another. Shall I not direct you to a thing which, if you do it, will foster love amongst you: give currency to (the practice of giving the salutation to one another by saying) "As-salamu alaikum" (meaning 'Peace be unto you').[3]

---

(1) The speaker: al-Bukhari – Source: Sahih al-Bukhari – page or number: 7382. Conclusion of the speaker: sound.

(2) The speaker: Muslim – Source: Sahih Muslim – page or number: 487. Conclusion of the speaker: sound.

(3) The speaker: Muslim – Source: Sahih Muslim – page or number: 54. Conclusion of the speaker: sound.

6. The Faithful - Al-Mu'min (المؤمن ﷻ)

The Faithful – He is the source of all faith and, through faith, believers are made secure and safe. See the Quranic verse above [59:23].

Abu Hurairah (may God be pleased with him) narrated that he heard Prophet Muhammad (pbuh) say, "The Muslim is the one from (the harm of) whose tongue and hand (other) Muslims are safe, and the believer is the one with whom the people trust their blood and their wealth."[1]

7. The Dominator - Al-Muhaymin (المهيمن ﷻ)

The Dominator – He dominates all things in the Heavens and on the earth, including the Unseen and the seen, with His knowledge; everything is under His domination and control. See the Quranic verse above [59:23].

8. The Mighty - Al-Aziz (العزيز ﷻ)

The Mighty – His Might and Command are powerful over all things. This name is mentioned eighty-eight times in the Quran. See the Quranic verse above [59:23].

❧*Ha. Meem. [1] The revelation of the Book from God, the Mighty, the All-Knowing ... [2]* ❧ *[Q 40:1-2]*

❧*(The believing man among Pharaoh's people said) "You call upon me to disbelieve in God and to ascribe as a partner to Him that whereof I have no knowledge, whereas I call you to the Mighty, the Forgiving."* ❧ *[Q 40:42]*

9. The Ever-Compelling - Al-Jabbar (الجبار ﷻ)

The name 'The Ever-Compelling' is mentioned once in the Quran. He has absolute power and command over His Kingdom and can compel any of His creatures as He Wills. This name can also include the meaning of restoring, repairing, and putting things back together after they have been damaged. See the Quranic verse above [59:23].

---

(1) The speaker: Tirmidhi – Source: Sunan al-Tirmidhi – page or number: 2627. Conclusion of the speaker: fair and sound.

10. The Lofty - Al-Mutakabbir (المتكبر ﷻ)

The Lofty – He is Exalted, Sublime and Majestic over all things. This name is mentioned once in the Quran, as shown in the verse below.

God is He save whom there is no god: the Absolute Ruler, the Holy, the Peace, the Faithful, the Dominator, the Mighty, the Ever-Compelling, the One, the Lofty. Utterly remote is God, in His limitless glory, from anything to which men may ascribe a share in His divinity! [Q 59:23]

Abu Hurairah (may God be pleased with him) narrated that he heard Prophet Muhammad (pbuh) say, "God the Most High says, 'Loftiness is my cloak and Majesty is my garment, and I shall throw him who vies with Me regarding one of them into Hell."[1]

11. The Creator - Al-Khaliq (الخالق ﷻ)

The Creator – He brings forth into existence whatsoever He wills, and when He decrees a matter, He says to it, 'Be' and it is. This name is mentioned many times in the Quran.

He is God, the Creator, the Maker, the Fashioner! His (alone) are the most beautiful names. All that is in the heavens and on earth extol His limitless Glory: for He alone is the Mighty, the Wise! [Q 59:24]

12. The Maker - Al-Bari (الباري ﷻ)

The Maker – this name describes God's infinitely creative power to shape whatsoever He Wills, and is mentioned once in the Quran.

He is God, the Creator, the Maker, the Fashioner! His (alone) are the most beautiful names. All that is in the heavens and on earth extol His limitless glory: for He alone is the Mighty, the Wise! [Q 59:24]

13. The Fashioner - Al-Musawwir (المصور ﷻ)

The Fashioner - He forms all of His creation as He wills.

He is God, the Creator, the Maker, the Fashioner! His (alone) are the most beautiful names. All that is in the heavens and on earth extol His limitless glory: for He alone is the Mighty, the Wise! [Q 59:24]

---

(1) The speaker: Abu Dawood – Source: Sunan Abu Dawood – page or number: 4090. Conclusion of the speaker: Did not comment [He wrote in his letter to the people of Mecca that whenever he did not comment, it is accepted].

The difference between these three names in the verse are: The Creator creates something from nothing, while the Maker shapes what He has created into the forms He Wills, while the Fashioner forms it into a unique and recognizable creature.

(God addresses all the angels) "... so when I have proportioned him (Adam) and breathed into him of My Spirit, fall down before him in prostration." [Q 15:29]

... assembling you in whatever form He willed? [Q 82:8]

14. The Ever-Forgiving - Al-Ghaffar (الغفار ﷻ)

The Ever-Forgiving will cover believers' sins and forgive them, for those who are sincere in repenting their sins.

"... the Lord of the heavens and the earth and all that is between them, the Mighty, the Ever-Forgiving." [Q 38:66]

He created the heavens and the earth in Truth. He wraps the night over the day and wraps the day over the night and has subjected the sun and the moon, each running (its course) for a specified term. Unquestionably, He is the Mighty, the Ever-Forgiving." [Q 39:5]

(The believing man among Pharaoh's people said) "You invite me to disbelieve in God and associate with Him that of which I have no knowledge, and I invite you to the Mighty, the Ever-Forgiving." [Q 40:42]

15. The Ever-Subduing - Al-Qahhar (القهار ﷻ)

The Ever-Subduing – this name describes God's dominance, according to His Justice and Wisdom, over those who deserve to have His divine law imposed on them. This name is mentioned six times in the Quran.

Say, "Who is the Lord and Sustainer of the heavens and the earth?" Say, "(It is) God." Say, "Have you then taken besides Him allies not possessing (even) for themselves any benefit or any harm?" Say, "Are the blind and the seeing equal? Or can darkness be equal to light? Or have they attributed to God partners who have created the like of His creation such that that creation seems alike to them?" Say, "God is the Creator of all things, and He is the One, the Ever-Subduing." [Q 13:16]

❝*Had God wanted to take a son, He would have chosen whatsoever He willed from that which He created. Glory be to Him; He is the One, the Ever-Subduing."*❞ [Q 39:4]

16. The Ever-Endowing - Al-Wahhab (الوهاب ﷻ)

The Ever-Endowing – this name describes God's attribute of unlimited bounty and blessings which He gives to His creation. He bestows His limitless bounty on whomsoever He wills.

❝*(... who say), "Our Lord, let not our hearts deviate after You have guided us, and grant us from Yourself mercy. Truly You are the Ever-Endowing.*❞ [Q 3:8]

❝*Or do they (think that they) own the treasures of your Lord's Grace – (the Grace) of the Mighty, the Ever-Endowing.*❞ [Q 38:9]

17. The Ever-Sustaining - Ar-Razzaq (الرزاق ﷻ)

Ar-Razzaq – this name describes God's attribute of providing the necessities of life for all His creatures. He is the best Provider and He Sustains everyone according to His Mercy and Wisdom.

❝*Truly God is the Ever-Sustaining, the Possessor of Strength, the Firm.*❞ [Q 51:58]

Jabir ibn 'Abdullah (may God be pleased with him) narrated that Prophet Muhammad (pbuh) said, "O people! Fear God and be moderate in seeking a living, for no soul will die until it has received all its provision, even if it is slow in coming. So reverence God and be moderate in seeking provision; take that which is permissible and leave that which is forbidden."[1]

18. The Ever-Opening - Al-Fattah (الفتاح ﷻ)

God opens the gates of forgiveness and mercy to His servants and the stores of His provision; He opens believers' hearts to greater faith in Him, and their minds to wisdom. He also opens the Heavens and provides needed rain to the earth.

❝*Say, "Our Lord will gather us all together (on the Day of Judgment); then He will decide between us, with Truth; and He alone is the Ever-*

---

(1) The speaker: al-Albani – Source: Sahih ibn Majah – page or number: 1756. Conclusion of the speaker: sound.

Opening, the All-Knowing." ❁ *[Q 34:26]*

19. The Omniscient - Al-ʿAlim (العليم ﷻ)

The Omniscient – He is the All-Knowing of the Unseen and the seen, and He Encompasses all with His knowledge. This name also includes the meaning of Vastness, and is mentioned one hundred and fifty-four times in the Quran.

❁ *And if they incline to peace, then incline to it (also) and rely upon God. Truly He is the All-Hearing, the Omniscient.* ❁ *[Q 8:61]*

❁ *Truly your Lord is the Omniscient Creator.* ❁ *[Q 15:86]*

20. The All-Hearing - As-Sami' (السميع ﷻ)

God hears all things, from the quietest whispers of a secret conversation to the loudest of sounds. Nothing escapes His Hearing. This name is mentioned forty-five times in the Quran.

❁ *And (mention) when (Prophet) Abraham raised the foundations of the House (the Kaaba in Mecca) and (with him) Ishmael, (saying), "Our Lord! Accept (this) from us. Truly You are the All-Hearing, the Omniscient."* ❁ *[Q 2:127]*

❁ *And if they believe in the same as you believe in, then they shall be (rightly) guided. And if they turn away, they are only in dissension, and God will suffice you against them. And He is the All-Hearing, the Omniscient.* ❁ *[Q 2:137]*

❁ *God decrees with Truth, while those on whom they call apart from Him do not decree by means of anything. Truly God is the All-Hearing, the All-Seeing.* ❁ *[Q 40:20]*

21. The All-Seeing - Al-Basir (البصير ﷻ)

God sees all things, wherever they are, at all times. The Prophet (pbuh) told believers, "Worship God as though you are seeing Him; and while you do not see Him, truly He sees you." This name is mentioned forty-one times in the Quran.

❁ *Glory be to Him Who carried His Servant by night from the Sacred Mosque (in Mecca) to the Farthest Mosque (in Jerusalem), whose precincts We have blessed, that We might show him some of Our signs. Truly He is the All-Hearing, the All-Seeing.* ❁ *[Q 17:1]*

❧And God decrees with Truth, while those on whom they call apart from Him decree not with anything. Truly He is the All-Hearing, the All-Seeing. ❧ [Q 40:20]

22. The Gracious - Al-Latif (اللطيف ﷻ)

God is Gracious to His servants; His Kindness is given in a subtle way and people may not be aware of it. He comprehends all sight, and He perceives all vision. He might turn hardship and calamity into ease and safety through His Grace. The name is mentioned twice in the Quran.

❧Does He Who creates not know, while He is the Gracious, the All-Knowing. ❧ [Q 67:14]

❧Vision perceives Him not, but He perceives (all) vision; and He is the Gracious, the All-Knowing. ❧ [Q 6:103]

23. The Knower - Al-Khabir (الخبير ﷻ)

God knows all things in His kingdom, whether it is visible or invisible. Wherever we are, He is with us, and knows what we do and where we are. He Knows and is Aware of all things in the heavens and on earth. This name is mentioned forty-five times in the Quran.

❧Sight comprehends Him not, but He comprehends all sight; and He is the Gracious, the Knower. ❧ [Q 6:103]

❧And it is He Who created the heavens and the earth in truth. And on the day He says, "Be!" and it is, His word is the Truth. And sovereignty is His on the Day when the trumpet is blown, Knower of the Unseen and the seen; and He is the truly Wise, the Aware. ❧ [Q 6:73]

❧Sight comprehends Him not, but He perceives [all] vision; and He is the Gracious, the Knower. ❧ [Q 67:14]

24. The Forbearing - Al-Halim (الحليم ﷻ)

He gives His servants many chances to repent and return to the straight path, from darkness to light; He does not punish in haste, but relents to those who ask for forgiveness; He is most Patient, Merciful, Clement and Forgiving to His servants.

❧ *Those of you who turned away on the day the two hosts met - Satan alone made them slip because of part of what they committed. And God certainly pardoned them; truly God is the Ever-Forgiving, the Forbearing.* ❧ [Q 3:155]

❧ *He will surely cause them to enter an entrance with which they shall be content. And truly God is the Omniscient, the Forbearing.* ❧ [Q 22:59]

Abdullah ibn Abbas (may God be pleased with him) narrated that Prophet Muhammad (pbuh) used to say at times of difficulty, "None has the right to be worshipped but God, the Majestic, the Ever-Forbearing. None has the right to be worshipped but God, the Lord of the Tremendous Throne. None has the right to be worshipped but God, the Lord of the Heavens and the Lord of the Honorable Throne." [1]

25. The Great - Al-Azim (العظيم ﷻ)

The scale of God's greatness is so vast that it is difficult for human minds to grasp or comprehend. His Perfection, Glory and Magnificence are unique and incomparable. This name is mentioned six times in the Quran.

❧ *His throne embraces the heavens and the earth. Protecting them tires Him not, and He is the Most High, the Great.* ❧ [Q 2:255]

❧ *So glorify the Name of your Lord, the Great.* ❧ [Q 69:52]

26. The Ever-Forgiving - Al-Ghafur (الغفور ﷻ)

His forgiveness is unlimited for all His creatures, and believers must be sincere in their repentance. Whatever wrongdoing that people have done, they should remember that God is the Ever-Forgiving and pray for His forgiveness. All people make mistakes, but we must admit our mistakes, feel regret, and be determined to not repeat them.

❧ *And if God should touch you with adversity, none can remove it save He; and if He desires some good for you, none can hold back His bounty. He causes it to reach whomsoever He wills among His servants. And He is the Ever-Forgiving, Most Merciful.* ❧ [Q 10:107]

---

(1) The speaker: al-Bukhari – Source: Sahih al-Bukhari – page or number: 7431. Conclusion of the speaker: sound.

❧*He (Prophet Jacob) said, "I shall indeed seek forgiveness for you (Jacob's sons) from my Lord. Truly He is the Ever-Forgiving, the Most Merciful."*❧ [Q 12:98]

❧*Say, "O My servants who have been prodigal to the detriment of their own souls! Despair not of God's mercy. Truly God forgives all sins. Truly He is the Ever-Forgiving, the Most Merciful."*❧ [Q 39:53]

27. The All-Thankful - Ash-Shakur (الشكور ﷻ)

God acknowledges and appreciates any good deeds we do to show our love for, and obedience to Him, and He rewards us in the here and the hereafter. Any good deed will be rewarded multiple times its value.

❧*... that He may pay them their rewards in full and increase them from His bounty. Truly He is the Ever-Forgiving, the Ever-Thankful.*❧ [Q 35:30]

❧*And they (the inhabitants of Paradise) will say, "Praise be to God, Who has removed from us (all) sorrow. Truly our Lord is the Ever-Forgiving, the Ever-Thankful.*❧ [Q 35:34]

28. The Most High - Al-Ali (العلي ﷻ)

Nothing is higher than God, and no one can describe how High He is, since it is beyond a human's mind to know this. His status is supreme and sublime. 'The Most High' is mentioned eight times in the Qur'ān.

❧*(The disbelievers will be told), "That is because when God alone was invoked as One, you disbelieved, and when partners were ascribed to Him, you believed. Judgment lies with God, the Most High, the Great."*❧ [Q 40:12]

❧*To Him belongs whatsoever is in the heavens and whatsoever is on the earth, and He is the Most High, the Grand.*❧ [Q 42:4]

29. The Grand - Al-Kabir (الكبير ﷻ)

God is Grand in His actions, which we can witness in His creation and His Power to do whatsoever He Wills. 'The Grand' is mentioned five times in the Qur'ān.

❧*(He is) Knower of the Unseen and the seen, the Grand, the Transcendent.*❧ [Q13:9]

❧*(The disbelievers will be told), "That is because when God alone was invoked as One, you disbelieved, and when partners were ascribed to Him, you believed. Judgment lies with God, the Most High, the Grand."* ❧ *[Q 40:12]*

30. The All-Preserving - Al-Hafiz (الحفيظ ﷻ)

This name means that God is the Guardian and Protector Who provides absolute protection of His creatures against dangers, threats and disasters.

❧*He (Prophet Jacob) said, "Should I entrust him (Benjamin) to you as I entrusted his brother (Joseph) to you before? But God is the All-Preserving, and He is the Ever-Merciful."* ❧ *[Q 12:64]*

❧*But if you turn away, (know that) I have delivered to you the message wherewith I have been sent by Him. My Lord will cause you to be succeeded by a people other than yourselves, and you harm Him not in the least. Truly my Lord is the All-Preserving over all things."* ❧ *[Q 11:57]*

❧*Truly it is We Who have sent down the Reminder (the Holy Quran), and surely We are its Preserver.* ❧ *[Q 15:9]*

31. The All-Providing - Al-Muqīt (المقيت ﷻ)

God provides for and sustains all His creatures with unlimited ability and those provisions can be physical or spiritual. He creates provisions which come from the heavens, as in rain, or from the earth in forms that keep evolving to meet the needs of His creation.

❧*There is no moving creature on earth but its sustenance depends on God.* ❧ *[Q 11:6]*

❧*And ever is God, over all things, the All-Providing.* ❧ *[Q 4:85]*

❧*And truly God is the best of providers.* ❧ *[Q 22:58]*

32. The All-Reckoning - Al-Hasib (الحسيب ﷻ)

With His infinite knowledge, ability and presence, every detail is recorded, and everyone is held responsible before Him for all their deeds.

❧*And whoever trusts in God, He is the All-Reckoning.* ❧ *[Q 65:3]*

❧ *This Day every soul shall be recompensed for what it has earned. No injustice today! Truly God is the All-Reckoning.* ❧ [Q 40:17]

❧ *Those to whom the hypocrites said, "Indeed the people have gathered against you, so fear them." But it (merely) increased them in faith, and they said, "Sufficient for us is God, (and He is) the All-Reckoning."* ❧ [Q 3:173]

❧ *(God praises) those who convey the messages of God and fear Him and do not fear anyone but Him. And sufficient is God as the All-Reckoning.* ❧ [Q 33:39]

Abdullah ibn Abbas (may God be pleased with him) narrated that Prophet Abraham (pbuh) said, "God is sufficient for us and He is the Best Disposer of affairs," when he was thrown into the fire by the idol-worshippers; and it was said by Prophet Muhammad (pbuh) when they (the hypocrites) told him, "A great army is gathering against you, therefore fear them," but it only increased him in faith and he recited: "Sufficient for us is God, (and He is) the All-Reckoning." (Q 3:173) [1]

33. The Munificent - Al-Karim (الكريم ﷻ)

God is the most generous towards His creatures and meets their needs whether they ask for them or not. Their prayer is answered without any intermediary, and He provides for them with unlimited generosity; His blessings are countless. When we are thankful to Him, He increases His Grace upon us.

❧ *So, exalted is God, the King; there is no god but He, Lord of the Munificent throne.* ❧ [Q 23:116]

❧ *O mankind! What has deceived you with regard to your Lord, the Munificent.* ❧ [Q 82:6]

34. The Watchful - Ar-Raqīb (الرقيب ﷻ)

Everything is under God's watch. Nothing escapes Him and He is the All-Knowing. He is Watchful over all His creatures and is ever vigilant. Nothing is hidden or unknown to Him. We should thus always seek God's protection and help since He is watching over everything and everyone.

---

(1) The speaker: al-Bukhari – Source: Sahih al-Bukhari – page or number: 4563. Conclusion of the speaker: sound.

❈I (Jesus) said nothing to them save that which You commanded me: 'Worship God, my Lord and your Lord.' And I was a witness over them, as long as I remained among them. But when You took me (to Yourself), it was You Who were Watchful over them. And You are the Witness.❈ [Q 5:117]

❈And God is Watchful over all things.❈ [Q 33:52]

35. The Answerer - Al-Mujib (المجيب ﷻ)

He is the One Who answers prayers and rewards us for asking Him. It can be an immediate answer in this life, or a reward that comes to us in the Hereafter, according to His infinite Wisdom and Mercy.

❈And indeed Noah cried out to Us. How excellent is the Answerer. [75]

❈We saved him and his people from great distress ...[76] ❈ [Q 37:75-76]

❈He, Who answers the one in distress when he calls upon Him and removes the evil, and makes you vicegerents of the earth? Is there a god alongside God? Little do you reflect! ❈ [Q 27:62]

36. The Broad - Al-Wāsi (الواسع ﷻ)

God is the Broad in the sense of being vast, all-embracing and all-encompassing in His Knowledge, Ability and Mercy, which have no limits. His broad power and wisdom encompass all things.

❈... those who avoid grave sins and indecencies, save what is slight; truly your Lord is of broad forgiveness. He knows you best, from when He brought you forth from the earth and when you were hidden in your mothers' wombs. So, do not deem yourselves purified. He knows best who are conscious of Him.❈ [Q 53:32]

❈(a group of the People of the Book said) "And believe none but him who follows your religion ...." Say, "Truly guidance is God's guidance." "... lest anyone be granted the like (knowledge) of what you were granted or dispute with you before your Lord." Say, "Truly, (all) bounty is in God's Hand. He grants it to whomsoever He will, and God is the Broad, the Omniscient."❈ [Q 3:73]

❈And God gives His sovereignty to whomsoever He will, and God is the Broad, the Omniscient."❈ [Q 2:247]

37. The Wise - Al-Hakim (الحكيم ﷻ)

All wisdom comes from God, and it is His greatest gift to man. He grants wisdom to whomsoever He Wills, and who is given wisdom has been given much good. He governs the Universe with utmost wisdom and mercy. All wisdom belongs to Him.

They (the angels) said, "Exalted are You; we have no knowledge except what You have taught us. Indeed, it is You Who is the Omniscient, the Wise." [Q 2:32]

(Prophet Abraham prayed) Our Lord! Send among them (his descendants) a messenger from themselves who will recite to them Your verses and teach them the Book and wisdom and purify them. Truly You are the Exalted in Might, the Wise." [Q 2:129]

It is He Who forms you in the wombs however He wills. There is no deity except Him, the Exalted in Might, the Wise." [Q 3:6]

38. The Affectionate - Al-Wadud (الودود ﷻ)

As a mercy in Islam, for righteous believers who abide by God's laws, He will reward them with affection and love. He is the One Who loves all His creatures. There is mutual love between Him and His righteous servants, and He gives His love to those who love one another for His sake. This name, the Affectionate, is mentioned twice in the Qur'an.

(Prophet Shu'ayb said) Truly my Lord is the Merciful, the Affectionate. [Q 11:90]

And He is the Ever-Forgiving, the Affectionate. [Q 85:14]

39. The Glorious - Al-Majid (المجيد ﷻ)

This name can be interpreted to include all His attributes of Greatness, Whose bounty is infinite, and Whose position is Most High. God's Glory has no equal, and His Glory extends to all things created by Him, and to His Names and His Holiness.

They (angels) said (to Prophet Abraham) "Do you marvel at the Command of God? The Mercy of God and His Blessings be upon you, O Family of the House! Truly, He is the (ever) Praised, the Glorious." [Q 11:73]

... Possessor of the Throne, the Glorious... [Q 85:15]

40. The Witness - Ash-Shahid (الشهيد ﷻ)

God witnesses everything, and no one can hide from Him in the Heavens or on the earth. Nothing can be hidden or kept secret from God since He is the All-Knowing. Whatever He witnesses of our actions will be recorded and used for or against each of us on the Day of Judgment.

❊*Say, "O People of the Book! Why do you disbelieve in God's signs, while God is Witness over all things?"*❊ *[Q 3:98]*

❊*To each We have appointed heirs from what parents and relatives leave. Those to whom you have given your oath, give them their share. Truly God is ever, over all things, the Witness.*❊ *[Q 4:33]*

❊*We will show them Our signs in the horizons and within themselves until it becomes clear to them that it is the truth. But is it not sufficient concerning your Lord that He is, over all things, the Witness?*❊*[Q 41:53]*

41. The Truth - Al-Haqq (الحـق ﷻ)

God is the Truth and what He revealed is the Truth. What He has promised is the Truth. He governs His Kingdom in Truth, and nothing else shares this attribute. He is the true Creator of the Heavens and the earth. This name is mentioned ten times in the Quran.

❊*So exalted is God, the King, the Truth; there is no god but He, the Munificent Lord.*❊ *[Q 23:116]*

❊*There the authority is (completely) for God, the Truth. He is best in reward and best in outcome.*❊ *[Q 18:44]*

42. The Advocate - Al-Wakil (الوكيل ﷻ)

He is the trustee of His creation in every aspect. All the affairs of His creation are entrusted to Him, and He guides their affairs with His utmost Mercy, Knowledge and Wisdom.

❊*That is God, your Lord; there is no god but He, the Creator of all things, so worship Him. And He is the One, the Advocate.*❊ *[Q 6:102]*

❊*God is the Creator of all things, and He is the One, the Advocate.*❊ *[Q 39:62]*

43. The Strong - Al-Qawī (القوي ﷻ)

All strength belongs to Him, and He is the source of all strength in the Heavens and on the earth. He is able to do whatsoever He Wills. This name is mentioned nine times in the Quran.

So when Our Command came, We saved (Prophet) Salih and those who believed with him, through a Mercy from Us, and (saved them) from the disgrace of that day. Truly your Lord, He is the Strong, the Mighty. [Q 11:66]

And they (the disbelievers) did not measure God with His true measure. Truly God is the Strong, the Mighty. [Q 22:74]

God is Kind to His servants; He Provides for whomsoever He will. And He is the Strong, the Mighty. [Q 42:19]

44. The Firm - Al-Matīn (المتين ﷻ)

God's firmness is seen in His absolute Strength, Power and Ability. The believer seeks His firmness to strengthen his faith and ability to go through tests and challenges in life. This name is mentioned once in the Quran.

Truly God is the Provider, the Possessor of Strength, the Firm. [Q 51:58]

45. The Patron - Al-Waliyy (الولي ﷻ)

God is the Patron of all believers and He takes care of their affairs. He protects them and provides for them, guides them with Love and Mercy, and answers their prayers as long as they are righteous and show gratitude to Him. This name is mentioned thirteen times in the Qur'an.

Or have they taken protectors apart from Him? Yet God, He is the Patron, and He gives life to the dead; and He is Powerful over all things. [Q 42:9]

He it is Who sends down the rain after they have despaired and spreads forth His Mercy. And He is the Patron, the Praiseworthy. [Q 42:28]

46. The Praiseworthy - Al-Hamid (الحميد ﷻ)

He is the only One Who deserves all our praise for His Grace, Mercy and Guidance. This name is mentioned in the Quran seventeen times.

❀*They (the angels) said (to Prophet Abraham), "Do you marvel at the Command of God? The Mercy of God and His blessings be upon you, O People of the House. Truly He is the Praiseworthy, the Glorious."*❀ [Q 11:73]

❀*And know that God is the Self-Sufficient, the Praiseworthy.*❀ [Q 2:267]

47. The Ever-Living - Al-Ḥayy (الحي ﷻ)

God has always existed and He is the eternally alive. He is the source of all life and to Him we will return. He has granted life to all His creation. He is the eternally Self-Sufficient. He begets not, nor was He begotten. This name is mentioned five times in the Holy Quran.

❀*God, there is no god but He, the Ever-Living, the Ever-Rising.*❀ [Q 3:2]

❀*And trust in the Ever-Living, Who dies not, and exalt (God) with His praise. And God suffices as (the) One (Who is) Aware of the sins of His servants.*❀ [Q 25:58]

48. The Ever-Rising - Al-Qayyum (القيوم ﷻ)

God rises over everything, and there is nothing above Him. He governs His Kingdom without help from anyone or anything. He rises above His servants' affairs. This name is mentioned three times in the Quran, always with His name, the Ever-Living.

❀*God, there is no god but He, the Ever-Living, the Ever-Rising.*❀ [Q 3:2]

❀*Faces will be humbled before the Living, the Ever-Rising. And whosoever bears wrongdoing will have failed.*❀ [Q 20:111]

❀*God, there is no god but He, the Ever-Living, the Ever-Rising.*❀ [Q 2:255]

49. The One - Al-Wahid (الواحد ﷻ)

He is the One, and there is nothing comparable to Him, and no multiple for Him. He is the Unique and indivisible. No-one is equal to Him. This name, the One, is mentioned twenty-one times in the Qur'an.

(Prophet Joseph said) 'O my fellow prisoners! Are diverse lords better, or God, the One, The Ever-Subduing? ...' [Q 12:39]

... Say, "God is the Creator of all things, and He is the One, The Ever-Subduing." [Q 13:16]

Buraidah (may God be pleased with him) narrated: "Prophet Muhammad (pbuh) heard a man say, 'O God! I ask of You by virtue of testifying that You are God, there is no god but You, the One, the Self-Sufficient Master, Who does not beget, and was not begotten, and to whom no-one is equal.' The prophet (pbuh) then said, 'He has asked God by His Names by which, when asked, He gives, and by which, when supplicated, He answers.'" [1]

50. The Indivisible - Al-Ahad (الأحد ﷻ)

He is the One and Only One and nothing can rival Him or be like Him in His attributes of Might and Holiness. This name is mentioned once in the Holy Quran.

Say, "He, God, is the Indivisible, [1] God, the Steadfast, [2] He begets not, nor was He begotten. [3] And none is like unto Him."[4] [Q 112:1-4]

51. The Steadfast - As-Samad (الصمد ﷻ)

God is the everlasting refuge, the eternal supporter of Creation, and the One free from all need. He is the Master of the Universe. Everyone seeks refuge in Him, and believers put their trust in Him. This name is mentioned once in the Holy Quran.

Say, "He, God, is the Indivisible, [1] God, the Steadfast, [2] He begets not, nor was He begotten. [3] And none is like unto Him."[4] [Q 112:1-4]

---

(1) The speaker: Tirmidhi – Source: Sunan al-Tirmidhi – page or number: 3475. Conclusion of the speaker: fair but strange.

52. The Powerful - Al-Qadir (القادر ﷻ)

He is the One Who has absolute authority, and is capable of anything. He sets the measures to rule the Universe with His limitless Knowledge and Wisdom. He brings these measures into force with His Mercy and Compassion. Nothing can stop Him from accomplishing His Will. This name is mentioned seven times in the Qur'an.

❀Say, "He is the Powerful, Who can send a punishment upon you from above you or from beneath your feet, or confound you as discordant factions and make you taste the might of one another." Behold how We vary the signs, that they may understand. ❀ [Q 6:65]

53. The Omnipotent - Al-Muqtadir (المقتدر ﷻ)

He is the One with full Authority and absolute Power over all of His creation. He is the supreme Ruler, and His divine decrees cannot be challenged. Nothing is beyond His Power. He brings into being whatever measures He wills. This name is mentioned twice in the Quran.

❀Set forth for them a parable of the life of this world: (it is) like rain We send down from the sky. Then it mixes with the vegetation of the earth. Then it becomes chaff, scattered by the winds. And God is, over all things, the Omnipotent. ❀ [Q 18:45]

❀They denied Our signs - all of them; so We seized them with the seizing of One Exalted in Might, the Omnipotent. ❀ [Q 54:42]

54. The First - Al-Awwal (الأول ﷻ)

55. The Last - Al-Akhir (الآخر ﷻ)

Since God is Eternal, He has always existed. His existence has no beginning and no end. The very fact of His existence excludes His absence. He is the One Who existed before the Heavens and the earth were created by Him. There is nothing before Him, and there is nothing after Him; He is the Everlasting.

❀He is the First and the Last, the Manifest and the Unmanifest, and He is, over all things, the Omniscient. ❀ [Q 57:3]

❀He is the First and the Last, the Manifest and the Unmanifest, and He is, over all things, The Omniscient. ❀ [Q 57:3]

56. The Manifest - Az-Zahir (الظاهر ﷻ)

57. The Unmanifest - Al-Batin (الباطن ﷻ)

He makes Himself evident without being seen. His signs are everywhere: "We shall show them Our signs in the horizons and in themselves, until it is clear to them that it is the Truth." [Q 41:53] He is Manifest in His actions, His words, His guidance and His Presence.

He encompasses and transcends place, time and space, appearance and reality. The realm of the Unmanifest or Unseen is His exclusive preserve.

❈*He is the First and the Last, the Manifest and the Unmanifest, and He is, over all things, The Omniscient.*❈ *[Q 57:3]*

❈*No vision can grasp Him, but His grasp is over all vision: He is above all comprehension, yet is Acquainted with all things.*❈ *[Q 6:103]*

Abu Hurairah (may God be pleased with him) reported: "The Messenger of God (pbuh) used to order that when any one of us was about to sleep, he should say: 'O God! Lord of the heavens and the earth! Our Lord and the Lord of everything, splitter of the grain-seed and date-stone, and Revealer of the Torah, the Injil and the Qur'an. I seek refuge in You from the evil of every evil one that You hold by the forelock. You are the First, there is nothing before You; You are the Last, there is nothing after You; and You are the Manifest, there is nothing above you, and You are the Unmanifest, there is nothing below You. Relieve me of my debt, and enrich me from poverty.'"[1]

58. The Transcendent - Al-Muta'ali (المتعال ﷻ)

He is the Perfect and is Exalted beyond anything in His creation. "To God applies the highest similitude: for He is the Exalted in Power, Full of Wisdom." [Q 16:60] To Him belongs the loftiest description in the Heavens and on the earth. This name is mentioned once in the Qur'an.

❈*(He is) Knower of the Unseen and the witnessed, the Grand, the Transcendent.*❈ *[Q 13:9]*

---

(1) The speaker: Tirmidhi – Source: Sunan al-Tirmidhi – page or number: 3481. Conclusion of the speaker: fair but strange.

59. The Beneficent - Al-Barr (البر ﷻ)

He is the One Who bestows all types of benefits upon His righteous servants. He is the Most Merciful, Kind and Generous. He also grants many kinds of blessings upon all His creation. This name is mentioned once in the Quran.

❀*Indeed, we used to supplicate Him before. Truly He is the Beneficent, the Merciful."* ❀ *[Q 52:28]*

60. The Ever-Accepting of Repentance - At-Tawwāb (التواب ﷻ)

God's Mercy and Forgiveness are limitless, and He opens the gates of forgiveness to those who sincerely and humbly repent their sins. This name is mentioned eleven times in the Holy Quran.

❀*Then Adam received from his Lord (some) words, and He accepted his (Adam's) repentance. Truly He is the Ever-Accepting of Repentance, the Merciful.* ❀ *[Q 2:37]*

❀*And (He also forgave) the three who were left behind (and regretted their error) until the earth, despite its breadth, closed in upon them, and their own souls closed in upon them, and they deemed there to be no refuge from God, save with Him. Then He relented to them, that they might repent. Truly God is the Ever-Accepting of Repentance, the Merciful.* ❀ *[Q 9:118]*

61. The Pardoner - Al-'Afuww (العفو ﷻ)

He is the One Who readily pardons all the sins committed by mankind. His forgiveness is so great that we should never lose hope of being forgiven, however many sins we have committed. The only sin that God does not forgive is that of setting up partners with Him. We should emulate this attribute by pardoning the mistakes made by others, and return others' kindness to us. This name is mentioned five times in the Quran.

❀*... Truly God is the Pardoner and the Ever-Forgiving.* ❀ *[Q 22:60]*

❀*Truly God is the Pardoner and the Ever-Forgiving.* ❀ *[Q 4:43]*

62. The Compassionate - Ar-Ra'ūf (الرؤوف ﷻ)

He is the One Who shows Compassion, Mercy and Kindness to all His creatures, and expresses this by protecting them from danger, providing everything they need, guiding them, caring for them, and pardoning their sins. His compassion is boundless. This name is mentioned ten times in the Quran.

❦ ... He Who created the heavens and the earth and whatsoever is between them in six days, then mounted the Throne, the Compassionate (is He) ...❦ [Q 25:59]

❦On the Day when every soul shall find presented the good it did (before it) and the evil it did, it will wish that there might be a great distance between it (the evil) and itself. And God warns you of Himself, and God is Compassionate to His servants."❦ [Q 3:30]

❦... He, Who created the earth and the high heavens. The Compassionate mounted the Throne. ❦ [Q 20:4-5]

63. The Rich - Al-Ghani (الغني ﷻ)

He is the One Who is free from all want, and does not need anything from His creatures. He is utterly Self-Sufficient. It is His creatures who depend on Him for all their needs and they are the poor. He bestows riches upon whomever He Wills, and these riches might be in the form of useful knowledge or wisdom. Whoever is given these is rich indeed. This name is mentioned eighteen times in the Qur'an.

❦O mankind! You are needful of God; and He is the Rich, the Praiseworthy. ❦ [Q 35:15]

❦They say, "God has taken a child." Glory be to Him! He is the Rich. To Him belongs whatsoever is in the heavens and whatsoever is on the earth. You have no authority for this (claim). Do you say about God that which you know not? ❦ [Q 10:68]

64. The Inheritor - Al-Wārith (الوارث ﷻ)

He will inherit all things in the Universe after everything has passed away, for there is no greater power than His. He will continue to rule over the heavens and the earth for all eternity, and His infinite Power and Might transcend time and space.

❧Surely it is We Who give life and cause death, and We are the Inheritor (after all else passes away).❧ [Q 15:23]

The above sixty-four Most Beautiful Divine Names of God are found in the Quran itself, and they satisfy the condition of being proper names or nouns.

As mentioned earlier, there is a Hadith (Prophetic Tradition) which states that the Most Beautiful Names of God are 99 in number. There is no dispute about the above sixty-four Names, and they are generally accepted by most scholars, since they are already mentioned in the Quran.

The religious scholars, over the centuries, have tried to identify the other thirty-five names, using different approaches and outcomes. One scholar, whose name is Walid Ibn Muslim, deduced the following names, from the Quran and Hadith to complete the list of 99 names. They are the most used names. Present-day scholars, however, have not yet come to an agreement about these last thirty-five names, and continue to debate them.

The next two names are taken from the Prophetic Tradition.

65. The Constrictor - Al-Qabid (القابض ﷻ)

66. The Expander - Al-Basit (الباسط ﷻ)

He is the One Who constrains the sustenance of whomsoever He Wills, and He decides the fate of each of His creatures according to His Mercy, Grace and Wisdom. At the same time, He expands the sustenance for whomsoever He pleases since He has the absolute Power to set the measures for all things in the Heavens and on earth.

Anas Ibn Malik, may God be pleased with him, said that the people asked the Prophet (pbuh) to set the price of goods. The Prophet (pbuh) said, "God sets the prices. He is the constrainer and the expander, and the Provider of sustenance. I hope that when I meet God Almighty, none of you would demand anything from me because of any injustice I may have committed against you concerning money and lives. [1]

---

(1) The speaker: Abu Dawood – Source: Sunan Abu Dawood – page or number: 3451. Conclusion of the speaker: accepted.

Abu Dawood reported a saying narrated by Abu Musa (may God be pleased with them) that the Prophet (pbuh) said: "God created Adam from the earth and He constricted particles from the whole earth, and this is why the children of Adam are as diverse as the earth, some of them are red, some white, some black and some between. And some of them are at ease, or sad, or good or ugly." [1]

Muslim reported a saying narrated by Abu Musa al-Ashari (may God be pleased with them) that the Prophet (pbuh) said: "God Almighty expands His Hand (of forgiveness) at night for the people to repent from the sins they have committed that day, and He expands His Hand (of forgiveness) during the day for the people to repent from the sins they have committed during the night, and He will continue to extend His Hand (of forgiveness) until the sun rises from the west" (which is a sign of the coming Day of Judgment). [2]

67. The Judge - Al-Hakam (الحكم ﷻ)

He decrees the laws to be followed by all His creatures, and these laws are unchangeable. He implements His laws which differentiate between truth and falsehood, right and wrong. He makes judgments for His creation and there is no doubt that His judgment is the best and encompasses His utmost Mercy and Wisdom.

Hani ibn Yazid said that when he came to the Prophet (pbuh) with a group of his people, they were calling him (Hani ibn Yazid) 'aba al-Haqam' (father of judgment). The Prophet (pbuh) asked him why his people were calling him this name – since only God is the Judge (Al-Haqam). This is part of a longer Hadith. [3]

68. The Advancer - Al-Muqaddim (المقدم ﷻ)

69. The Delayer - Al-Mu'akhkhir (المؤخر ﷻ)

He advances the righteous believers through blessing them with wisdom and greater understanding. He promoted the Prophet (pbuh) to be the best among His servants. He advances and promotes whomever He Wills according to His Wisdom and Knowledge.

---

(1) The speaker: Abu Dawood – Source: Sunan Abu Dawood – page or number: 4693. Conclusion of the speaker: accepted.

(2) The speaker: Muslim – Source: Sahih Muslim – page or number: 2795. Conclusion of the speaker: sound.

(3) The speaker: Ibn Hibban – Source: Sahih Ibn Hibban – page or number: 504. Conclusion of the speaker: He included it in his Sahih Ibn Hibban.

Just as God can advance people and events, He can also, in His ultimate Wisdom and Mercy, delay such things as punishment, giving His servants more time to repent. He can also delay death, based on His judgment and Mercy, and defer events for a more suitable time in the future.

Bukhari narrated, based on what Abdullah ibn Abbas (may God be pleased with them) had told him, that the Prophet (pbuh), when he rose at night to pray (the Tahajjud prayer) would say, "O God, praise be to You, You are the Ever-Rising over the heavens and the earth. You are the Advancer and the Delayer. Forgive me for what I advanced and what I delayed; there is no god except You, and no God but You." [1]

❧*Do not suppose that God is heedless of the deeds of the wrongdoers; He merely grants them a delay until the Day when eyes will stare transfixed.*❧ *[Q 14: 42]*

70. The Demoter - Al-Khāfid (الخافض ﷻ)

He is the One Who demotes and lowers the status of those who transgress, disbelieve, show disobedience and disregard for God and His laws. He also promotes whomsoever He wills of His sincere believers.

71. The Promoter - Ar-Rafi (الرافع ﷻ)

❧*God will promote in degrees those among you who believe and those who have been given knowledge. God is Aware of whatsoever you do.*❧ *[Q 58:11]*

72. The Exalter - Al-Mu'izz (المعز ﷻ)

73. The Humiliator - Al-Mudhill (المذل ﷻ)

He is the One Who exalts whomever He pleases by empowering and supporting them, and He humiliates whoever He wishes because of their arrogance, envy, ingratitude and disobedience.

❧*Say, "O God, Master of Sovereignty, You give sovereignty to whomsoever You will, and take away sovereignty from whomsoever*

---

(1) The speaker: al-Bukhari – Source: Sahih al-Bukhari – page or number: 1120. Conclusion of the speaker: sound.

You will. You exalt whomsoever You will, and humiliate whomsoever You will. In Your hand is (all) good. Truly You are Powerful over all things." [Q 3:26]

74. The Just - Al-`Adl (العدل ﷻ)

God's justice is perfect and He urges His servants to be just among themselves. Whatever He Wills is utterly just. The Islamic way of life is most equitable and just.

And the Word of your Lord finds its fulfillment in Truth and in Justice. None can alter His Words, for He is the All-Hearing, the All-Knowing. [Q 6:115]

75. The Majestic - Al-Jalil (الجليل ﷻ)

He is the Owner of Majesty as He is the Most High, the Glorious. God's Majesty is evident in His Perfection and Greatness.

Blessed is the Name of your Lord, Possessed of Majesty and Bounty. [Q 55:78]

76. The Resurrector - Al-Bā'ith (الباعث ﷻ)

He is the One Who will resurrect all His creatures on the Day of Resurrection.

Only those who hear will respond. As for the dead, God will resurrect them, and to Him they shall be returned. [Q 6:36]

77. The Accounter, The Reckoner - Al-Muḥṣī (المحصي ﷻ)

He is the One Who keeps a numbered count of all things.

... that he may know that they (the prophets) have indeed conveyed the messages of their Lord. And He encompasses whatsoever is with them and keeps a numbered count of all things. [Q 72:28]

78. The Initiator - Al-Mubdi' (المبديء ﷻ)

79. The Restorer - Al-Mu'īd (المعيد ﷻ)

God initiates whatsoever He Wills, and is the initiator of all creation. His Will is the source of all being. On the Day of Resurrection He will restore all that was dead before that day.

❝He it is Who initiates creation; then restores it, and that is most easy for Him. To Him belongs the loftiest description in the heavens and on the earth, and He is the Mighty, the Wise. ❞ [Q 30:27]

❝God initiates creation, then restores it; then to Him shall you be returned.❞ [Q 30:11]

80. The Life-Giver - Al-Muḥyi (المحي ﷻ)
81. The Life-Taker - Al-Mumīt (المميت ﷻ)

He gives life and takes life. He restores life to the earth after it was dead. It is He Who gives us life, and He determines when we shall die.

❝His is the Dominion of the heavens and the earth. He gives life and causes death, and He is competent over all things.❞ [Q 57:2]

❝He it is Who gives life and causes death; and when He decrees a matter, He but says to it, "Be," and it is.❞ [Q 40:68]

82. The Finder, The Founder, The Author - Al-Wajid (الواجد ﷻ)

God is the founder of the universe, the author of its measures, and He can find everything. Nothing can be hidden from Him, and He is capable over everything He founds, and it is under His Will. He rules the universe according to His Wisdom and Mercy. Nothing escapes Him and He is close to everything.

❝ Did He not find you an orphan and shelter (you), [6] find you astray and guide (you), [7] and find you in need and enrich (you)? [8] ❞ [Q 93:6-8]

❝ ... whatever good you send forth for your souls, you will find it with God better and greater in reward ... ❞ [Q 73:20]

83. The Glory-Giver - Al-Majid (الماجد ﷻ)

All glory belongs to God and He gives it to whomsoever He Wills.

Abu Zar al-Ghafari (may God be pleased with him) narrated that the Prophet (pbuh) said, "God, Glory be to Him, says, 'I am the Generous, the Glorious, and the Glory-Giver. What I give and how I punish is by My Word. And if I want something, I tell it, 'Be', and it is.'" (1)

84. The Ordainer, The Protector - Al-Wali (الوالي ﷻ)

God is the Ordainer and Protector of whoever He Wills, according to His Mercy and Wisdom.

❦*God is the Protector of those who believe. He brings them out from darkness into the light. And those who disbelieve - their allies are the evil ones. They take them out of the light into darkness. Those are the companions of the Fire; they will abide eternally therein.*❧ [Q 2:257]

85. The Avenger - Al-Muntaqim (المنتقم ﷻ)

God will avenge the wrong-doers after He has given them ample opportunities to repent. And for the transgressors He will avenge them after giving them warnings.

❦*O you who believe, do not kill game while you are in the state of 'Ihram' (performing the pilgrimage in Mecca). And whoever of you kills it intentionally - the penalty is an equivalent from sacrificial animals to what he killed, as judged by two just men among you as an offering (to God) delivered to the Kaabah, or an expiation: the feeding of needy people or the equivalent of that in fasting, that he may taste the consequence of his deed. God has pardoned what is past; but whoever returns (to violation), then God will take revenge against him. And God is Exalted in Might, the Avenger.*❧ [Q 5:95]

86. The Owner of Dominion - Malik al-Mulk (مالك الملك ﷻ)

The whole universe belongs to God and He is the One Who holds absolute power over everything; He governs the Heavens and the earth and is the supreme ruler of His creation.

❦*Say, "O God, the Owner of Dominion, You give sovereignty to whom You will and You take sovereignty away from whom You will. You honor whom You will and You humble whom You will. In Your Hand is (all) good. Truly You are, over all things, Competent."*❧ [Q 3:26]

---

(1) The speaker: Shuaib Al Arna'ut – Source: Musnad Ahmed – page or number: 21367. Conclusion of the speaker: sound.

87. The Majestic and Bounteous One - Dhu-al-Jalal wa-al-Ikram (ذو الجلال والإكرام ﷻ)

He is the sole possessor of absolute Glory and Perfection, and His Majesty and Bounty are infinite.

❝Blessed is the name of your Lord, the Majestic and Bounteous One.❞ [Q 55:78]

88. The Equitable - Al-Muqsiṭ (المقسط ﷻ)

He is the Just, the Judge, the Equitable. He is the One Who is perfectly just and fair in His judgments. This gives believers peace of mind to know that their fate is in the hands of the Lord Who is Most Merciful, Ever-Forgiving, and Ever-Pardoning.

❝And if each soul that has wronged had everything on earth, it would offer it in ransom. And they will be filled with regret when they see the punishment; and they will be judged with equity, and they will not be wronged.❞ [Q 10:54]

89. The Gatherer - Al-Jami' (الجامع ﷻ)

He is the One Who gathers and brings together whomsoever and whatsoever He Wills, and this is easy for Him. He will gather all of mankind on the Day of Judgment.

❝God - there is no god but Him. He will surely gather you for [account on] the Day of Resurrection, about which there is no doubt. And who is more truthful than God?❞ [Q 4:87]

90. The Enricher - Al-Mughnī (المغني ﷻ)

God is the One Who grants wealth and riches to whomsoever He Wills and His Bounty is infinite. He is the Rich and enriches his servants as He pleases. Whoever wishes to be rich, he should ask the Enricher for it, and contentment makes believers the richest of the rich in terms of spiritual wealth.

❝… and (did He not) find you in need and enrich (you)?❞ [Q 93:7]

❝And if you fear privation, God will enrich you from His bounty if He wills. Indeed, God is Knowing and Wise.❞ [Q 9:28]

91. The Preventer - Al-Mani' (المانع ﷻ)

God prevents harm from reaching believers by protecting their lives, and no one can stop what He has ordained for His servants.

92. The Benefiter - Al-Nāfi' (النافع ﷻ)

93. The Distresser - Ad-Darr (الضار ﷻ)

God is the source of all forms of benefit for His creatures, based on His Wisdom and Mercy. His Benevolence is infinite, and no one can prevent it from reaching you.

Distress comes to people as part of God's tests and trials and He is the Only One Who can relieve you from them.

If God touches you with distress, there is none who can remove it but He; if He designs some benefit for you, there is none who can keep back His favour: He causes it to reach whomsoever of His servants He pleases. And He is the Ever-Forgiving, the Most Merciful. [Q 10:107]

Say, "I hold not for myself (the power of) benefit or distress, except what God has willed." [7: 188]

94. The Light - An-Nur (النور ﷻ)

God is the Light of the heavens and the earth, and He illuminates the whole universe with His Light. He enlightens His servants by guiding them from darkness to the light.

God is the Light of the heavens and the earth. The example of His light is like a niche within which is a lamp, the lamp is within glass, the glass as if it were a pearly (white) star lit from (the oil of) a blessed olive tree, neither of the east nor of the west, whose oil would almost glow even if untouched by fire. Light upon light. God guides to His Light whom He wills. And God presents examples for people, and God is All-Knowing. [Q 24:35]

God is the Protector of those who believe. He brings them out of the darkness into the light. [Q 2:256]

95. The Guide - Al-Hadi (الهادي ﷻ)

He guides believers to the straight path by His guidance in the Quran; He guides believers, through their hearts, to contentment. He guides the community of believers to peace. His guidance is the best and wisest guidance on which all mankind should depend.

❦ *That is the guidance of God by which He guides whomever He wills of His servants. But if they associate others with God, then worthless for them would be whatsoever they have done.* ❦ *[Q 6:88]*

❦ *... Say, "Truly, guidance is God's Guidance." "... Say, "Truly bounty is in God's Hand. He grants it to whomsoever He Will, and God is All-Encompassing, Knowing."* ❦ *[Q 3:73]*

96. The Originator - Al-Badi' (البديع ﷻ)

He is the One Who originates all things with perfection, beauty and ease. As the Originator, He creates whatsoever He Wills.

❦ *The Originator of the heavens and the earth. When He decrees a matter, He only says to it, "Be," and it is.* ❦ *[Q 2:117]*

97. The Ever-Lasting - Al-Bāqī (الباقي ﷻ)

He alone is the Eternal, the Infinite; He will endure forever. His Presence has no beginning and no end.

❦ *(Pharaoh's magicians said) "Indeed, we have believed in our Lord that He may forgive us our sins and what you (Pharaoh) compelled us (to do) of magic. And God is best and the Ever-Lasting."* ❦ *[Q 20:73]*

98. The Guide to Sound Judgment - Ar-Rashid (الرشيد ﷻ)

God guides believers to rectitude – to the right and straight path - with sound judgment to distinguish easily between right and wrong. True guidance is God's Guidance.

❦ *... "Truly we have heard a wondrous Quran [1] that guides to sound judgment; ... " [2]* ❦ *[Q 72:1-2]*

❦ *He whom God guides is the (rightly) guided, but he whom He leaves astray - never will you find a protector to guide him to the right path.* ❦ *[Q 18:17]*

99. The Most Patient - As-Ṣabūr (الصبور ﷻ)

God is fully aware of those who sin or disbelieve, but He gives them ample opportunities to repent, and He delays punishment because He is the Most Patient. He is also the Forbearing, and the Relenting.

Abu Musa al-Ash'ari (may God be pleased with him) narrated that the Messenger of God (pbuh) said, "None is more forbearing in listening to the most irksome things than God, the Exalted. They associate rivals with him, attribute a son to Him, but in spite of this He provides them sustenance, grants them safety, and confers upon them so many things. [1]

5-3-8 From the Prophetic Tradition

'Aisha (may God be pleased with her) narrated that the Messenger of God (pbuh) used to say: "O God, grant me health in my body, and health in my sight, and make these the inheritor from me; none has the right to be worshipped but God, the Clement, the Bountiful. Glory be to God, the Greatest, Lord of the Throne, and all praise is due to God, the Lord of all the worlds." " [2]

Abdullah ibn 'Abbas (may God be pleased with him) reported that God's Messenger (pbuh) used to say at times of distress: "There is no deity but God, the Greatest, the Most Forbearing; there is no deity but God, the Lord of the Throne, the Greatest; there is no deity but God, Lord of the Earth, Lord of the Throne, the Most Generous." [3]

Abdullah ibn Umar (may God be pleased with him) reported that God's Messenger (pbuh) used to say, "O God! I ask You for pardon and well-being in this life and in the Hereafter. O God! I ask You for pardon and well-being in my religion and worldly affairs, and my family and my wealth. O God! Veil my 'awrah' (my shameful matters) and set at ease my dismay. O God! Preserve me from the front, the back (behind me), my right, my left and from above, and I seek refuge in Your Greatness against being attacked from below." [4]

---

(1) The speaker: Muslim – Source: Sahih Muslim – page No. 835 Hadith number: 2804 (c). Conclusion of the speaker: sound.

(2) The speaker: Tirmidhi – Source: Sunan al-Tirmidhi – page or number: 3480. Conclusion of the speaker: fair but strange.

(3) The speaker: al-Albani – Source: Sahih al-Jaami' – page or number: 4940. Conclusion of the speaker: sound.

(4) The speaker: al-Albani – Source: Sahih al-Adab al-Mufrad – page or number: 912. Conclusion of the speaker: sound.

Anas ibn Malek (may God be pleased with him) narrated that he heard the Messenger of God (pbuh) say: "What prevents you from hearing what I recommend you to say when you enter the morning and when you enter the evening: 'The Ever-Living, the Ever-Rising, of Your Mercy I call for help. Put in order my whole state of affairs and do not leave me to myself for a single blink of the eye.' " [1]

5-4 Praying for the Prophet (pbuh) sincerely and frequently

❈*Truly God confers blessings upon the Prophet, and His angels (ask Him to do so). O you who believe, ask (God to confer] blessing upon him and ask (God to grant him) peace.* ❈ *[Q 33:56]*

'Abdullah ibn Mas'ud (may God be pleased with him) narrated that the Messenger of God (pbuh) said, "Those who are nearest to me on the Day of Resurrection will be those who invoked many prayers upon me." [2]

God Almighty informs His servants that His angels pray for the Prophet (pbuh) and He orders the believers to do the same. If people are in a gathering and do not pray for the Prophet (pbuh), they will regret it.

For those who keep the Prophet (pbuh) in their prayers, they will be among the closest to him in Paradise. The way to enter Paradise is to follow the Prophet's Guidance, as mentioned in the Hadith below.

Abu Hurairah (may God be pleased with him) narrated that God's Messenger (pbuh) said, "All my followers will enter Paradise except those who refuse." The Companions of the Prophet (pbuh) said, "O God's Messenger! Who will refuse?" He (pbuh) said, "Whoever obeys me will enter Paradise, and whoever disobeys me is the one who refuses (to enter Paradise)." [3]

Abu Mas'ud al-Badri (may God be pleased with him) reported the following: "We were sitting in the company of Saad ibn Ubada when the Messenger of God (pbuh) joined us. Bashir ibn Saad said: "O

---

(1) The speaker: al-Albani – Source: Sahih al Targhib– page or number: 661. Conclusion of the speaker: fair.

(2) The speaker: Ibn Hibban – Source: Boulough al-Maram – page or number: 455. Conclusion of the speaker: sound

(3) The speaker: al-Bukhari – Source: Sahih al-Bukhari – page or number: 280. Conclusion of the speaker: sound.

Messenger of God! God has commanded us to supplicate for you, but how should we do that?" The Messenger of God (pbuh) kept silent. We were much perturbed over his silence and we wished that Bashir had not asked him this question. The Messenger of God (pbuh) then said, 'Say: 'O God, exalt the mention of Muhammad and the household of Muhammad as You exalted the household of Abraham. And bless Muhammad and the household of Muhammad as You blessed the household of Abraham. You are the Praiseworthy, the Glorious,' and the method of greeting (i.e., Salam) is as I have taught you." [1]

Abu Hurairah (may God be pleased with him) reported that the Messenger of God (pbuh) said, "Whenever someone greets me, God returns my soul and I return his greeting." [2]

Abu Hurairah (may God be pleased with him) narrated that he heard the Prophet (pbuh) say: "Pray on the prophets and messengers of God, for God sent them as He has sent me." [3]

Abu Imam al-Bahli (may God be pleased with him) narrated that the Prophet (pbuh) said: "Increase me in prayer every Friday. My nation's prayer is offered to me every Friday. Whoever prays the most for me will be the closest one to me in Paradise. [4]

Al-Hassan ibn Ali (may God be pleased with him) narrated that he heard the Prophet (pbuh) say, "Do not make your houses as graves, and do not make my grave a place of festivity. But invoke blessings on me, for your blessings reach me wherever you may be." [5]

Abdullah ibn Amr ibn al-Aas (may God be pleased with him) reported God's Messenger (pbuh) as saying: "When you hear the caller to prayer (the Mu'adhdhin), repeat what he says, then invoke a blessing on me, for everyone who invokes a blessing on me will receive ten blessings from God. Then request from God Al-Wasila for me, which is a rank in Paradise that is fitting for only one of God's

---

(1) The speaker: Muslim – Source: Sahih Muslim – page or number: 405. Conclusion of the speaker: sounds like the prayer is veiled until the Prophet is given the due prayer.
(2) The speaker: Abu Dawood – Source: Sunan Abu Dawood – page or number: 2041. Conclusion of the speaker: Did not comment [accepted].
(3) The speaker: al-Suyuti – Source: al-Jaami' al-Saghîr – page or number: 5034. Conclusion of the speaker: fair
(4) The speaker: al-Suyuti – Source: al-Khasais al-Kubra – page or number: 2/261. Conclusion of the speaker: fair
(5) The speaker: al-Suyuti – Source: al-Jaami' al-Saghîr – page or number: 3768. Conclusion of the speaker: sound

servants, and I hope that I may be that one. If anyone asks that I be given Al-Wasila, he will be assured of my intercession."[1]

Abdullah ibn Umar (may God be pleased with him) narrated that the Messenger of God (pbuh) said: "The best of your days is Friday. On that day Adam was created and passed away, on it the Trumpet will be blown; on it all creatures will swoon. So, send a great deal of peace and blessings upon me on that day, for your peace and blessings will be presented to me." A man asked, 'O Messenger of God! How will our peace and blessings be shown to you when you are decayed?' He (pbuh) answered: 'God has forbidden the earth to consume the bodies of the Prophets.'[2]

We can conclude from this that continuous prayer for the Prophet (pbuh) is a great blessing and benefit in the here and the Hereafter.

5-5 The mission of Satan and his followers is to prevent us from remembering God

As explained above, continuous remembrance of God will keep believers under God's protection and guidance. The mission of Satan and his followers is to lead believers astray, and they focus on preventing us from connecting with God through prayer and remembering Him. They use whatever means they can, such as through intoxicants (alcohol, drugs) or gambling, as the verse below shows.

❖*Satan wants only to cause between you animosity and hatred through intoxicants and gambling and to avert you from the remembrance of God and from prayer. So will you not desist?* ❖ [Q 5:91]

Continuous remembrance of God will lead to a prosperous, good life, while turning away from this remembrance will result in the opposite effect. Remembering God is the light one sees with, while turning away from God's light will make one like a blind person, as mentioned in the verse below.

❖*And whoever turns away from My remembrance - indeed, he will have a depressed life, and We will gather him on the Day of*

---

(1) The speaker: Muslim – Source: Sahih Muslim – page or number: 384. Conclusion of the speaker: sound.

(2) The speaker: Ibn Hibban – Source: Sahih Ibn Hibban – page or number: 2454. Conclusion of the speaker: He included it in his Sahih Ibn Hibban.

Resurrection blind." [124] He will say, "My Lord, why have you raised me blind while I was (once) seeing?" [125](God) will say, "Thus did Our signs come to you, and you forgot them; and thus will you this Day be forgotten." [126] [Q 20:124-126]

The ones who remember God are with Him, and He is with them. The one who does not remember God has taken a devil as his companion, as shown in the verses below.

And whoever is blind to remembrance of the Most Merciful - We appoint for him a devil, and he is to him a companion. [Q 43:36]

This has been the mission of Iblis (Satan) ever since he was banished from Paradise for his arrogance and disobedience. Satan and his followers do whatever they can, by all means, to prevent believers from remembering God and from being thankful for God's bounty and grace. The only way for believers to safeguard themselves is to be very aware of Satan and his followers and protect themselves by seeking God's protection and guidance.

(Satan) said, "Because You have put me in error, I will surely sit in wait for them on Your straight path. [16] Then I will come upon them from before them and from behind them and on their right and on their left, and You will not find most of them grateful (to You)." [17] [Q 7:16-17]

And never let Satan avert you. Truly he is to you a clear enemy. [Q 43:62]

It is mentioned forty-three times, in forty-two verses of the Quran, that Satan (the Devil) will try to avert believers from the remembrance of God, as shown in the above two verses. Nineteen of these verses were revealed in Mecca, and twenty-three in Medina, in different contexts. All have the same message, that through the continuous remembrance of God you are protected from Satan. Believers should always keep this in mind and be aware that Satan is our avowed enemy.

5-5-1 Satan's attempts to turn believers away from the straight path

Believers must safeguard themselves by being constantly aware that Satan will never stop trying to turn us away from the remembrance of God. Believers must be equally on guard against Satan's followers, who have gone astray, even though this may not be obvious to the believer.

❦*He (Satan) led me away from the remembrance (of God) after it had come to me. And ever is Satan, to man, a deserter.* ❦ [Q 25:29]

❦*Truly those who disbelieve spend their wealth to avert (people) from the way of God. So they will spend it; then it will be for them a (source of) regret; then they will be overcome. And those who have disbelieved - to Hell they will be gathered.* ❦ [Q 8:36]

God has promised that what the disbelievers spend to avert believers from the way of God, they will regret and be the losers in this world and in the Hereafter.

❦*And do not be like those who came forth from their homes insolently, to be seen by people and to avert (them) from the way of God. And God encompasses all that they do.* ❦ [Q 8:47]

Furthermore, disbelievers will dedicate their lives to leading believers astray. Even though their behavior is corrupt and sinful, they believe they are doing good. They can only be judged against Islamic principles.

❦*O you who believe! Truly many of the scholars and monks devour the wealth of people unjustly and avert (them) from the way of God. And those who hoard gold and silver and spend it not in the way of God - give them tidings of a painful punishment.* ❦ [Q 9:34]

❦*And indeed, the devils avert them from the way (of guidance) while they think that they are (rightly) guided.* ❦ [Q 43:37]

❦*And when it is said to them, "Do not cause corruption on the earth," they say, "We only want to make peace." [11] Unquestionably, it is they who are the corrupters, but they perceive (it) not.[12]* ❦ [Q 2:11-12]

5-6 Summary and Conclusions

In this chapter we have reviewed the various types of remembrance (known as 'dhikr'), such as saying 'There is no deity but God' (known as 'Tahlil') and 'All power and ability belong to God alone' (known as 'Hawqala'), as well as prayers for the Prophet (pbuh), prayers for forgiveness, prayers for the glorification of God, reading the Holy Quran - which is the foundation of worship, and especially prayers that include His Most Beautiful Divine Names. A brief presentation of these

Divine Names is given because of their blessings, and because God urges believers to ask Him for their needs while addressing Him by these Names. Also included are the prayers of God's prophets as given throughout the Quran. Every good deed that is done for the sake of God is a remembrance of Him and a source of reward. In the next chapter we will discuss thankfulness since being thankful, and having a heart free of envy, are major sources of contentment.

Chapter 6

Thankfulness for what you have and overlooking what others have of worldly splendour

❦... 'If you give thanks, I shall surely grant you increase ...❧
[Q 7:14]

❦And never turn your eyes (with longing) towards whatever
splendour of this world's life We may have allowed so many
others to enjoy in order that We might try them thereby:
for the sustenance which your Sustainer provides
(for you) is better and more enduring.❧
[Q 20:131]

بِسْمِ اللَّهِ الرَّحْمَنِ الرَّحِيمِ

﴿وَأَسْبَغَ عَلَيْكُمْ نِعَمَهُ ظَاهِرَةً وَبَاطِنَةً﴾

﴿وَلَا تَتَمَنَّوْا مَا فَضَّلَ اللَّهُ بِهِ بَعْضَكُمْ عَلَى بَعْضٍ﴾

وان تعدوا
نعمة الله
لا تحصوها

صدق الله العظيم

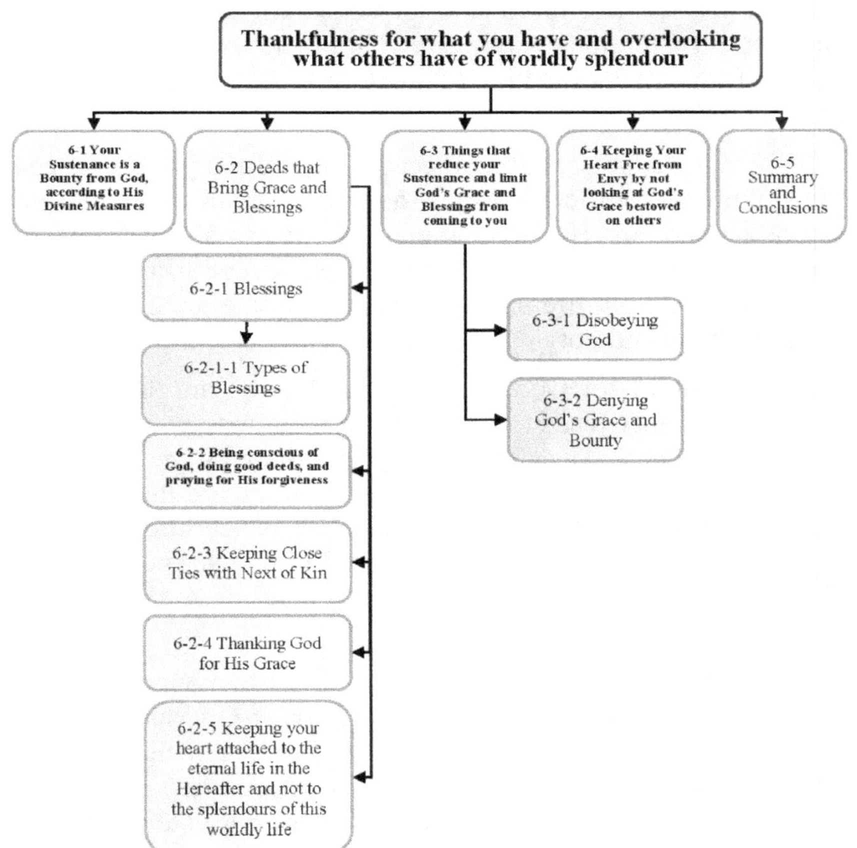

Fig. 1: Structure of Chapter 6

6-0 Introduction

Praising God and thanking Him for His Grace will bring His contentment and blessings on what He has bestowed upon us. God's Bounty is infinite, and some of it is apparent, some not. When we realize this and are grateful to God for everything we have been given, it will turn our attention away from what others have, and will purify our hearts from envy – the kind of heart every believer needs when he meets his Lord.

This chapter addresses the subject of God's Bounty, sustenance and blessings and their different forms, and what believers should do to keep God's Grace and Bounty coming to them, and also continue to be blessed, which is a source of contentment. Believers' hearts need to be focused on the eternal life in the Hereafter and the great rewards that await them there, and not on the splendours of this world.

Being thankful for God's Grace and Bounty, and being content with your sustenance leads to God being content with you and blessing you with more Grace. The Grace of God is infinite. Some of this Grace can be seen, while other sources of God's Grace are hidden and not obvious. For example, if God gives you wealth and children, people can see this. Other types of Grace that cannot be seen are peace of mind, wisdom, and contentment. If you are thankful, you will have a contented heart.

Lowering your gaze – that is, not desiring or envying what others have – will cause you to be satisfied with what God has given you. Never concern yourself with what others have, and never compare yourself to others. This will purify your heart and free it from envy, jealousy and resentment. This is a pre-requisite for entering Paradise. However, thoughts and attitudes when one becomes envious, lead to severing of social ties and prevents one from achieving a heart free of evil. Count your blessings and God will increase them because of your gratitude and acknowledgement of His Grace upon you.

If you try to count all your blessings, you will not be able to as they are so many. He provides for you, and delays punishment for those who are unthankful.

God provides for us with set measures and all of these are written in the Mother of the Book (Um al-Kitāb), as are all other Godly measures. He distributes His provision as He wills, and He is the All-Knowing, the Ever-Wise. We should rest assured that He is our Sponsor and Patron, and He will amply provide for us from His limitless bounty.

You might like something that is bad for you, but dislike something that is good for you, and then pray for things that are unsuitable or inappropriate for your life. People pray for whatever they think is good for them since they do not know the future. This is why believers should always place their trust in God and ask Him to bless the outcome that is best for them. Being ever thankful to God, the Sustainer, for all the things He provides for you will increase His blessings on you. Believers should rely on God's limitless Mercy, Knowledge and Wisdom.

❊... it may be that you hate a thing though it is good for you, and it may be that you love a thing though it is not good for you. God knows, and you know not. ❊ [Q 2:216]

❊And man supplicates for evil as he supplicates for good, and man is ever hasty. ❊ [Q 17:11]

❊Indeed, your Lord extends provision for whomsoever He wills and restricts (it). Indeed He is, concerning His servants, All-Aware and All-Seeing. ❊ [Q 17:30]

❊And enjoin prayer upon your family (and others) and be steadfast therein. We ask you not for provision; We provide for you, and the (best) outcome is for (those of) righteousness. ❊ [Q 20:132]

❊And in heaven is your provision and whatever you are promised. Then by the Lord of Heaven and Earth, indeed, it is truth – just as (sure as) it is that you are speaking. ❊ [Q 51: 22-23]

Whatever God promises of fortune and misfortune is written in His Book, and all these measures are included. Almighty God fulfils His promises, and we should be sure of this and trust completely in God's infinite Goodness and Mercy.

❊And I did not create the jinn (unseen beings) and mankind except to worship Me. [56] I do not want from them any provision, nor do I want them to feed Me. [57] Truly it is God Who is the (continual) Provider, the Firm Possessor of Strength. [58] ❊ [Q 51:56-58]

The verses above show that God created us to be dedicated to His worship and service, so anything we do should have this intention. We need to continuously keep Him in our hearts and minds, appreciate His Grace and Bounty, and think about His Signs. God's Grace and Blessings are given mercifully and wisely according to His measures.

6-1 Your Sustenance is a Bounty from God, according to His Divine Measures

Sustenance is not only wealth, but also spiritual and material blessings. Some of this grace will be addressed here, and is outlined in the Quranic verses and Traditions of the Prophet (pbuh) shown below.

A. <u>General Grace</u>

1. Living in a safe and secure place

One of God's bounties is that you live in a peaceful place, not threatened by war, disease or famine, and where you feel safe in your home.

❃And (remember) when (Prophet) Abraham said, "My Lord! Make this land secure, and keep me and my children from worshipping idols…"❃ [Q 14:35]

❃And they (the Prophet's people of Mecca) say, "If we follow guidance along with you, we shall be snatched away from our land." Have We not established for them a secure Sanctuary, to which the fruits of all things are brought, as a provision from Our Presence? But most of them know not. ❃ [Q 28:57]

❃… and by this land (Mecca) made safe … ❃ [Q 95:3]

❃Or have they not considered that We have made a secure sanctuary while people are snatched away all around them? ❃ [Q 29:67]

❃So when they (Prophet Joseph's parents and brothers) entered upon Joseph, he drew his parents close to himself and said, "Enter Egypt in security, if God wills!" ❃ [Q 12:99]

As can be seen from the above verses, it is a great grace from God to live in a safe and secure place. One important condition to living in safety and security is that you live where there is law and order, and that is why the following hadith emphasize the importance of having an equitable and impartial system of justice.

Abu Huraira (may God be pleased with him) narrated that the Prophet (pbuh) said, "God will give shade to seven (types of people) on the Day when there will be no shade but His. (These seven are) a just ruler; a youth who has been brought up in the worship of God (i.e. worships God sincerely from childhood); a man whose heart is attached to the mosques (i.e. he prays the compulsory prayers in the mosque in congregation); two persons who love each other only for God's sake and they meet and part in God's cause only; a man who refuses the call of a charming woman of noble birth for illicit relations with her and says: 'I am afraid of God; a man who gives charitable gifts so secretly that his left hand does not know what his right hand has given (i.e. nobody knows how much he has given in charity); and a person who remembers God in seclusion and his eyes are then flooded with tears." [1]

'Abdullah ibn 'Umar (may God be pleased with him) reported that the Messenger of God (pbuh) said, "Behold! The dispensers of justice will be seated on pulpits of light beside God, on the right side of the Merciful, Exalted and Glorious. Either side is the right side, both being equally meritorious. (The dispensers of justice are) those who maintain justice in their rule, in matters relating to their families and in all that they undertake to do. [2]

Salamah ibn 'Ubaidullah ibn Mihsan al-Khatmi narrated from his father - and he was a Companion - (may God be pleased with them) who reported that he heard the Messenger of God (pbuh) say, "Whoever among you wakes up in the morning secure in his dwelling, healthy in his body, having his food for the day, then it is as if the world has been gathered for him.'" [3]

Believers should seek to live in a place of peace and security, and pray that these conditions prevail, not only in their own country but also throughout the world.

2. The Natural World is subservient to mankind

❂He made subservient to you whatsoever is in the heavens and whatsoever is on the earth — all together. Truly in that are signs for a people who reflect. ❂ [Q 45:13]

❂Have they not looked upon the sky above them, how We built it and adorned it, and (how it) has no rifts? [6] The earth We spread out, and

---

(1) The speaker: al-Bukhari – Source: Sahih al-Bukhari – page or number: 660. Conclusion of the speaker: sound.

(2) The speaker: Muslim – Source: Sahih Muslim – page or number: 1827. Conclusion of the speaker: sound.

(3) The speaker: Tirmidhi – Source: Sunan al-Tirmidhi – page or number: 2346. Conclusion of the speaker: fair.

cast therein firm mountains, and caused every delightful kind to grow therein, [7] as a source of insight and a reminder for every penitent servant. [8] And We sent down blessed water from the sky whereby We grew gardens and the harvested grain, [9] and the date palms towering with layered spathes as provision for His servants ... [10] [Q 50:6-10]

And cattle has He created for you, in which there is warmth and (other) uses, and whereof you eat. [Q 16:5]

And (He has created) horses, mules, and asses, that you may ride them, and as adornment, and He creates that which you know not. [Q 16:8]

... who, were We to establish them upon the earth, would perform the prayer, give the alms, and enjoin right and forbid wrong. And to God is the end of all affairs. [Q 22:41]

As can be seen, the Grace of God is all around us, from the earth and the heavens, in all different forms. We should reflect and be thankful for them, use them wisely and preserve them for future generations.

B. Personal Grace

In addition to the general grace and bounty of God, there is grace and bounty of a personal nature, which is given to individuals to enable them to carry out their mission as entrusted to them by God. These include such things as one's health, knowledge, wisdom, marriage and children, and they are provided to us over our lifespan with the utmost wisdom and mercy of God. Some examples of personal grace and bounty are a good and righteous spouse, and a marriage that is blessed by love, mercy and understanding.

1. A Righteous Spouse

And among His signs is that He created mates for you from among yourselves, that you might find rest in them, and He established love and tenderness between you. Truly in that are signs for a people who reflect. [Q 30:21]

... and who pray: "O our Sustainer! Grant that our spouses and our offspring be a joy to our eyes, and cause us to be foremost among those who are conscious of You." [Q 25:74]

Abu Huraira (may God be pleased with him) narrated that the Prophet (pbuh) is reported to have said, "The believer whose faith is most complete is the one whose character is the best; and the best among you are those who are best to their wives." [1]

'Abdullah ibn Amr (may God be pleased with him) reported the Prophet (pbuh) as saying, "The whole world is a provision, and the best object of benefit in the world is the pious woman." [2]

Abu Huraira (may God be pleased with him) narrated that the Prophet (pbuh) said, "A woman is married for four things, i.e., her wealth, her family status, her beauty, and her religion. So you should marry the religious woman, (otherwise) you will be losers." [3]

2. Good Offspring

It is a great grace from God to be given righteous offspring who will continue your good works, propagate the word of God, pray for you and do good deeds. That was the prayer of the Prophets.

❧*These were some of the prophets upon whom God bestowed His blessings – (prophets) whom We caused to be carried (in the ark) with Noah, and of the seed of Abraham and Israel (Jacob): and (all of them were) among those whom We had guided and elected; (and) whenever the messages of the Most Compassionate were conveyed to them, they would fall down (before Him), prostrating themselves and weeping.*❧ [Q 19:58]

❧*And he (Prophet Abraham) prayed: "O my Lord! Bestow upon me the gift of (a son who shall be) one of the righteous!"*❧ [Q 37:100]

❧*To (Prophet) David We gave Solomon (for a son) – how excellent in Our service! Ever did he turn (to Us)!*❧ [Q 38:30]

❧*In that self-same place (where Mary lived) (Prophet) Zachariah prayed to his Lord, saying: "O my Lord! Bestow upon me (too) out of Your grace, the gift of goodly offspring; for You, indeed, hear all prayer."*❧ [Q 3:38]

---

(1) The speaker: al-Albani – Source: Jami` at-Tirmidhi – page or number: 1162. Conclusion of the speaker: fair and sound.

(2) The speaker: Muslim – Source: Sahih Muslim – page or number: 1467. Conclusion of the speaker: sound.

(3) The speaker: al-Bukhari – Source: Sahih al-Bukhari – page or number: 5090. Conclusion of the speaker: sound.

Abu Huraira (may God be pleased with him) reported God's Messenger (pbuh) as saying: "When a man dies, his acts come to an end, except for these three: recurring charity, or knowledge (by which people benefit), or pious offspring who pray for him (for the deceased). [1]

3. Wisdom as a Grace from God

God is the Most Wise, and this is one of His 99 Most Beautiful Divine Names. Part of His grace to His servants is the bestowing of wisdom on whom He wills, and it is a great grace from Almighty God.

❊ *(Prophet Abraham and his son Ishmael prayed:) "O our Lord! Raise up from the midst of our offspring an apostle from among themselves, who shall convey to them Your messages, and impart to them revelation as well as wisdom, and cause them to grow in purity: for truly, You alone are Almighty, truly Wise."* ❊ *[Q 2:129]*

God answered the prayer of Abraham and Ishmael, as shown in the following verse:

❊*... even as We have sent to you an apostle from among yourselves to convey to you Our messages, and to cause you to grow in purity, and to impart to you revelation and wisdom, and to teach you that which you knew not ..* ❊ *[Q 2:151]*

❊*He grants wisdom to whomsoever He will. And whosoever is granted wisdom has been granted much good. Yet none remember save the possessors of intellect.* ❊ *[Q 2:269]*

4. Guidance as a Grace from God

God is the Guide, and His guidance, love and contentment are wonderful gifts bestowed by Him upon whom He wills, in His utmost Mercy, especially for those who seek the guidance given in the Holy Quran. Believers can find guidance by following the straight path outlined in God's messages.

❊*Whomsoever God guides, he is rightly guided; and whomsoever He leads astray, it is they who are the losers.* ❊ *[Q 7:178]*

❊*Whomsoever God guides, he is rightly guided; and whomsoever He leads astray, you will find no protectors for them apart from Him.* ❊ *[Q 17:97]*

---

(1) The speaker: Muslim – Source: Sahih Muslim – page or number: 1467. Conclusion of the speaker: sound.

❀*Say (O Prophet), "Truly guidance is God's Guidance."* ❀ *[Q 3:73]*

❀*God increases in guidance those who are rightly guided. And that which endures – righteous deeds – are better in reward with your Lord, and better in return.* ❀ *[Q 19:76]*

❀*But those who are (willing to be) guided, He increases them in guidance and causes them to grow in God-consciousness.* ❀ *[Q 47:17]*

5. Knowledge as a Grace from God

Almighty God is the All-Knowing, the All-Aware, and He gives knowledge to people as a test to see how they use this knowledge, and they will be judged accordingly. It is a type of gift that must be used very carefully, in righteous ways, and seeking God's guidance in order to make this knowledge useful and beneficial to oneself and to humanity.

❀*The Compassionate [1] has imparted this Quran (to man); [2] He has created man; [3] He has imparted to him articulate thought and speech.[4]* ❀ *[Q 55:1-4]*

❀*Recite in the Name of your Lord Who has created, [1] created man from a blood clot. [2] Recite! Your Lord is most Noble, [3] Who has taught (man) the use of the Pen, [4] taught man that which he knew not. [5]* ❀ *[Q 96:1-5]*

❀*... even as We sent among you a messenger from among you, who recites Our signs to you and purifies you, and teaches you the Book and Wisdom, and teaches you what you knew not.* ❀ *[Q 2:151]*

❀*And remain conscious of God, since it is God Who teaches you, and God has full knowledge of everything.* ❀ *[Q 2:282]*

❀*He it is Who has sent down the Book upon you; therein are signs determined ... And none know its interpretation save God and those firmly rooted in knowledge. They say, "We believe in it; all is from our Lord." And none remember, save those who possess intellect.* ❀ *[Q 3:7]*

❀*God bears witness that there is no god but He, as do the angels and the possessors of knowledge, upholding justice. There is no god but He, the Mighty, the Wise.* ❀ *[Q 3:18]*

❦No, it is only clear signs in the hearts of those who have been given knowledge, and none reject Our signs, save the wrongdoers. ❦
[Q 29:49]

6. Good Health as a Grace from God

Good health is a gift from God that should be maintained to serve the cause of God. We must be thankful for this gift, look after it, and use it wisely.

❦ "Truly God has raised up Saul for you as king." They (the Children of Israel, after Moses) said, "How shall he have sovereignty over us while we have more right to sovereignty than he, and he has not been given abundant wealth?" He (Prophet Samuel) said, "Truly God has chosen him over you, and has endowed him abundantly with knowledge and bodily perfection." ❦ [Q 2:247]

❦… and when I fall ill, (He) is the One Who restores me to health." ❦
[Q 26:80]

Anas ibn Malik (may God be pleased with him) narrated that a man came to the Prophet (pbuh) and said: "O Messenger of God, which supplication is the best?" He (pbuh) said: "Ask God for pardon and good health (al-Afuww wa al-Afiyah)." [1]

7. Wealth as a trial from God

Wealth in different forms is given by God to whomsoever He wills, and it is one of the toughest tests that people can face. Many fail it but, even so, many people still desire to have much wealth. The believer should be very aware that this is a difficult test, and try to use whatever wealth is bestowed on him in the cause of God. He should also keep in mind that he will be judged on the Day of Reckoning for what he did with his wealth.

❦Made to seem fair to mankind is the love of passions, among them women, children, hoarded heaps of gold and silver, horses of mark, cattle, and tillage. Those are the enjoyment of the life of this world. And God, with Him is the beautiful return. ❦ [Q 3:14]

❦Wealth and children are the adornment of the life of this world, but that which endures — righteous deeds — are better in reward with your

---

(1) The speaker: Tirmidhi – Source: Sunan al-Tirmidhi – page or number: 2346. Conclusion of the speaker: fair.

Lord, and better (as a source of) hope. ❧ *[Q 18:46]*

Sahl ibn Saad (may God be pleased with him) reported, "I heard Ibn al-Zubair, who was on the pulpit at Mecca, delivering a sermon; he said, "O men! The Prophet used to say, 'If the son of Adam were given a valley full of gold, he would love to have a second one, and if he were given the second one, he would love to have a third, for nothing fills the belly of Adam's son except dust (when he is buried in his grave). And God forgives he who repents to Him.' [1]

8. Sovereignty as a trial from God

He is the Sovereign Lord, and He appoints kings and removes kings as He wills. When He entrusts one with such high status, it is merely a test and he will be judged on his performance in this capacity, whether he used his kingdom for good or evil, for forces of justice or for forces of darkness.

❧*Say, "O God, Master of Sovereignty, You give sovereignty to whomsoever You will, and wrest sovereignty from whomsoever You will. You exalt whomsoever You will, and abase whomsoever You will ..."* ❧ *[Q 3:26]*

❧*When they (two shepherds) entered upon (King) David, he was frightened of them. They said, "Fear not! We are two disputants: one of us has transgressed against the other; so judge between us with truth. Be not unjust, and guide us to the right path. * ... He (David) said, "Truly many associates transgress against one another, save those who believe and perform righteous deeds. Yet how few are they!" And David understood that We had tried him; so he sought forgiveness from his Lord, fell down kneeling, and repented.* ❧ *[Q 38: 22-24]*

It is the duty of all believers to appreciate the different forms of bounty and grace that God has bestowed upon them and be thankful to Him. We should pray that He sustains His bounty and grace, and blesses it for us.

In the following section we discuss the concept of God's blessings and how these blessings are part of what God bestows upon His servants.

---

(1) The speaker: al-Bukhari – Source: Sahih al-Bukhari – page or number: 6438. Conclusion of the speaker: sound.

6-2 Deeds that bring Grace and Blessings

6-2-1 Blessings

God is the source of all blessings in everything, and they are a divine gift. He bestows His blessings with His ultimate Wisdom and Mercy. When He blesses anything, its value and benefits are magnified. The best blessing for anyone is the contentment of God, and it comes only from Him. The believer, when he asks for anything, should ask for it to be blessed by God, so that it will have the utmost benefit in the here and in the Hereafter. We ask God to bless our health, our parents and children, our knowledge, our wealth, our country, and all aspects of our lives. Receiving His blessings will generate contentment and have the utmost usefulness.

Blessed is He Who sent down the Criterion (the Quran) upon His servant (Prophet Muhammad) that he may be a warner to the worlds. [Q 25:1]

Blessed is He in Whose Hand lies sovereignty, and He is Powerful over all things. [Q 67:1]

That is God, your Lord; so blessed is God, Lord of the worlds. [Q 40:64]

Blessed is God, the best of creators! [Q 23:14]

As the giver of all blessings, God blesses some things and not others – different places and different people, based on His unlimited Knowledge and Mercy. There are so many sources of blessings that God has bestowed upon mankind, and some of them are mentioned below.

6-2-1-1 Types of Blessings

A. Blessed Sustenance

Without the blessings of God, the value or usefulness of any sustenance will be diminished. With His blessings, our sustenance will be useful and rewarding. For example, when God blesses your time, it means that you can achieve meaningful, fruitful work. When he blesses your life in this world, it will be filled with good deeds. When He blesses your knowledge, it will be useful for humanity. When he blesses your wealth, it provides for you and will be a source of help to many people. When he blesses your food and drink, it will be useful for your health. When He blesses your health, you will stay healthy and well. When He blesses your house, it will be a house of contentment, love and tranquility. When he blesses your marriage, it will be a source of love, understanding and support. When he blesses your children, they will be kind and obedient. Anything that is blessed by God will have a positive and happy outcome, in this world and in the Hereafter.

One of the sources of great blessings is rain, as mentioned below.

❖And We sent down blessed water from the sky whereby We grew gardens and the harvested grain ❖ [Q 50:9]

B. Blessed Revelation

❖ (This is) a blessed Book that We have sent down upon you (O Muhammad), that they may contemplate His signs and that those possessed of intellect may reflect. ❖ [Q 38:29]

❖And this is a blessed Book that We have sent down, confirming that which came before it ❖ [Q 6:92]

❖And this is a blessed Book that We have sent down; so follow it and be conscious of God, that perhaps you may receive mercy. ❖ [Q 6:155]

C. Blessings from the Quran

Believers who read and recite the Quran will be blessed, and those who follow the guidance of the Quran will experience a blessed life in the here and the Hereafter, and in all aspects of human life.

Abu Umama (may God be pleased with him) narrated that he heard God's Messenger (pbuh) say: "Recite the Qur'an, for on the Day of Resurrection it will come as an intercessor for those who recite it. Recite the two bright ones, Surahs al-Baqarah and Al-Imran (Chapters 2 and 3), for on the Day of Resurrection they will come as two clouds or two shades, or two flocks of birds in ranks, pleading for those who recite them. Recite Surah al-Baqarah (Chapter 2), for to take recourse to it is a blessing and to give it up is a cause of grief, and the magicians cannot confront it. [1]

D. Blessings upon the Prophets

Following the guidance of God's prophets (peace be upon them) is a source of blessing, since they conveyed the messages of the Holy Books and how people can live by God's guidance, and following them is a source of blessing in one's life.

---

(1) The speaker: Muslim – Source: Sahih Muslim – page or number: 804. Conclusion of the speaker: sound.

It was said, "O Noah! Disembark (from the Ark) with peace from Us, and blessings upon you and upon the communities that (will arise) from those with you and upon the communities for whom We shall grant enjoyment. Then a painful punishment from Us shall befall them." [Q 11:48]

She (Prophet Abraham's wife Sarah) said, "Oh, woe is me! Shall I bear a child when I am an old woman, and this husband of mine is an old man? That would surely be an astounding thing." [72] They (the angels) said, "Do you marvel at the Command of God? The mercy of God and His blessings be upon you, O Family of the House! Truly He is Praised, Glorious." [73] [Q 11:72-73]

*He (Jesus) said, "Truly I am a servant of God. He has given me the Book and made me a prophet. * He has made me blessed wheresoever I may be, and has enjoined upon me prayer and almsgiving so long as I live, * and [has made me] dutiful toward my mother. And He has not made me domineering or wretched. * Peace was upon me the day I was born, and (will be upon me) the day I die, and on the day I am raised alive!" That is Jesus, son of Mary — a statement of the truth, which they doubt.* [Q 19:30-34]

E. Places that are blessed

Almighty God draws our attention to places He has blessed, so that we can visit them to gain blessings from them. When we visit them we should take the opportunity to increase our prayers and good deeds and remember why these places became holy and blessed, and learn from the history of such places.

Truly the first house (of worship) established for mankind was that at Mecca, full of blessing and a guidance for the worlds. [Q 3:96]

Glory be to Him Who carried His servant (Prophet Muhammad) by night from the Sacred Mosque (at Mecca) to the Farthest Mosque (at Jerusalem), whose precincts We have blessed, that We might show him some of Our signs. Truly, He (alone) is the all-Hearing, the all-Seeing. [Q 17:1]

(Remember) when Moses said to his family, "Truly, I perceive a fire. I will bring you some news from there or a burning brand that you may warm yourselves." [7] Then when he came to it, a call came to

him, "Blessed is the One in the fire, and the one around it. And glory be to God, Lord of the worlds! [8] O Moses! Truly, it is I, God, the Mighty, the Wise!" [9] ❧ *[Q 27:7-9]*

❧ Then when Moses had completed the term and set out with his family, he perceived a fire on the side of the Mount. He said to his family, "Stay here. I perceive a fire. Perhaps I will bring you some news from there, or a firebrand, that you may warm yourselves." [29] And when he came upon it, he was called from the right bank of the valley, at the blessed site, from the tree, "O Moses! Truly I am God, Lord of the worlds!" [30] ❧ *[Q 28:29-30]*

❧ We said: "O Fire! Be cool and (a source of) inner peace for Abraham." [69] And whereas they sought to do evil to him, We caused them to suffer the greatest loss: [70] for We saved him and Lot (his brother's son, by guiding them) to the land that We have blessed for all peoples, [71] ❧ *[Q 21:69-71]*

❧ And to Solomon [We made subservient] the wind blowing violently: it ran by his command to the land which We had blessed. And We know all things. ❧ *[Q 21:81]*

F. Times that are blessed

God, in His infinite Wisdom and Mercy, blessed certain times, as shown below. Believers should take advantage of such times to intensify their prayers and good deeds and earn the blessings associated with them, with the understanding that the rewards at that time will be more, and prayers at such times will be given greater reward.

❧ Truly We sent it (the Holy Quran) down on a blessed night – truly We are ever warning (mankind). ❧ *[Q 44:3]*

❧ The Night of Power is better than a thousand months. ❧ *[Q 97:3]*

Abu Huraira (may God be pleased with him) reported that the Messenger of God (pbuh) said, "The best day on which the sun has risen is Friday. On it Adam was created, and on it he was made to enter Paradise. On it he was expelled from Paradise. And the Last Hour will take place on no day other than Friday." [1]

---

(1) The speaker: Muslim – Source: Sahih Muslim – page or number: 854. Conclusion of the speaker: sound.

Aws ibn Aws (may God be pleased with him) narrated that the Prophet (pbuh) said: "Among the most excellent of your days is Friday; on it Adam was created, and on it he died. On it the Last Trumpet will be blown, and on it the Shout will be made, so invoke more blessings on me that day, for your blessings will be submitted to me." The people asked, 'Messenger of God, how can it be that our blessings will be submitted to you while your body is decayed?' He replied, "God, the Exalted, has prohibited the earth from consuming the bodies of (His) Prophets." [1]

Praying for God's Grace and Blessings

All believers seek God's grace and blessings in every aspect of their lives, and the Prophet (pbuh) urged believers to pray for God's blessing in everything they do.

Abu Hurairah (may God be pleased with him) narrated that the Prophet (pbuh) congratulated a man on his marriage by saying, "May God bless everything for you, and may He bless you, and combine both of you in good (works)."[2]

Abdullah ibn Busr (may God be pleased with him) reported that when he and the Prophet (pbuh) had been invited for a meal, the Prophet (pbuh) offered the following prayer for the host: "O God, bless them in what You have provided them as sustenance, and forgive them and have mercy on them". [3]

6-2-2 Being Conscious of God, doing good deeds, and praying for His forgiveness

In order to increase one's sustenance, believers should be ever conscious of God, follow His orders, and observe His laws as obedient servants. Those who deny Him will reap what they have sown. Be constant in practising your religion and spending your sustenance in lawful ways, and you will earn more of God's blessings and grace.

---

(1) The speaker: Abu Dawood – Source: Sunan Abu Dawood – page or number: 1047. Conclusion of the speaker: No comment [He wrote a letter to the people of Mecca: Whenever I do not comment, it is accepted].

(2) The speaker: Abu Dawood – Source: Sunan Abu Dawood – page or number: 2130. Conclusion of the speaker: No comment [He wrote a letter to the people of Mecca: Whenever I do not comment, it is accepted].

(3) The speaker: Muslim – Source: Sahih Muslim – page or number: 2042. Conclusion of the speaker: sound.

❖ *And if only the people of the cities had believed and been conscious of God, We would have opened upon them blessings from the heaven and the earth; but they denied (the messengers), so We seized them for what they were earning.* ❖ *[Q 7:96]*

❖ *And (God revealed) that if they had remained on the straight way, We would have given them abundant provision.* ❖ *[Q 72:16]*

Be conscious of God at all times, do good deeds and pray for forgiveness. These actions will earn God's reward of increased sustenance and blessings in one's life.

❖ *And O my people, ask forgiveness of your Lord and then repent to Him. He will send (rain from) the sky upon you in showers and increase you in strength (added) to your strength. And do not turn away, (being) criminals.* ❖ *[Q 11:52]*

❖ *I (Prophet Noah) said (to my people): 'Ask forgiveness of your Lord. Indeed, He is ever a Perpetual Forgiver. [10] He will send (rain from) the sky upon you in (continuing) showers [11] and give you increase in wealth and children and provide for you gardens and rivers. [12]* ❖ *[Q 71:10-12]*

Hasan al-Basri, a famous religious scholar, was sitting with his companions, and a man came to him to complain of a lack of sustenance from God. He told him, "Pray for forgiveness." Another man came to him and complained about his children and Hasan told him, "Pray for forgiveness." A third man came to him to complain about too much rain. He also told him, "Pray for forgiveness." He then recited to them the verse shown above.

God's sustenance can include health, knowledge, guidance and protection, such as preventing bad things from coming to you, such as hardship or ill-health. Sustenance is not counted by how much or how little it is, but by how blessed it is. Even if it is small, but is blessed, one can live in comfort and happiness.

Sakhr al-Ghamidi (may God be pleased with him) narrated that the Prophet (pbuh) said: "O God, bless my people in their early mornings." [1]

---

(1) The speaker: Abu Dawood – Source: Sunan Abu Dawood – page's number:352. Hadith number: 2606. Conclusion of the speaker: Did not comment [He wrote in his letter to the people of Mecca that whenever he did not comment, it is accepted].

Umar ibn al-Khattab (may God be pleased with him) reported that the Messenger of God (pbuh) said, "Eat together, and do not separate. For the food of one is sufficient for two, and the food of two is sufficient for three or four. They can then all eat together and not separate. There is blessing in congregation. [1]

As mentioned earlier, when putting one's trust in God, one should consult God, before proceeding with any new matter, by praying two rounds (rakat) of prayer for consultation ('istikhara') and saying the prayer mentioned in Chapter 4. This is a source of blessing, since you are asking God to bless something if it will be good for you.

6-2-3 Keeping Close Ties with Next of Kin

All of us should maintain close personal ties with our relatives and give them moral and material support whenever we can. This is one reason for God giving His blessings and increasing our sustenance, as mentioned in the Qur'anic verse and hadith (Prophetic saying) below.

And those who believed after (the initial emigration) and emigrated and fought with you - they are of you. But those of (blood) relationship are more entitled (to inheritance) in the decree of God. Indeed, God is the All-Knowing, All-Aware. [Q 8:75]

Anas ibn Malik (may God be pleased with him) narrated, "The Messenger of God (pbuh) said, 'He who desires ample provisions and his life prolonged should maintain close ties with his blood relations (next of kin)." [al-Bukhari and Muslim] [2]

6-2-4 Thanking God for His Grace

Being thankful to God involves acknowledging His Grace in all its forms and doing what pleases Him, as can be seen in the Qur'anic verses below. Thanking God for his Grace also includes praising Him Who bestows His Grace upon whomsoever He wills. Our sincere thanks and praise perpetuate His grace.

"... And (remember the time) when your Lord made (this promise) known: 'If you are grateful (to Me), I shall most certainly give you more and more; but if you are ungrateful, truly, My chastisement will be severe indeed!'" [Q 14:7]

---

(1) The speaker: al-Albani – Source: Sahih al-Jaami'– page or number: 4501. Conclusion of the speaker: fair.

(2) The speaker: al-Bukhari – Source: Sahih al-Bukhari – page or number: 2067. Conclusion of the speaker: sound

Yes, indeed, (O men,) We have given you a (bountiful) place on earth, and appointed thereon means of livelihood for you: (yet) how seldom are you grateful! [Q 7:10]

And if you should count the favours of God, you could not enumerate them. Indeed, God is Ever-Forgiving, Most Merciful. [Q 16:18]

Have you not considered that God has made whatsoever is in the heavens and whatsoever is on the earth subservient to you and has poured His blessings upon you, both outwardly and inwardly? Among mankind are those who dispute concerning God without knowledge, without guidance, and without an illuminating Book (from Him). [Q 31:20]

God gives us His Grace and Bounty in this life as long as we are grateful, thank Him and appreciate all His blessings; He will also give us more in this life and in the Hereafter, as He is the Most Generous, Possessed of Tremendous Bounty.

6-2-5 Keeping your heart attached to the eternal life in the Hereafter and not to the splendours of this worldly life

Believers should yearn for Paradise and the Hereafter, and not for this world, since this worldly life is where we are all tested and tried and, in terms of time, our life here is very brief. We come into this world with nothing, and leave it with nothing. It is therefore best that our hearts be detached from the life of this world and instead be completely attached to the Hereafter - our final dwelling place with God - hoping for the highest rank and closeness to God.

Performing good deeds and purifying our souls will help to elevate our status with God in the life to come.

The Prophet (pbuh) said, "The path to Paradise is full of difficulties and trials, while the path to Hell is full of lusts and desires."

We should strive always to be patient, forgiving, truthful, charitable, ever thankful to God, and sincere in our efforts to earn God's contentment.

❖*Are you content with the life of this world over the Hereafter? Yet the enjoyment of the life of this world, compared with the Hereafter, is but (very) little.* ❖ [Q 9:38]

❖*Made to seem fair to mankind is the love of passions, among them women, children, hoarded heaps of gold and silver, horses of mark, cattle and tilled land. Those are the enjoyments of the life of this world. And God, with Him is the beautiful return.* ❖ [Q 3:14]

❖*Say, "Shall I inform you of what is better than that? For those who are conscious of God, there will be with their Lord Gardens with rivers running below - they will abide eternally, and spouses made pure, and Contentment from God. And God is All-Seeing of His servants.*❖ [Q 3:15]

❖*Say, "Scant is the enjoyment of this world, and the Hereafter is better for those who are conscious of God. And you will not be wronged so much as the thread of a date stone."* ❖ [Q 4:77]

The Almighty provides many allegorical examples in the Holy Qur'an to make clear to people its meaning, and He blesses whomsoever He wills.

❖*The parable of the life of this world is that of water which We send down from the sky: the earth's vegetation, from which men and cattle eat, mingles with it until, when the earth has taken on its luster and is beautified, and its people think they have gained mastery over it, Our Command comes upon it by night or by day, whereupon We make it as a harvest, as if it had not flourished yesterday. Thus do We explain in detail the signs for a people who reflect.* ❖ [Q 10:24]

❖*Know that the life of this world is but amusement, diversion, adornment, boasting to one another and competition in increase of wealth and children - like the example of a rain whose (resulting) plant growth pleases the tillers; then it dries and you see it turned yellow; then it becomes (scattered) debris. And in the Hereafter is severe punishment and forgiveness from God and approval. And what is the worldly life except the enjoyment of delusion.* ❖ [Q 57:20]

Abu Hurairah (may God be pleased with him) narrated that the Messenger of God (pbuh) said, "Indeed, God the Most High says, 'O son of Adam! Devote yourself to My worship, and I will fill your heart with riches and alleviate your poverty. And if you do not do so, I will fill your hands with problems and not alleviate your poverty." [1]

Zaid ibn Thabit (may God be pleased with him) reported that he heard the Messenger of God (pbuh) say, "Whoever is focused only on this world, God will confound his affairs and make him fear poverty constantly, and he will not get anything of this world except that which has been written for him. Whoever is focused on the life to come, God will settle his affairs for him and make him feel content with his lot, and his provision and worldly gains will undoubtedly come to him." [2]

6-3 Things that can reduce your Sustenance and limit God's Grace and Blessings from coming to you

Things that will limit your sustenance include disobeying God, being ungrateful to Him, becoming sinful and corrupt, and not acknowledging or being thankful for God's Grace.

6-3-1 Disobeying God

In Chapter 18 of the Quran we find the parable of two men, each of whom owned a garden. One of them boasted that he was greater in wealth and stronger in men than the other, and that his own garden would never perish. He also expressed doubt about the Day of Judgment and the Hereafter. As a result of his pride and not acknowledging God's grace and bounty, he wronged himself. Consequently, his garden was destroyed.

When you entered your garden, why did you not say, '(This is) as God wills. There is no strength except in God' ... [Q 18:39]

Do they not see how many a generation We have destroyed before their time – (people) whom We had given a (bountiful) place on earth, the like of which We never gave to you, and upon whom We showered heavenly blessings abundant, and at whose feet We made running waters flow? And yet We destroyed them for their sins, and gave rise to other people in their stead. [Q 6:6]

---

(1) The speaker: Tirmidhi – Source: Sunan al-Tirmidhi – page or number: 2466. Conclusion of the speaker: fair but strange.
(2) The speaker: al-Albani – Source: Sahih al-Targhib– page or number: 3168. Conclusion of the speaker: fair and sound.

❦*Have they, then, never journeyed about the earth and beheld what happened in the end to those (deniers of the truth) who lived before their time? Greater were they in power than they are, and in the impact which they left on earth: but God took them to task for their sins, and they had none to defend them against God.* ❧ *[Q 40:21]*

❦*And how many have We destroyed from the generations after Noah. And sufficient is your Lord, concerning the sins of His servants, as He is well Acquainted with all things and is All-Seeing.* ❧ *[Q 17:17]*

❦*And how many a community that (once) exulted in its wanton wealth and ease of life have We destroyed, so that those dwelling places of theirs – all but a few – have never been dwelt in after them: for it is indeed We alone Who shall remain when all else will have passed away!* ❧ *[Q 28:58]*

6-3-2 Denying God's Grace and Bounty

The Qur'an also gives the story of Qarūn (Korah), an extremely wealthy man at the time of Moses, who claimed that his great fortune was the result of his own knowledge. He did not acknowledge that it had been given to him by God, so He destroyed him and his wealth due to his ingratitude (see the two verses below). When we are thankful and grateful for everything we have, however small or large it is, we should also acknowledge God's Grace and Bounty, feel blessed by Him, and realize that God Alone is the source of all good.

❦*He said, "I was only given it (great wealth) because of knowledge I have." Did he (Qarūn) not know that God had destroyed before him generations of those (arrogant ones) who were greater than him in power and greater in accumulation (of wealth)? And the guilty will not be questioned about their sins.* ❧ *[Q 28:78]*

In this case, God will not question the guilty about their sins because He is fully aware of all that they did, since He is the All-Knowing, the All-Aware, the All-Hearing, All-Seeing, and the Witness to all things.

❦*Then We caused the earth to engulf him (Qarūn) and his house. And he had no party who could help him against God, nor could he help himself.* ❧ *[Q 28:81]*

6-4 Keeping your heart free from envy by not looking at God's Grace bestowed on others

❀*And do not extend your eyes toward that by which We have given enjoyment to (some) categories of them, (its being but) the splendour of worldly life by which We test them. And the provision of your Lord is better and more enduring.* ❀ *[Q 20:131]*

❀*... turn not your eyes (longingly) towards the worldly benefits which We have granted to some of those (who deny the truth). And neither grieve over those (who refuse to heed you), but spread the wings of your tenderness over the believers ...* ❀ *[Q 15:88]*

❀*And do not wish for that by which God has made some of you exceed others. For men is a share of what they have earned, and for women is a share of what they have earned. And ask God of His bounty. Indeed God is All-Knowing.* ❀ *[Q 4:32]*

One source of discontent and corruption of the heart and soul is looking at what others have and then envying them for it. God has ordered us not to do this – we should never envy other people – since this is how jealousy begins and it then corrupts people's hearts. Envying what other people have may lead you to be unthankful, and destroy your relationship with those you envy. Never compare yourself with anyone else. God knows each person's needs before they themselves even become aware of them, since God is the All-Knowing, All-Aware, and Ever-Merciful.

❀*"... and (protect us) from the evil of an envier when he envies."* ❀ *[Q 113:5]*

❀ *"... the Day on which neither wealth will be of any use, nor children, [88] (when) only he (will be happy) who comes before God with a sound heart (free from evil)!" [89]* ❀ *[Q 26:88-89]*

❀*So bear patiently that which they say, and glorify your Lord before the rising of the sun and before its setting; and during periods of the night (glorify Him) and at the ends of the day, that you may be content. [130] And do not extend your eyes toward that by which We have given enjoyment to (some) categories of them, (its being but) the splendor of worldly life by which We test them. And the provision of your Lord is better and more enduring. [131] And enjoin prayer upon your family (and others) and be steadfast therein. We ask you not for provision; We provide for you, and the (best) outcome is for (those of) righteousness. [132]* ❁ *[Q 20:130-132]*

Abu Hurairah (may God be pleased with him) narrated that the Prophet (pbuh) said, "Avoid envy, for envy devours good deeds just as fire devours kindling wood or (he said) 'grass'." [1]

❁*And (there is a share for) those who came after them, saying, "Our Lord, forgive us and our brothers who preceded us in faith and put not in our hearts (any) resentment toward those who have believed. Our Lord, indeed You are Kind and Merciful."* ❁ *[Q 59:10]*

❁*And We will remove whatever is in their hearts of resentment, (so they will be) brothers, on thrones facing each other.* *[Q 15:47]*

Abdullah ibn Amr ibn al-Aas (may God be pleased with him) reported the following: "It was said to the Messenger of God (pbuh): 'Which of the people is best?' He (pbuh) answered: 'Everyone who is pure of heart and sincere in speech.' They said: 'Sincere in speech, we know what this is, but what is pure of heart?' He (pbuh) replied: 'It is the heart that is pious and pure, with no sin, injustice, hatred or envy in it.'" [2]

Anas ibn Malik (may God be pleased with him) narrated, "We were sitting in the company of the Prophet (pbuh) when he said, 'Soon there will appear before you a person from among the dwellers of Paradise.' Soon thereafter, a person from the Ansar (Helpers of Medina) appeared – his beard was dripping with water which he had used to perform ablution, and he was holding his sandals in his left hand. The next day, the Prophet (pbuh) said the same thing and the same person appeared in the same manner (as he had appeared the first time). On the third day, the Prophet (pbuh) said the same thing

---

(1) The speaker: Abu Dawood – Source: Sunan Abu Dawood – page or number: 4903. Conclusion of the speaker: Did not comment [He wrote in his letter to the people of Mecca that whenever he did not comment, it is accepted].

(2) The speaker: Al-Mundhiri – Source: al-Targhib Wat Tarhib – page or number: 4/33. Conclusion of the speaker: Conclusion of the speaker: sound.

again, and the same person appeared in the same manner as he had appeared the previous two times. "When the Prophet (pbuh) got up and left, Abdullah ibn Amr al-Aas followed the man and said to him, 'I had a dispute with my father and so I took an oath that I will not go to him for three days. (Now that I have no place to stay) Is it possible for you to accommodate me until the three days pass?' The man replied, 'Yes.' Anas continued: "Abdullah ibn Amr said he stayed with the man for three days. He did not see him get up at night for night prayers. However, when he used to toss and turn in his bed, he would engage in the remembrance of God and say 'God is Great' (Allahu Akbar). He would eventually get up for the pre-dawn prayer (Fajr salah). Abdullah ibn Amr added: "However, I never heard him say anything but good. When the three days passed and I was on the verge of considering his good deeds to be very few and insignificant, I said to him, 'O servant of God! There was neither any dispute nor any separation between me and my father. Rather, I heard the Prophet (pbuh) say on three occasions about you: 'Soon there will appear before you a person from among the dwellers of Paradise.' And on each of these three occasions, it was you who appeared. I therefore decided to live with you to see what deeds you do so that I can emulate you. However, I did not see you doing many good deeds. How, then, have you reached the rank concerning which the Messenger of God (pbuh) said about your being from among the dwellers of Paradise?' "The man replied, 'I do not do anything more than what you have seen. However, I am never deceitful towards anyone, nor do I envy anyone for the good which God has given him.' "Abdullah ibn Amr said, 'These are the qualities that have raised you to such a high rank.'" [1]

❧*Do they envy men on account of what God has given them of His bounty? We gave the House of Abraham the Book and Wisdom, and We granted them a mighty sovereignty.* ❧ [Q 4:54]

Abu Hurairah (may God be pleased with him) narrated that God's Messenger (pbuh) said, 'Beware of suspicion, for it is the worst of

---

(1) The speaker: al-Haytami al-Makki – Source: Az-Zawajr – page or number: 1/56. Conclusion of the speaker: Based on the condition of the two Sheikhs (al-Bukhari and Muslim).

false tales; do not look for the other's faults; do not spy on others; do not hate one another, and do not cut your relations with one another. O God's servants, be brothers!" (See Hadith No. 90)[1]

Al-Zubair ibn al-'Awwam (may God be pleased with him) narrated that the Prophet (pbuh) said, "The disease of the nations before you is creeping towards you: envy and hatred - it is the cutting blade. I do not speak of what cuts the hair, but what severs the religion. By the One in Whose Hand is my soul! You will not enter Paradise until you believe, and you will not believe until you love each other. Shall I tell you about what will strengthen that for you? Spread peace among one another." [2]

Damra ibn Tha'laba (may God be pleased with him) reported that the Messenger (pbuh) said: "People will remain in peace unless they envy each other." [3]

Salem, son of Abdullah ibn 'Umar, is reported to have said, on the authority of his father (may God be pleased with them), that the Messenger (pbuh) remarked: "Envy is not justified except in the case of two persons only: one who, having been given (knowledge of) the Qur'an by God, recites it during the night and the day (and acts upon it), and the person who, having been given wealth by God, gives it in charity during the night and the day." [4]

Anas ibn Malik (may God be pleased with him) reported, "The Messenger (pbuh) said, "Do not stop talking to one another, do not nurse hatred towards one another, do not be jealous of one another, but become servants of God as brothers. It is not lawful for a Muslim to ignore his (Muslim) brother for more than three days." [5]

---

(1) The speaker: Muslim – Source: Sahih Muslim – page or number: 2563. Conclusion of the speaker: sound.

(2) The speaker: Tirmidhi – Source: Sunan al-Tirmidhi – page or number: 2510. Conclusion of the speaker: weak.

(3) The speaker: Damra ibn Tha'laba – Speaker: al-Munziri - Source: al-Targhib wat Tarhib – page or number: 4/31. Conclusion of the speaker: his narrators are entrusted.

(4) The speaker: Muslim – Source: Sahih Muslim – page or number: 815. Conclusion of the speaker: sound.

(5) The speaker: al-Albani – Source: Sahih al-Tirmidhi – page or number: 1935. Conclusion of the speaker: fair and sound.

Abdullah ibn Abbas (may God be pleased with him) reported that the Messenger of God (pbuh) said, "There are three things, if any man has not adopted them, God the Exalted will forgive whatever else he has committed: he who dies having no partner with God, he who is not a magician nor practises black magic, and he who holds no grudge against his brother." [1]

6-5 Summary and Conclusions

One source of contentment for the believer is to be thankful for and appreciative of God's Grace. The reward of God for being thankful and appreciative of His bounty is that He will maintain His reward in this life and in the Hereafter. In addition to being thankful to God, being conscious of Him and being close to Him through piety and good deeds also strengthens one's contentment. Being discontent with God's Grace and not adhering to the straight path will produce the opposite result.

Other important aspects of contentment are for the believer to not extend his gaze to the bounties and grace which God has bestowed on others. This will corrupt his heart and harm his relationship with others. Harbouring envious thoughts will prevent him from attaining contentment in this life and in the Hereafter.

(1) The speaker: al-Tabarani – Source: al-Mu'jam al-Awsat – page or number: 1/281.

Chapter 7

Being Forgiving and Patient, and Repelling Evil with Good

❲… who spend (in His way) in times of plenty and in times of hardship, and hold in check their anger, and pardon their fellow-men because God loves the doers of good …❳
[Q 3:134]

❲… God loves those who are patient in adversity …❳ [Q 3:146]

❲… and who are patient in adversity out of a longing for their Sustainer's countenance, and are constant in prayer, and spend on others, secretly and openly, out of what We provide for them as sustenance, and (who) repel evil with good. It is these who shall find their fulfilment in the Hereafter. ❳ [Q 13:22]

بِسْمِ اللَّهِ الرَّحْمَنِ الرَّحِيمِ

﴿ وَلَا تَسْتَوِي الْحَسَنَةُ وَلَا السَّيِّئَةُ ادْفَعْ بِالَّتِي هِيَ أَحْسَنُ فَإِذَا الَّذِي بَيْنَكَ وَبَيْنَهُ عَدَاوَةٌ كَأَنَّهُ وَلِيٌّ حَمِيمٌ وَمَا يُلَقَّاهَا إِلَّا الَّذِينَ صَبَرُوا وَمَا يُلَقَّاهَا إِلَّا ذُو حَظٍّ عَظِيمٍ ﴾

إن الله يحب الصابرين

صدق الله العظيم

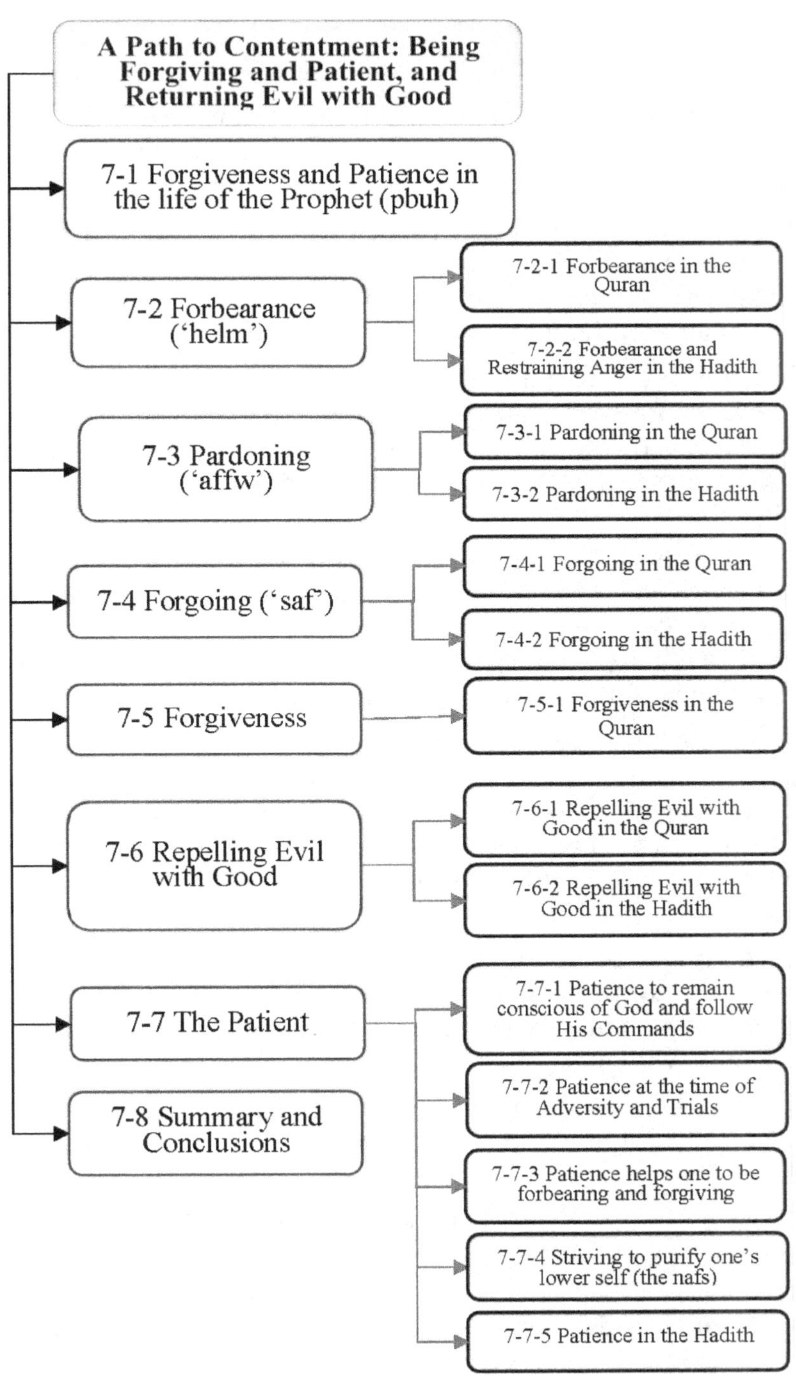

Fig. 1: Structure of Chapter 7

7-0 Introduction

Forgiveness in Islam involves four stages or levels:

The first stage is forbearance (in Arabic, 'hilm'), when you control your anger and do not act in haste. You show restraint and self-control, and hold back any negative reactions.

The second is pardoning ('afw'), when you refrain from blaming or complaining about the person who has wronged you, do not mention it, and do not make an issue about the wrong done to you. You excuse, look the other way, let it go, and show tolerance.

The third is forgoing ('saf'), when you overlook what has happened, do not seek retaliation or compensation against the person who has wronged you, and keep the matter entirely private. You refrain from taking revenge, you pass over it, ignore it, and take no notice of the offence.

The fourth is forgiveness ('mughfira'), when you forgive and forget, behave as if the person has not wronged you, and that nothing has happened between you and the other person. You let the other person off the hook, so to speak, you wipe the slate clean, let bygones be bygones, and forbear, pardon, overlook, and excuse.

The attribute of being forbearing means that you do not become angry, but remain calm and keep your emotions under control. This is one of the many virtuous character traits that belonged to all the prophets, in which they made sound decisions while keeping control of their emotions. They were not hasty in taking actions they might later regret.

In addition to being forbearing, they also pardoned others for what they had done to them. Pardoning includes the sense of not blaming others or complaining about them, which helps all parties to act in a calm manner, without rushing to take action.

God wants us to go beyond pardoning and also not hold a grudge against anyone who mistreats or abuses us, and not pursue revenge against anyone.

Being forgiving means that one does not look for retribution, and forgives for the sake of God. In Islam, believers are told to take one step further in forgiving, and be good to those who are bad to them, returning evil with good. This is the ultimate level of goodness, which goes beyond forgiveness. Such conduct will cause God to be content with you, and you will be content with yourself and others, which leads to a life of contentment.

To conduct oneself this way requires patience, and being patient helps one to be forgiving. All aspects of acquiring contentment need patience. The Quran tells us that God is with the patient, and that He loves the patient. So believers must cultivate patience, and be always conscious of God, so that they can do what He wants us to do. Being patient in adversity helps us during different tests and trials, and enables us to pass them successfully. Patience is needed to continuously remember God and stay close to Him. Be patient and thankful to God, and accept His Will. Patience is the foundation upon which one can build all other virtues needed to obtain God's contentment and then your own contentment.

In this chapter we outline different aspects of the believer's character which lead to contentment. Before we do that, we will visit some incidents in the life of the Prophet (pbuh) which show how patient and forgiving he was, and how he returned bad with good. We should take him (pbuh) as an example to follow.

7-1 Forgiveness and Patience in the life of the Prophet (pbuh)

Almighty God caused the prophets (peace be upon them) to endure many severe trials so that they could give us examples of the highest level of conduct in adversity, and how they bore considerable hardships in the cause of their mission; they were always forgiving and kind to their enemies.

Muhammad (pbuh) was forty years old when he became a prophet, and spent an additional thirteen years in Mecca before moving to Medina. The idol-worshippers of Mecca put him through numerous hardships and trials, starting with his uncle, Abu Lahab, who was one of the chiefs of the Quraish. He used to throw garbage in front of the Prophet's door every morning and the only thing he would say to him was, "O child of Abd al-Manaf! Who would do this to their neighbor?" The disbelievers of Mecca accused the prophet (pbuh) of being bewitched and of unsound mind.

The wife of Abu Lahab used to spread branches with thorns in front of the Prophet's door, hoping that he would injure his feet by stepping on them. She also used to verbally abuse him, spread lies about him, and urge others to act against him. There is a chapter in the Quran that directly addresses Abu Lahab and his wife, who were among those who most fiercely opposed the Prophet (pbuh) and persecuted his followers. These verses are shown below.

❁*May the hands of Abu Lahab perish, and may he perish! [1] His wealth avails him not, nor what he has earned. [2] He shall enter a blazing Fire. [3] And his wife, carrier of firewood, [4] upon her neck is a rope of palm fiber. [5]* ❁ *[Q 111:1-5]*

❁*And yet, they (who deny the truth) say, "O you to whom this reminder has (allegedly) been bestowed from on high, truly, you are mad! ..."* ❁ *[Q 15:6]*

❁*Now these (people) deem it strange that a warner should have come to them from their own midst — and (so) the deniers of the truth are saying: "A (mere) spellbinder is he, a liar!"* ❁ *[Q 38:4]*

❁ *"No," they say, "(Muhammad propounds) the most involved and confusing of dreams!" — "No, but he has invented (all) this!" — "No, but he is (only) a poet!" — (and,) "Let him, then, come to us with a miracle, just as those (prophets) of old were sent (with miracles)!"* ❁ *[Q 21:5]*

❁*Moreover, those who are bent on denying the truth are wont to say, "This (Quran) is nothing but a lie which he (himself) has devised with the help of other people, who thereupon have perverted the truth and brought a falsehood into being." [4] And they say, "Fables of ancient times which he has caused to be written down, so that they might be read out to him at morn and evening!" [5]* ❁ *[Q 25:4-5]*

The disbelievers among the Prophet's community in Mecca received the messages with great resentment and hostility, as outlined in the verses shown above. They continued to spread rumors, false allegations and lies, including making loud noises whenever the Prophet (pbuh) tried to speak with people in public.

❁*Now those who are bent on denying the truth say (to one another): "Do not listen to this Quran, but rather talk frivolously about it, so that you might gain the upper hand!"* ❁ *[Q 41:26]*

The Prophet (pbuh) was also subjected to physical abuse by the idol-worshippers of Mecca, and he remained patient in the face of such treatment from them.

Urwa ibn al-Zubair (may God be pleased with him) narrated that he said to Ibn Amr ibn Al-Aas, "Tell me the worst thing that the pagans did to the Prophet." He said, "While the Prophet (pbuh) was praying in the Hijr of the Kaaba, Uqba ibn Abi Mu'ait came and put his garment around the Prophet's neck and throttled him violently. Abu Bakr came and caught him by his shoulder, pushed him away from the Prophet (pbuh) and said, "Do you want to kill a man just because he says, 'My Lord is God'?" [1]

Abdullah ibn Masood (may God be pleased with him) reported that when the Messenger of God (pbuh) was lying prostrate in prayer and around him were some people from the Quraish, Uqba ibn Abu Muait brought the (dead) foetus of a she-camel and threw it on the back of the Messenger of God (pbuh). He did not raise his head until Fatima (the Prophet's daughter) arrived, removed it from his back and cursed him who had done that. He (the Prophet, pbuh) said, "O God, it is for You to deal with the chiefs of the Quraish." [2]

The tribe of Quraish made a pact against the Prophet (pbuh) and his family, essentially ostracizing them by not doing business with them, not sitting with them or talking to them, and not marrying from them. Their pact contained one condition: they would desist only if the Prophet's family handed him over to them, in which case they would kill him. The prophet's family refused to yield to this threat. The prophet's supporters had to live outside of Mecca under siege for three years, where they suffered starvation, and the Prophet stood his ground and eventually emigrated to Medina.

After the Prophet (pbuh) left to Medina, which is 500 kilometers north of Mecca, the disbelievers of Mecca continued to launch wars against him, trying to uproot him from Medina so that they could kill him. The Prophet (pbuh) and his supporters in Medina had to defend themselves in various battles, such as the Battles of Badr and Uhud, some of which were very violent, where many companions of the Prophet (pbuh) were killed and their bodies mutilated. The disbelievers wanted to inflict the greatest harm on him and his followers. The prophet (pbuh) was so badly injured in the Battle of Uhud, that he was unable to stand. The disbelievers then gathered men from all the Arab Tribes around Medina to launch a decisive battle, hoping to finally

---

(1) The speaker: al-Bukhari – Source: Sahih al-Bukhari – page or number: 3856 Conclusion of the speaker: sound.

(2) The speaker: Muslim – Source: Sahih Muslim – page or number: 1794 Conclusion of the speaker: sound.

finish off the Prophet (pbuh) and his companions. As they were about to attack, a very powerful wind storm came and blew away the attacker's tents and scattered them, causing them to abandon their positions and return to Mecca. Some of the Prophet's companions emigrated to Abyssinia to escape persecution by the disbelievers.

At the end of twenty-three years of persecution and all sorts of ordeals, the Prophet (pbuh) returned to Mecca victorious, without shedding a drop of blood. When he entered the city, the people who had fought him for so many years were expecting that he would take revenge on them but, as he entered, he said to them, "What do you think I am going to do with you?" They replied, "You are a generous brother and cousin, you do only good." The prophet replied, "You are free, and no harm will come to you."

Prophet Joseph (pbuh), whose brothers had thrown him into a well to die when he was a boy, was rescued from the well by traders on their way to Egypt. He was sold as a slave in Egypt and underwent many trials before he eventually became the Treasurer of Egypt. At that time, a great famine occurred in the surrounding countries and his brothers came to Egypt asking for charity. He recognized them and they eventually recognized him. He gave them food and shelter and was very generous to them, despite what they had done to him as a child.

The essence of prophethood is to forgive and do good towards those who are bad to you, which is the essence of righteousness and the sign of a contented soul, with no anger and no desire to settle accounts. Forgiveness and doing good is reflected in one's inner soul, which will bring contentment.

In the Quran, God urges believers to have the character traits, or attributes, of patience, forbearance and forgiveness, and to repel evil with good. These are very important virtues in gaining contentment and they are complemented by the virtue of patience, as we will explain in this chapter.

7-2 Forbearance ('hilm')

Being forbearing is a quality where we are in control of our emotions and behave in a calm manner, avoiding becoming angry and irrational. We restrain ourselves, a quality which the prophets had, in order to convey their message and persevere in the face of opposition. They were able to avoid anger or the seeking of revenge, which is a great grace given by God. Their forbearance resulted in maintaining harmonious relations among the believers, which increased the love amongst them.

7-2-1 Forbearance in the Quran

God describes Himself as the Most Forbearing, as can be seen in the following two verses, and it is one of His Most Beautiful Divine Names. The prophets are also described as being forbearing, as shown in the verses below.

❖And do not make (your oath by) God an excuse against doing good or acting rightly, or making peace between people, for God is the All-Hearing, the All-Knowing. [224] God will not call you to account for thoughtlessness in your oaths, but He will call you to account for the intention in your hearts. And God is Most Forgiving and Forbearing. [225]❖ [Q 2:224-225]

❖Kind words and the covering of (other's) faults are better than an act of charity followed by injury. And God is the Self-Sufficient, the Forbearing. ❖ [Q 2:263]

❖... for (Prophet) Abraham was most tender-hearted and forbearing.❖ [Q 9:114]

❖So We gave him (Prophet Abraham) the glad tiding of a forbearing son (Ismail). ❖ [Q 37:101]

7-2-2 Forbearance and Restraining Anger in the Prophetic Traditions

Anas ibn Malik (may God be pleased with him) narrated that the Prophet (pbuh) said: "Doing things with care is from God, while haste is from the devil. No one is more accepting of excuses than God, and nothing is dearer to God than forbearance. [1]

Abu Hurairah (may God be pleased with him) narrated that a man addressed the Prophet (pbuh), saying: "O Messenger of God, advise me." The Messenger of God answered him by stating: "Do not become angry." The man repeated his request several times, and the Prophet (pbuh) replied each time, "Do not become angry." [2]

---

(1) The speaker: al-Albani – Source: Sahih al-Targhib – page or number: 2677. Conclusion of the speaker: fair.

(2) The speaker: al-Bukhari – Source: Sahih al-Bukhari – page or number: 6116 Conclusion of the speaker: sound.

Abu Huraira (may God be pleased with him) reported that it was said to God's Messenger (pbuh): "Invoke curse upon the disbelievers," whereupon he (pbuh) said: "I have not been sent as the invoker of curse, but as a mercy." [1]

Abu Huraira (may God be pleased with him) narrated that God's Messenger (pbuh) said, "The strong is not the one who overcomes the people by his strength, but it is the one who controls himself when he is angry." [2]

7-3 Pardoning ('afw')

Pardoning is when you forgo blaming or complaining about the person who has wronged you, not mentioning it, not making an issue about it. Instead, you excuse him, look the other way, let it go, and show tolerance. You remain patient in the hope that God will also pardon you for your mistakes.

7-3-1 Pardoning in The Quran

❦*... whoever pardons and makes reconciliation, his reward is (due) from God ...* ❦ *[Q 42:40]*

❦*... and to pardon (by forgoing) what is due to you is nearer to God-consciousness. And do not forget (that you are to act with) grace towards one another. Truly, whatever you do, God sees it (all).* ❦ *[Q 2:237]*

❦*And the retribution for an evil act is an evil one like it, but whoever pardons and makes reconciliation - his reward is [due] from God. Indeed, He does not love wrongdoers.* ❦ *[Q 42:40]*

❦*Many among the followers of earlier revelation would like to bring you back to disbelief, from their selfish envy, after you have believed, (even) after the Truth has become clear to them; but pardon and forgive until God accomplishes His purpose. Truly, God has power over all things.* ❦ *[Q 2:109]*

---

(1) The speaker: Muslim – Source: Sahih Muslim – page or number: 2599 Conclusion of the speaker: sound.

(2) The speaker: al-Bukhari – Source: Sahih al-Bukhari – page or number: 6114 Conclusion of the speaker: sound.

❈*... those who spend (in His way) in time of plenty and in time of hardship, and hold in check their anger, and pardon their fellow-men because God loves the doers of good.* ❉ [Q 3:134]

❈*It is part of the mercy of God, (O Muhammad), that you deal gently with them. If you had been severe or harsh-hearted with them, they would have disbanded from about you. So pardon (their faults), and ask for (God's) forgiveness for them; and consult them in affairs (of moment). Then, when you have taken a decision, put your trust in God. Truly, God loves those who put their trust (in Him).* ❉ [Q 3:159]

❈*But pardon them and forgive (their misdeeds). Indeed, God loves the doers of good.* ❉ [Q 5:13]

❈*Take to pardoning, and enjoin right, and turn away from the ignorant.*❉ [Q 7:199]

7-3-2 Pardoning in the Prophetic Traditions

Anas ibn Malik (may God be pleased with him) reported that he asked the Prophet (pbuh): "What are the three highest morals in Islam?" The Prophet (pbuh) replied: "Pardon those who have been unjust to you, help those who have denied you help, and keep in contact with those who have cut you off." [1]

Abdullah ibn Sarjis al-Muzam (may God be pleased with him) narrated that the Messenger of God (pbuh) said: "Being of good character, and being kind and decent, is a part of the twenty-four parts of Prophethood." [2]

Ibn Jarir and Ibn Abu Hatim narrated that Yunus told us Sufyan ibn Ayna, on the authority of Ummai, said: "When God Almighty revealed to the Prophet (pbuh), "Be pardoning, follow the traditions and disregard the ignorant," the Prophet asked Archangel Gabriel what was meant by this. Gabriel said: "God commands you to

---

(1) The speaker: al-Suyuti – Source: al-Jaami' al-Saghîr – page or number: 3510. Conclusion of the speaker: fair

(2) The speaker: Tirmidhi – Source: Sunan al-Tirmidhi – page or number: 2010. Conclusion of the speaker: fair and strange.

pardon those who have been unjust to you, help those who have denied you help, and keep in contact with those who have cut you off." [1]

7-4 Forgoing ('saf')

Forgoing means overlooking what has happened, not bringing up the issue, not seeking retaliation or compensation against the person who has wronged you, and keeping the matter entirely private. It also includes refraining from taking revenge, and passing over it, ignoring it, and taking no notice of the wrong done to you.

7-4-1 Forgoing in the Holy Quran

❀*And We have not created the heavens and the earth and all that is between them but for just ends. And the Hour is surely coming (when this will be manifest). So overlook (any human faults) with gracious forgoing. [85] For truly your Lord is the Master Creator, the All-Knowing. [86]* ❀ [Q 15:85-86]

❀*... let them pardon and forgo; do you not desire that God forgives you? For God is Most Forgiving and Most Merciful.* ❀ [Q 24:22]

❀*But pardon them and forgo (their misdeeds). Indeed, God loves the doers of good.* ❀ [Q 5:13]

❀*Many among the followers of earlier revelation would like to bring you back to disbelief after you have believed, from selfish envy (even) after the Truth has become clear to them; but pardon and forgo until God accomplishes His purpose. Truly, God has power over all things.*❀ [Q 2:109]

❀*And hasten in the race for forgiveness from your Lord, and for a Garden as vast as the heavens and the earth, prepared for those who remain conscious of God ...* ❀ [Q 3:133]

❀*And the Hour is surely coming. So overlook (any human faults) with gracious overlooking.* ❀ [Q 15:85]

❀*... overlook what they do, and say, "Peace." For soon they will know.*❀ [Q 43:89]

---

(1) Tafsir Ibn Kathir.

7-5 Forgiveness ('mughfira')

Forgiveness means forgiving and forgetting, behaving as if the person has not wronged you, and that nothing has happened between you and the other person. You let the other person off the hook, you wipe the slate clean, let bygones be bygones, and forbear, pardon, overlook and excuse.

7-5-1 Forgiveness in the Quran

The first verse shown below mentions the stages involved in reaching full forgiveness.

But if you pardon and forgo and forgive - then indeed, God is the Ever-Forgiving, the Merciful. [Q 64:14]

Those who avoid shameful deeds and, when they are angry, they readily forgive. [Q 42: 37]

He (Prophet Joseph) said (to his brothers), "No blame will there be upon you today. God will forgive you; and He is the most Merciful of the merciful!" [Q 12:92]

Say (O Muhammad) to all those who believe, to forgive those who do not look forward to the Days of God: it is for Him to recompense (for good or ill) each people according to what they have earned. [Q 45:14]

7-6 Repelling Evil with Good

God urges believers to go beyond forgiveness by repelling evil with good, rather than taking revenge, as can be seen from the Quranic verses below.

7-6-1 Repelling Evil with Good in the Quran

These it is who shall receive a twofold reward for having been patient in adversity, and having repelled evil with good, and having spent on others out of what We provided for them as sustenance. [Q 28:54]

and repel evil with good – for such there is the final attainment of the (Eternal) home. [Q 13:22]

... but (since) good and evil cannot be equal, repel (evil) with something that is better (good) – and lo! he between whom and

yourself was enmity (may then become) as though he had (always) been close (to you), a true friend! [34] Yet (to achieve) this is not given to any but those who are patient in adversity: it is not given to any but those endowed with the greatest good fortune! [35] ❧ *[Q 41:34-35]*

❧ *Repel (their) evil by (means of) what is best (good). We are well-acquainted with (all) the things they say.* ❧ *[Q 23:96]*

By displaying such a high level of conduct, the believer hopefully causes the wrong-doer to reflect and think about what he has done, feel ashamed, and then change his behavior when he sees other people whom he wronged returning his wrongdoing with good. We hope it will create an environment of harmony, peace and contentment among society. The doer of good hopes to be rewarded in the Hereafter for such conduct, as is promised in various Quranic verses. They hope that those rewards will help them to achieve the highest rank possible in the Hereafter, which is our final destination.

The following verse is used as a prayer that believers repeat when they want to express their complete trust in God, hoping that He will manage their affairs; it is called 'Hasbi Allah' (God is sufficient for me):

❧ *But if those (who are bent on denying the truth) turn away, say "God suffices me! There is no god but He. In Him have I placed my trust, and He is the Lord of the mighty throne.* ❧ *[Q 9:129]*

The Prophet (pbuh) recommended that believers recite this verse every morning and evening, meaning that the believer entrusts his affairs to God and whatever bad happens to him, he will leave it to God and the Day of Judgment, and whatever good he does, he hopes to be rewarded for that.

Many believers would rather be rewarded for their patience and forgiveness in the Hereafter which, for them, is much greater and more permanent than anything in this temporary world.

7-6-2 Repelling Evil with Good in the Prophetic Traditions

Abu Huraira (may God be pleased with him) reported God's Messenger (pbuh) as saying: "Do you know who is bankrupt?" The Companions of the Prophet (pbuh) said: "A bankrupt man amongst us is one who has neither dirham with him nor wealth." The Prophet (pbuh) said: "The bankrupt of my community will be he who comes on the Day of Resurrection with prayers and fasts and Zakat, but he will find himself bankrupt on that day as he will have exhausted his fund of virtues since he had hurled abuse upon others, brought calumny against others, unlawfully consumed the wealth of others, shed the blood of others and beat others, and his virtues will be credited to the account of one who had suffered at his hand. And if his good deeds fall short to clear the account, then the sins of those he mistreated will be entered into his account and he will be thrown into the Hell-Fire. [1]

Uqba ibn `Amir (may God be pleased with him) narrated that he met the Prophet (pbuh) and asked him: "O Messenger of God, tell me which deeds are most virtuous." He (pbuh) said, "O Uqba, keep in contact with those who have cut you off, help those who have denied you help, and pardon those who have been unjust to you" [2]

Abdullah ibn Masood (may God be pleased with him) narrated that he saw the Prophet (pbuh) talking about one of the prophets whose nation had beaten him and caused him to bleed and, while cleaning the blood off his face, he said, "O God! Forgive my nation, for they have no knowledge." [3]

7-7 Patience

Patience is the foundation of all virtues, and this work focuses on one of these virtues, namely contentment, by presenting the different keys and approaches to achieving contentment. These include loving God, His messengers, and your fellow believers, remaining conscious of God at all times, accepting His Will and Wisdom, being sincere, and putting your complete trust in God alone. Also, being thankful for what you have, being forgiving, and being good to those who have been bad to you.

For the believer to practice all these virtues over his lifetime, he must have patience and persistence. In the following verses it is shown how believers should cultivate patience in order to gain the contentment of God. One of the virtues that all the prophets shared was patience in adversity.

---

(1) The speaker: Muslim – Source: Sahih Muslim – page or number: 2581 Conclusion of the speaker: sound.

(2) The speaker: Al-Mundhiri – Source: al-Targhib wa-al-Tarhib – page or number: 3/310

(3) The speaker: al-Bukhari – Source: Sahih al-Bukhari – page or number: 6929 Conclusion of the speaker: sound.

Patience is very important for those who seek contentment, through the various elements that have been presented in this and previous chapters, and to patiently persevere throughout one's lifetime to attain contentment. We are told in many places throughout the Quran that God is with the patient, that He loves the patient, He supports them, and that they will be given the highest reward. We will outline how patience is tied to the virtues mentioned earlier.

These shall be rewarded with a high station (in Paradise) for what they patiently endured, and they will be received therein with greetings and (words of) Peace. [Q 25:75]

Peace be upon you for what you patiently endured. And excellent is the final home (in the Hereafter). [Q 13:24]

7-7-1 Patience to remain conscious of God and follow His Commands

O you who believe! Seek aid in steadfast patience and prayer, for, behold, God is with those who are patient. [Q 2:153]

Patience is mentioned jointly with prayer, and is always attached to good deeds; this emphasizes that good deeds need to be done continuously throughout the believer's life, while also practising patience.

And seek help through patience and prayer, and indeed, it is difficult for all but the humbly submissive (to God). [Q 2:45]

(And thus it is with most men) - except those who are patient in adversity and do righteous deeds: it is they whom forgiveness of sins awaits, and a great reward. [Q 11:11]

Then he will be of those who believe, and who enjoin upon one another patience in adversity and deeds of kindness and compassion. [17] Such are they who have attained to righteousness. [18] [Q 90:17-18)

(Luqman the sage said) O my dear son! Perform the prayer, enjoin what is right, forbid what is wrong, and bear patiently whatever may befall you. That is indeed a course worthy of resolve. [Q 31:17]

As mentioned earlier, it is very important to keep remembering God and keep praying for His forgiveness; this should be a continuous practice throughout one's life, and requires patience and perseverance, as shown in the verses below.

❖... hence, remain patient in adversity – for, truly, God's promise always comes true – and ask forgiveness for your sins, and extol your Lord's glory and praise by night and by day. ❖ [Q 40:55]

❖Say, "Shall I tell you of better things than those (earthly joys)? For those who are conscious of God there are, with their Lord, gardens through which running waters flow, therein to abide, and spouses pure, and God's goodly acceptance." And God sees all that is in (the hearts of) His servants, [15] those who say, "Our Lord! Behold, we believe (in Thee); forgive us, then, our sins, and keep us safe from suffering through the fire" - [16] those who are patient in adversity, and true to their word, and truly devout, and who spend (in God's way), and pray for forgiveness from their innermost hearts. [17] ❖ [Q 3:15-17]

❖They (Prophet Joseph's ten brothers) exclaimed: "Why – is it indeed you who are Joseph?" He answered: "I am Joseph, and this is my brother (Benjamin). God has indeed been gracious to us. Truly, if one is conscious of Him and patient in adversity – behold, God does not fail to requite the doers of good!" ❖[Q 12:90]

❖If good fortune comes to you, it grieves them (the disbelievers); and if evil befalls you, they rejoice in it. But if you are patient in adversity and conscious of God, their scheming cannot harm you in the least: for, truly, God encompasses (with His Might) all that they do. ❖ [Q 3:120]

❖Say, "(Thus speaks God): 'O you servants of Mine who have attained to faith! Be conscious of your Lord! Ultimate good awaits those who persevere in doing good in this world. And remember: vast is God's earth, (and) truly they who are patient will be given their reward in full, beyond all reckoning!'" ❖ [Q 39:10]

7-7-2 Patience during times of adversity and trials

As explained in Chapter 3 of this work, believers will be exposed to various trials in life and they must persevere and be patient to be successful in these trials. It is a path to contentment, as outlined in the following verses.

❖ *True piety does not consist in turning your faces towards the east or the west – but truly pious is he who believes in God, and the Last Day, and the angels, and revelation, and the prophets, and spends his substance – however much he himself may cherish it – upon his next of kin, and the orphans, and the needy, and the wayfarer, and the beggars, and for the freeing of human beings from bondage, and is constant in prayer, and renders the purifying dues, and (truly pious are) they who keep their promises whenever they promise, and are patient in misfortune and hardship and in time of peril: it is they who have proved themselves true, and it is they, they who are conscious of God.* ❖ *[Q 2:177]*

❖ *You shall most certainly be tried in your possessions and in your persons; and indeed you shall hear many hurtful things from those to whom revelation was granted before your time, as well as from those who have come to ascribe divinity to other beings beside God. But if you remain patient in adversity and conscious of Him – this, behold, is something to set one's heart upon.* ❖ *[Q 3:186]*

❖ *And most certainly shall We try you by means of danger, and hunger, and loss of worldly goods, of lives and of (labour's) fruits. But give glad tidings to those who are patient in adversity [155] - who, when calamity befalls them, say, "Truly to God do we belong and, truly, to Him we shall return." [156]* ❖ *[Q 2:155-156]*

❖ *(But) do you think that you could enter paradise without having suffered like those (believers) who passed away before you? Misfortune and hardship befell them, and so shaken were they that the apostle, and the believers with him, would exclaim, "When will God's help come?" Oh, truly, God's help is (always) near!* ❖ *[Q 2:214]*

❖*... and most certainly We shall try you all, so that We might mark out those of you who strive hard (in Our cause) and are patient in adversity: for We shall put to a test (the truth of) all your assertions.*❖ [Q 47:31]

7-7-3 Patience helps one to be forbearing and forgiving

Patience is one of the most important attributes of a believer's character. Being patient, forbearing and forgiving are qualities that will help believers to repel bad deeds with good deeds. These traits are all tied to patience, which is needed to acquire contentment. Patience is the foundation of virtuous behaviour. From the Quran we know that God loves those who are patient, and that He is with the patient.

Hence, if you have to respond to an attack (in argument), respond only to the extent of the attack levelled against you; but to bear yourselves with patience is indeed far better for (you, since God is with) those who are patient in adversity. [126] Endure, then, with patience (all that they who deny the truth may say) – always remembering that it is none but God Who gives you the strength to endure adversity – and do not grieve over them, and neither be distressed by the false arguments which they devise.{127} Truly, God is with those who are conscious of Him, and those who are virtuous (doers of good). [128]❖ [Q 16:126-128]

7-7-4 Striving to purify one's lower self (the 'nafs')

Throughout one's life, one is striving to purify one's lower self to prevent it from making bad decisions and choices. We rely on patience to be successful in this struggle with our inner self.

❖*And yet (said Prophet Joseph), I am not trying to absolve myself: for, truly, man's inner self does incite (him) to evil, and saved are only they upon whom my Sustainer bestows His grace. Behold, My Lord is much-forgiving, a dispenser of grace!* ❖ [Q 12:53]

❖*As for those who strive hard in Our cause - We shall most certainly guide them onto paths that lead to Us: for, behold, God is indeed with the doers of good.* ❖ [Q 29:69]

❀*Then indeed your Lord, for those who emigrated after being oppressed, then strove (in God's cause) and were patient, surely your Lord thereafter is Ever-Forgiving, Most Merciful!* ❀ [Q 16:110]

❀*And be patient, for truly, God does not allow to be lost the reward of those who do good.* ❀ [Q 11:115]

❀*So he went forth before his people in all his adornment. Those who cared only for the life of this world said, "Oh, if only we had the like of what Qārūn has been given. Indeed, he is one of great fortune." [79] But those who had been granted true knowledge said (to them): "Woe to you! Merit in the sight of God is by far the best for any who attains to faith and does what is right: but none save the patient can ever achieve this (blessing)." [80]* ❀ [Q 28:79-80]

❀*And how many a prophet has had to fight (in God's cause), followed by many men devoted to God, and they did not become faint of heart for all that they had to suffer in God's cause, and neither did they weaken, nor did they abase themselves (before the enemy), since God loves those who are patient.* ❀ [Q 3:146]

❀*O you who believe! Be patient, and vie in patience with one another, and be ever ready (to do what is right), and remain conscious of God, so that you may prosper.* ❀ [Q 3:200]

❀*And obey God and His Messenger, and fall not into disputes with one another, lest you lose heart and your moral strength departs; and be patient and persevering: for God is with those who patiently persevere.* ❀ [Q 8:46]

❀*And (as) We raised among them leaders who, so long as they bore themselves with patience and had sure faith in Our messages, guided (their people) in accordance with Our Command.* ❀ [Q 32:24]

7-7-5 Patience in the Prophetic Traditions

The Prophetic Tradition also emphasizes the importance of patience, as can be seen from the following Hadith.

Suhayb ibn Sinan (may God be pleased with him) narrated that he heard the Prophet (pbuh) say, "Strange are the ways of a believer, for there is good in every affair of his, but this is not the case with anyone else except in the case of a believer, for if he has an occasion to feel happy, he thanks God, thus there is good in it for him, and if he faces hardship and shows resignation (endures it patiently), there is also good in it for him. [1]

Abu Sa`id al-Khudri (may God be pleased with him) narrated that some Ansari people asked for something from God's Messenger (pbuh) and he (pbuh) gave it to them. They again asked him for something and again he gave it to them. And then they asked him again and he gave them again until all that was with him was finished. And then he (pbuh) said, "If I had anything, I would not keep it away from you. Remember, whoever abstains from asking others, God will make him contented, and whoever tries to make himself self-sufficient, God will make him self-sufficient. And whoever remains patient, God will make him patient. No-one can be given a blessing better and greater than patience." [2]

Abu Malik al-Ash'ari (may God be pleased with him) reported: "The Messenger of God (peace be upon him) said: 'Cleanliness is half of faith' and 'All praise is due to God alone' (Al-Hamdu Lillah) fills the scale, and 'Glory be to God alone' (Subhan Allah) and 'All praise is due to God alone' (Al-Hamdu Lillah) fill up what is between the heavens and the earth, and prayer is a light, and charity is proof (of one's faith) and patience is a brightness, and the Holy Qur'an is a proof on your behalf or against you. All men go out early in the morning and dedicate themselves to either the good or the bad, thereby setting themselves free or destroying themselves." [3]

---

(1) The speaker: Muslim – Source: Sahih Muslim – page or number: 2999 Conclusion of the speaker: sound.

(2) The speaker: Muslim – Source: Sahih Muslim – page or number: 1053 Conclusion of the speaker: sound.

(3) The speaker: Muslim – Source: Sahih Muslim – page or number: 223 Conclusion of the speaker: sound.

Abdallah ibn Masood (may God be pleased with him) narrated that the Prophet (pbuh) said, "Patience is half of faith and full conviction (certainty) is the whole of faith." [1]

7-8 Summary and Conclusions

Cultivating the virtues of forbearance, pardoning and forgiveness bring God's love and contentment. Islam urges believers to follow this path and, as they hope that God will forgive them and pardon them, they should also forgive and pardon others. Many Quranic verses not only urge believers to forgive those who have been unjust to them, but to go beyond this and repel evil with good. This is a very high level of conduct that God, in His Holy Book, says can be achieved by those who are patient, and that it is a great triumph of righteous conduct.

This work has presented various ways to reach contentment: through loving God, and earning His love and contentment with you. A starting point is to do only those things which God loves, and avoid all things that He does not love. Then to be conscious of God at all times, accept His will and wisdom, be sincere and put your whole trust in Him. Giving thanks for all His blessings, never extending your gaze to the bounty He has given others, keeping your heart free from envy and anger, and, finally, in this chapter, being forbearing, forgiving, and repelling evil with good. All these noble actions need believers to be patient and persevering, since patience is the foundation of all the actions needed to reach contentment.

---

(1) The speaker: Al-Bayhaqi– Source: Shu`ab al-Iman – page or number: 7/3180

Summary

Contentment is a gift from God to those with whom He is content. With such contentment, believers will have a prosperous, righteous life, peace of mind, and a heart and soul at rest. And, in the Hereafter, they will be with those with whom God is content; this is the ultimate triumph.

Believers who have faith in God's Book will find guidance to the path that leads to contentment.

O mankind! There has now come to you an admonition from your Lord, and a cure for all (the ill) that may be in men's hearts, and guidance and grace to all who believe (in Him). [Q 10:57]

God, in His unlimited mercy, sent His messenger to guide humanity and show them the righteous, contented life.

(And as for you,) O Prophet – behold, We have sent you as a witness (to the truth), and as a herald of glad tidings and a warner, [45] and as one who summons (all men) to God by His leave, and as a light-giving beacon. [46] And (so,) convey to the believers the glad tiding that a great bounty from God awaits them; [47] [Q 33:45-47]

The guidance of the Prophet (pbuh) shows the Quranic guidance and the Prophetic Tradition will show the ways to contentment. As the Qur'an informs us, God warns us that the Devil and his party, as the arch-enemy of mankind, will try to divert them from such a path.

O you who believe! Surrender yourselves wholly to God, and follow not Satan's footsteps, for, truly, he is an open enemy to you. [Q 2:208]

The Qur'an portrays the Devil as envious, arrogant, and unthankful to God, despite what God had bestowed on Him, and having rejected what God had willed. This is the path of Satan, and mankind must be very aware of this and try to be of those who are always thankful to God and are humble.

"… (remember that) few are the truly grateful (even) among My servants!" [Q 34:13]

The main protection for mankind against Satan's attempts to misguide them is the continuous remembrance of God.

And should a temptation from Satan provoke you, seek refuge in God. Truly He is the All-Hearing, All-Knowing. [200] Truly those who are conscious of God, whenever any dark suggestion from Satan touches them, they remember (Him) – then, behold, they see (things) clearly [201]… and then they cannot fail (to do what is right). [202] [Q 7:200-202]

In addition to Satan and his party, the believer must also be aware of his own lower self and its lust for worldly splendour which may tempt him from the straight path.

*… by the soul and the One Who fashioned it * and inspired it as to what makes it iniquitous or reverent (conscious of God). Indeed, he prospers who purifies it (one's soul). And indeed he fails who obscures it.* [Q 91:7-10]

If believers want to attain the supreme triumph in the Hereafter, they should be sincere in seeking the contentment of God so that He will be content with them.

God said, "This is the Day wherein the truthful shall benefit from their truthfulness. For them shall be Gardens with rivers running below, abiding therein forever. God is content with them, and they are content with Him. That is the great triumph." [Q 5:119]

The approach of this book has been to search within the Holy Qur'an and the Prophetic Traditions to find the different ways and means to obtain God's contentment so that one will be content.

The first path to contentment is the love between believers and God.

Surely those who believe and perform righteous deeds, for them shall the Compassionate ordain love. [Q 19:96]

Believers' love of God and His Messenger is the way to obtain God's love. When God loves you, you will receive the bounty of His love, and the reward is mutual love between God and the believer. To obtain such love, believers need to do the things that God loves, and refrain from doing what God does not love. This leads to love between God and the believer, and the reward is mutual love.

❧... God will bring a people whom He loves and who love Him, humble toward the believers, stern toward the disbelievers, striving in the way of God, and fearing not the blame of any blamer. That is the Bounty of God, which He gives to whomsoever He will. And God is All-Encompassing, Knowing. ❧ [Q 5:54]

Being conscious of God will bring God's love.

❧... Truly God loves those who are conscious of Him. ❧ [Q 9:4]

God created everything according to measures and, when He wills, those measures will be manifested with His utmost wisdom and mercy. The manifestation of these measures will result in trials, and how we deal with these trials forms the basis of judgment on the Day of Judgment.

Being patient and persevering during these trials will bring God's mercy and reward, and will strengthen the believer's faith, helping him to become a better person. He should repent and pray that the outcome of these trials will be good for him in this life and the Hereafter. By accepting and being content with God's measures and what He has ordained will bring contentment, stability, and a peaceful life. Also, focusing on doing good deeds and living a righteous life will bring God's mercy and contentment.

❧... that you not despair over what has passed you by, nor exult in that which He has given to you. And God loves not any vainglorious boaster, ❧ [Q 57:23]

The path to contentment is through doing righteous deeds that will bring God's love. Such deeds should be devoted entirely to God, to gain God's contentment, without setting up partners with God since He does not accept any partners.

❧... not as payment for any favor received; [19] save for seeking the Face of His Lord, the Most High, [20] and surely he shall be content. [21] ❧ [Q 92:19-21]

When believers put their complete trust in God, everything they do will bring God's love and contentment.

❖*... when you have decided upon a course of action, place your trust in God: for, truly, God loves those who place their trust in Him.* ❖ *[Q 3:159]*

Trusting in God and seeking refuge in Him will protect believers against the efforts of Satan and his party to make them deviate from the straight path.

❖*... seek refuge in God from the outcast Satan. [98] Truly he (Satan) has no authority over those who believe and trust in their Lord. [99]* ❖ *[Q 16:98-99]*

God promises those who are sincere in their deeds and place their trust in Him that He will look after them.

❖*... And whosoever trusts in God, He suffices him. ...* ❖ *[Q 65:3]*

When believers act with sincerity, placing their complete trust in God, and with the intention to gain His contentment, this will help in assuring them of God's contentment.

The deed which will always bring the believer closer to God is remembrance of Him. This remembrance can be done by the heart, the tongue, or by good deeds, where the believer's actions are done with devotion and the sincere intention of attaining God's contentment. Remembrance can take the form of glorifying God, acknowledging His Oneness, praying for forgiveness, acknowledging His glory and greatness, reading the Holy Qur'an, offering supplications, and praying to God using His Most Beautiful Divine Names, which bring blessings and closeness to God.

Being thankful for God's limitless Grace will cause Him to increase your sustenance, bless it for you, and make you contented with it. Other actions that will help you to be contented include not extending your gaze to what others have of worldly splendours, and instead being thankful for what you have, and focusing on the great reward you will receive in the Hereafter.

Being forbearing, pardoning, forgoing and forgiving others for any wrong done to you is a very important aspect of the character of believers, and it is a way to receive God's forgiveness and contentment with you. Islam encourages believers to repel evil with good.

❋ The good deed and the evil deed are not equal. Repel by that which is better; then behold, the one between whom and you there is enmity shall be as if he were a loyal, protecting friend. [34] Yet none shall receive it, save those who are patient; and none shall receive it, save those who possess great fortune. [35] ❋ [Q 41:34-35]

All that is mentioned above is a path to contentment, such as doing the deeds that God loves, avoiding the deeds he does not love, remaining conscious of Him at all times, making the relationship between you and God one of love, and loving one another.

Accept God's will, patiently persevere in the various trials in life, be sincere, put your trust in God, be thankful for His Grace, and set your heart towards the Gardens of the Hereafter rather than this worldly life and its splendours. Finally, be forgiving and repel evil with good. All of this needs patience and perseverance, and this is why patience is the basis of all good deeds. This is why God loves the patient and will bestow on them His contentment, the greatest reward that believers can receive – it is the supreme triumph.

❋ God is content with them, and they are content with Him: this is the supreme triumph. ❋ [Q 5:119]

Appendix 1: Ibn Arabi Prayers

(يا رحمن) ارحمني بسبوغ نعمك وآلائك وبلوغ الأمل في دفع شدائدك وبلوائك.

O The Rahman, have mercy on me by amply bestowing Your grace and divine acts, and in the attainment of the hope to ward off Your adversities and afflictions.

(يارحيم) ارحمني بدخول جنتك والتنعم بقربك ورؤيتك.

O The Merciful, have mercy on me by entering your Garden, enjoying being close to You and seeing You.

(يا مالك) الدنيا والآخرة ملكاً تاماً كاملاً اجعلني في الوصول إلى جنة النعيم والملك الكبير جاداً عاملاً.

O The King, of the Lower Life and of the Last Life; full and complete sovereignty; make me in my progress toward the Garden of Bliss and grand sovereignty serious and diligent.

(يا قدوس) قدسني من العيوب والآفات وطهرني من الذنوب والسيئات.

قدسني من العيوب: أي طهرني من كل ما لا يليق بي.

O The Holy, make me holier than being blemished by defects and afflictions, purify me from sins and wrong-doings.

(يا سلام) سلمنى من كل وصف ذميم واجعلني ممن يأتيك بقلب سليم.

O The Peace, make me safe from any blameworthy description, and make me of those who come to you having a safe heart.

(يا مؤمن) أمني يوم الفزع الأكبر وارزقني من مزيد الإيمان بك الحظ الأكبر.

O The Faithful, make me safe on the Day of the Greatest Scare, and make my share of more belief in You the greatest.

(يا مهيمن) اجعلني لهيمنتك شاهداً ورائياً ولأماناتك وعهدك حافظاً وراعياً.

O The Dominator, make me for Your domination bear witness and have sight, and for Your trust and promise a keeper and preserver.

(ياعزيز) اجعلني بعزتك من الأذلين بين يديك واستعملني بأعمال الآخرة لديك.

O The Mighty, make me by Your might of the lowest before You, and use me by the acts of the Last Day that are Yours.

(يا جبار) اجبر حالى بموافقة مرادك ولا تجعلني جباراً على عبادك.

O The Ever-Compeller, set right my state by making it in compliance with Your will, and make me not tyrannical in attitude with Your slaves.

(يا متكبر) اجعلني من المتواضعين لكبريائك الخاضعين لحكمك وقضائك.

O The Lofty, make me of those who are humble in the face of Your loftiness, subjecting themselves to Your judgement and decrees.

(يا خالق) اخلق في قلبي توفيقاً للطاعة واعصمني بين خلقك من كل ظلامة وتباعة.

O The Creator, create in me success in obedience, and grant me infallibility among your creation against any act of injustice and its consequences.

(يا بارئ) اجعلني من خير البرية وخلقني بأخلاق حسنة مرضية.

O The Maker, make me of the best of those You created, and bestow upon me good and pleasing manners.

(يا مصور) صورني بصورة عبوديتك ونورني بأنوار معرفتك.

O The Fashioner, fashion me in the image of being a slave to You, and make me enlightened with the lights of those who know You.

(يا غفار) اغفر لي جميع الكبائر والصغائر وهواجم الغفلات وهواجس الضمائر.

O The Ever-Forgiving, forgive all my sins, great and venial, the onsets of inattention and the scruples of what is there in the innermost concealed.

(يا قهار) أشهدني قهرك ولا تؤمني مكرك.

O The Ever-Subduing, let me be a witness to Your subduing acts, and feel not safe against that which is Your craft.

(يا وهاب) هب لي من جزيل هبتك ما يبلغني إلى مرضاتك.

O The Ever-Endowing, lavishly bestow on me that which will make me attain to You being pleased with me.

(يا رزاق) ارزقني علماً نافعا ورزقاً حلالاً واسعاً.

O The Ever-Sustaining, provide me with the knowledge that is useful and the provision that is religiously admissible and abundant.

(يا فتاح) افتح لي أبواب السعادة وحققني بحقائق الإرادة.

O The Ever-Opening, open up for me the doors of happiness and make me live the truths of those who have the will.

(يا عليم) علمني من علمك ما ترضى به عنى ولا تؤاخذني بما تعلمه مني.

(يا سميع) اسمعني بلطائف أسماع من علمت فيه الخير واجعلني من الراغبين لسمعك وبصرك في نهي وأمر.

O The All-Hearing, let me listen to the subtleties of the hearkening ears of those You know are good and make me of those who seek to listen to You and know that You see them in what not to do and what to do.

O The Omniscient, let me learn of Your omniscience what will make You pleased with me, and do not hold it against me what You know is from me.

(يابصير) اجعلني بصيراً في دينك عند اشتباه الأمور ذا بصيرة تامة في اجتناب كل محظور.

O The All-Seeing, make me endowed with an insight into Your religion when there are matters indistinctive, and endowed with full insight in avoiding that which is prohibited.

(يا لطيف) ألطف بي في قدرك وقضائك واقسم لي من جزيل برك وآلائك.

O The Gracious, shower Your grace upon me in that which You decreed and destined, and let me have a good share of Your beneficence and acts of grace.

(يا خبير) اجعلني خبيراً بخفيات عيوبي مستغفراً من جميع ذنوبي.

O The Knower, make me knowing of that which is not manifest of my demerits, and asking for forgiving of all my sins.

(يا حليم) خلقني بخلق الحلم وحققني بحقائق العلم.

O The Forbearer, bestow upon me the good traits of forbearance, and make me truly cognizant of the truths of omniscience.

(يا عظيم) بعظمة لا تحيط بها أوهام المتفكرين اجعلني عظيم الهمة في الترقي في مقامات المتمكنين أهل التمكين.

O The Great, with a greatness that is beyond the grasp of the illusions of those pretending to be thinkers, make me of a great stamina in being promoted to the status of those who are of a competent standing among the people of standing.

(يا غفور) اغفر لي جميع الخطايا والذنوب وبلغني من رضوانك غاية المرغوب.

O The All-Forgiving, forgive all my sins and wrongdoings, and of Your being pleased with me, let me attain the end of the traveler to the end.

(يا شكور) اجعلني شكوراً لما أنعمت على من نعمائك ذَكُوراً لإحسانك وآلائك.

O The All-Thankful, let me be thankful for the acts of grace You have bestowed on me, always remembering how good You are to me and Your grace is lavishly bestowed on me.

(يا علي يا كبير) اجعلني عبداً من الأعلى عليين في درجات الكمال يا من لا كبيراً إلا وهو بالإضافة إلى كبريائه حقير اجعلني من الأكابر المختصين بالملك الكبير.

O The High One, O The Grand, make me a slave of the most high ones in the ascending grades of perfection, You other than Whom there is no grand and in comparison to His loftiness will be humble, make me of the grand who are assigned the grand dominion.

(يا حفيظ) احفظني من موافقة موجبات عذابك واجعلني حفيظاً لما استحفظتني من كتابك.

O The All-Preserving, preserve us against that which will incur Your torture, and make me memorizing what You made me preserve of Your Book.

(يا مقيت) أقتني باطناً وظاهراً بأحسن الأقوات وأعنى على طاعتك في جميع الحالات.

O The All-Providing, provide me in that which is manifest and unmanifest in me with the best provision, and help me to obey You in all cases.

(يا حسيب) استعملني بالمحاسبة قبل الحساب والسؤال وكن حسبي في جميع الأحوال.

استعملني بالمحاسبة: اعمِل فكري بالمحاسبة، أي اجعلني احاسب نفسي وأراقبها.

O The All-Reckoning, use me by accountability before the Reckoning and the Calling to Account, and let it be You that is sufficient unto me in all cases.

(يا كريم) اجعلني من المكرمين بطاعتك ومحبتك وأكرمني بالنظر إلى وجهك الكريم في جوارك وجنتك.

O The Munificent, make me of those by reason of Your obedience and love are of the honored, and honor me by letting me look at Your generous Face in Your neighborhood and garden.

(يا رقيب) ارزقني من مراقبتك ما يمنعني من العصيان ومن مشاهدة قربك ما يذهب بدواعي الغفلة والنسيان.

O The Watchful, of Your watchfulness provide me with what will preclude me from disobedience, and of watching Your closeness what will drive away the causes of inattention and forgetfulness.

(يا مجيب) استجب لي دعاك بأسمائك الحسنى وسناك واجعلني ممن أجاب دعوتك واتبع رسلك.

O The Answerer, answer my prayers in virtue of Your Most Beautiful Names and Your resplendence, and make me of those who answered Your call and followed Your messengers.

(يا واسع) وسعت كل شيء رحمةً وعلماً أوسع لي من الرحمة والعلم .

O The Broad, You comprehend everything in Your mercy and omniscience, give me of the broadness of mercy and omniscience the greatest share and the most lavish provision.

(يا حكيم) حكمته لا يشذ شيء عنها هب لي حكمة تحملني على محاسن الأحوال والأفعال وترك القبائح منها. محاسن الأحوال: كل ما يستحسن من أحوال المرء.

O The Wise, His wisdom allows for no exception, bestow upon me that wisdom which will take me to the best conditions and acts and away from any despicable condition or act.

(يا ودود) يا ود أوليائه وأصفيائه المقربين، اجعل في قلبي وداً لك أو اجعل لي وداً في قلوب المؤمنين.

O The Affectionate, by the affection of His saints and the select who are brought near, make in my heart affection for You, and make for me affection in the hearts of the faithful.

(يا مجيد) بمعنى عظيم الشأن عميم الإحسان ارزقني من المجد ما هو غاية الإمكان في طاقة الإنسان.

O The Glorious, You the Great, You of the bounty for all, provide me of the glory that beyond which no man can attain.

(يا شهيد) اجعلني لشهادتك متيقناً وبعلمك مكتفياً.

O The All-Witness, make me of Your witnessing ascertained and of Your omniscience sufficed.

(يا حق) حقق رجائي في بلوغي حقيقة من حقائق توحيدك واستعملني للقيام بحقك والوقوف على جودك.

O The Truth, make my prayers that I attain a truth of Your oneness come true, and use me that I may rise up to what serves You right and grasp Your generosity.

(يا وكيل) اجعلني من المتوكلين عليك في الأمور كلها ولا تكلني إلى نفسي طرفة عين ولا أقل من ذلك.

O The Advocate, make me of those who have trust in You in all matters, and let me not be left unto myself a twinkling of the eye, nor even less than that.

(يا قوي) قوني على العمل بكل طاعة وبر وقني شر نفسي وشر كل ذي شر.

O The Strong, give me the power to work obediently and with beneficence, and protect me against myself and against the evil of all that is evil.

(يا متين) اجعل ديني متيناً ويقيني قوياً مكيناً.

O The Firm, make my religion firm, and my firm belief strong and deep.

(يا ولي) اجعلني بولايتك إياي ولياً وبرعاية حقك وفياً.

O The Patron, make me by Your patronage to me a saint, and by being able to observe the right of sainthood fulfilling.

(يا حميد) اجعلني من الحامدين لك والشاكرين واحشرني تحت لواء الحمد في زمرة النبيين والصديقين والشهداء والصالحين.

O The Praiseworthy, make me of those singing Your praise and of the thankful, and gather me under the Banner of Divine Praise among the prophets, the Friends, the martyrs and the righteous ones.

(يا حي) احيني حياة طيبة واسقني من شراب محبتك أعذبه.

O The Living, give me a good life, and let me drink of the drink of Your love its best.

(يا قيوم) هب لي من معرفة قيوميتك ما أستريح به من كدر التدبير ومن مشاهدة لطائفك ما يتيسر لي به كل عسير.

O The Ever-Rising, endow me with the knowledge of Your being Ever-Rising that which will make me relieved of the burden of management, and of the watching of Your acts of grace that with which You facilitate for me that which is difficult.

(يا واحد) اجعلني موحداً بوجود وحدانيتك مؤيداً بشهود فردانيتك.

O The One, make me believing in the oneness of the existence of Your monotheism, supported by witnessing Your individualness.

(يا صمد) ارزقني صمدية تقضى دوام الحصول واجعلني ممن يصمد إليك بهمته في جميع الأمور.

O The Steadfast, provide me with a steadfastness that requires everlasting occurrence and make me of a steadfast stamina in all matters.

(يا قادر) إخلق لي قدرة صالحة لاكتساب الطاعات وقوة مانعة عن ارتكاب المخالفات.

O The Powerful, create for me a power good for acquisition of acts of obedience and a strength that stands against committing any act of disobedience.

(يا مقتدر) اجعلني بشهود اقتدارك وهيبته ممن يقارب بين يديك في سكونه وحركته.

O The Omnipotent, make me by witnessing Your omnipotence and reverence of those give in to You in their quietness or movement.

(يا أول يا آخر) اكتبني عندك في أوائل السابقين.

O The First, O The Last, write my name in Your book as among the first of those who go first.

(يا ظاهر يا باطن) احفظ باطني وظاهري مما لا ترضاه ولا ترضى به عن عبد أتاك.

O The Manifest, O The Unmanifest, preserve that which is manifest and that which is unmanifest in me against what pleases You not and what You does not make You pleased regarding a slave who has come to You.

(يا متعال) ارزقني من شهود تعاليك ما ينور الظلمات ويوضح المشكلات.

O The Transcendent, Provide me by the witnessing of Your transcendence that which will give light to the darkness and clarification to problems.

(يابر) اجعلني عندك باراً نقياً وبمن نزل بي براً حفياً مرضياً.

O The Beneficent, make me of those to You are beneficent and to those who are there beneficent, concealed and pleased.

(يا تواب) ارزقني إليك توبة نصوحاً لا تدع لي إلى المخالفة ميلاً ولا جنوحاً.

O The Ever-Accepting of Repentance, provide me with a sincere repentance unto You that will toward disobedience allow liking nor inclination.

(يا عفوُّ) اعف عنى بفضلك وإحسانك وعاملني بكرمك وامتنانك.

O The Pardoner, by Your grace and charitable giving grant me pardon and by Your bounty and favor do to me.

(يا رؤوف) كن بي في الدارين رءوفاً رحيماً واقسم لى من الرأفة بالمؤمنين قسماً وافراً وحظاً عظيماً.

O The Compassionate, be to me in the two abodes compassionate and merciful and in being compassionate to the faithful give me a big and great share.

(يا غنى) اجعلني غنياً بافتقاري إلى كرمك وأفضالك وكن بى حفياً يوم ورودى
عليك بإحسانك وإجمالك.

O The Rich, O The Enricher, make me rich by being in need of Your bounty and favors and by Your charitable and gracious acts be unto me ever-welcoming the day I come to you.

(يَا وَارِثُ) خُصَّني مِنْ وِرَاثَةِ خَوَاصِّكَ بِمَقَامٍ كَرِيْمٍ وَاجْعَلْني بَفَضْلِكَ مِنْ وَرَثَةِ
جَنَّةِ النَّعِيْمِ.

O The Inheritor, of those who inherit Your intrinsic attributes, assign for me an honorable standing and make me with Your grace one of those who inherit the Garden of Bliss.

(يا قابض يا باسط) اقبضني عن مسابقة دواعي النفس وابسط عليَّ نسيم
نفحات الأُنس.

O The Constrictor, O The Expander, let my hastiness toward what the self calls me to do be constricted, and let the breeze of the gifts of intimacy be spread over me.

(يا حكم) اجعلني لحكم إرادتك مسلماً ولأحكام شريعتك معظماً.

O The Judge, make me for the judgement of Your will committing myself to that will, and holding the rulings of Your Law in high esteem.

(يا مقدم يا مؤخر) قدمني في حلبة السابقين إلى دار السلام ولا تؤخرني مع
الهالكين باجترام أي بارتكاب المعاصي والآثام.

O The Advancer, O The Delayer, make me in the advance ornament of those who go first to the Garden of The Abode of Peace, and let me not be delayed with those perished by commitment of sins.

(يا خافض يا رافع) اخفض لي هوائي بموافقة كتابك وارفعني بقربك فهويتي
إلى جنابك.

O The Demoter, O The Promoter, let my whims be lowered by my acting in compliance with Your Book, and raise me up by being brought close to You, because my identity is by Your lofty side.

(يا معز يا مذل) أعزني بعز التوحيد والإيمان ولا تذلني بإتباع خطوات
الشيطان.

O The Exalting, O The Humiliator, make me cherished by the might of monotheism and humiliate me not by following the footsteps of Satan .

(يا عدل) اجعلني ممن يقوم بالعدل في جميع عمله ويبلغ بالترقي في درجات الإحسان غاية أمله.

O The Just, make me of those who administer justice in whatever I do, and in being promoted up the ascending grades of well-doing attain the highest of my hopes.

(يا جليل) فلا جليل إلا وهو في الجلالة له مستكين اجعلني من هيبتك وجلالك في مقام مكين.

O The Majestic, there is no Majestic except Him, in His majesty He is therein, of Your reverence and majesty make me in a standing of command.

(يا باعث) ابعث لي خواطر الخير من خزائن السر وثبتني يوم البعث بجزيل الأجر وجميل البر.

O The Resurrector, resurrect in me the thoughts of good from the treasures of the secret, and make me firm on the Day of Resurrection by the generous reward and the best beneficence.

(يا محصي) كل شيء عدداً وإحاطة وقدراً اجعلني من المحصين لأسمائك عقداً وطاقة وحصراً.

O The Reckoner, of everything in number, in comprehension and in worth, make me of those who comprehend Your Names in connectedness, power and enumeration.

(يا مبدئ يا معيد) اجعلني ممن يبدأ بمخالفة نفسه على مراده واختياره ويعود إلى بابك بصدق اجتهاده واعتماده وافتقاره.

O The Initiator, O The Restorer, make me of those who begin by acting in contravention with the dictates of the desires and choices of their selves and go back to Your door by the truthfulness of their striving, dependence and want of You.

(يا محيي يا مميت) أحيي قلبي بمعرفتك وأمت نفسي بشهود عظمتك وهيبتك.

O The Life-Giver, O The Life-Taker, give life to my heart by knowing You and let my self be dead by witnessing Your greatness and reverence.

(يا واجد) أوجد لي من جودك وجداً بالغاً وجوداً وأنلني من عرفان واجديتك عطاءً سابغاً وجوداً.

O The Author, bring into existence for me by Your existence an ecstasy for love that is great and bounteous, and let me attain by the knowledge of Your being existent a lavish giving and generosity.

(يا ماجد) أوصافه مجد وأسماؤه حسنى أعطني من محاذاة الهمة ما أرقى به إلى المحل الأسنى.

O The Glory-Giver, His attributes are glory and His Names are Beauty, give me by observing to have the stamina that with which I be promoted to the best place.

(يا والي) تولني بهدايتك واجعلني من أهل ولايتك وخاصتك.

O The Ordainer, be my patron by Your guidance and make me of those under Your patronage and those who are Yours.

(يا منتقم) لا تنتقم مني باقتراف الذلل ووفقني للقبول والعمل.

O The Avenger, take no revenge from me by letting me slip into sins and be my guide toward acceptance and diligence.

(يا مالك الملك) والأملاك أعوذ بك من مسالك الهلاك.

O The Owner of Dominion, and all property. I seek refuge in You from the roads to perdition.

(ياذا الجلال والإكرام) أعذني من الضلال والإجرام.

O The Majestic and Bounteous One, I take refuge in You from being led astray and from culpability.

(يا مقسط) استعملني بالقسط في جميع الأحوال ولا تعاملني بقسطك وعدلك.

O The Equitable, use me in equitability in all cases and by Your favor do not do to me as per Your equitability and justice.

(يا جامع) اجمع متفرقات كوني في جمع الجمع بين يديك وارزقني يوم الجمع قربك والنظر إليك.

O The Gatherer, bring together the severalty of my being in the assemblage of the collectivity and bestow on me on the Day of Assemblage being close to You and looking at You.

(يا مانع) امنعني عن العوالم كلها بانقطاعي إليك وأعنى على أموري بصدق التوكل عليك.

O The Preventer, prevent me from all the worlds by being fully dedicated unto You and help me with my affairs by being truly putting my trust in You.

(يا نافع) اجعلني ممن يضر بدنياه لطلب الآخرة ويذر هداه في مناه لشهود المنافع الفاخرة.

(يا ضار) امنعني بلطائف عنايتك من شر الأشرار واحفظني بحسن عنايتك من اقتحام الأوزار.

O The Benefiter, make me of those who in pursuit of the last life are distressed in the Lower life and would let go what he hoped for in order to witness the luxurious benefits.

O The Distresser, prevent me by the grace of Your care from the evil of the evil people and preserve me by Your good care from storming into sins.

(يا نور) السماوات والأرض بمعنى الهداية لأهلها والإرشاد اجعل لي نوراً أمشي به في العباد.

O The Light of the Heavens and the Earth, give me light with which I may live with Your servants.

(يا هادى) اهدني لأحسن الأعمال.

O The Guide, guide me to the best of deeds.

(يا بديع) السماوات والأرض حكمتك ما ينفى كل التباس ويوضح كل إشكال.

O The Originator, of the heavens and the earth with no like or example, show me of the greatness of Your wisdom that which clarifies any ambiguity and elucidates any problematic affair.

(يا باقي) فلا انتهاء لنهايتك ولا آخر أسهم لي من مقام البقاء بك الحظ الوافر.

O The Ever-Lasting, there is no end to Your end nor an extreme point, let me have the biggest share of the standing of everlastingness by Yours.

(يا رشيد) أرشدني إلى طاعتك ومحبتك واجعلني مرشداً لعبادك إلى طريق توحيدك ومعرفتك.

O The All-Guided, guide me toward Your obedience and love and make me a guide to Your slaves on the road of believing in Your oneness and knowing You.

(يا صبور) صبرني على طاعتك واجعلني صبورا في بلواك وعافيتك.

O The All-Patient, make me be patient in Your obedience and patient for better or for worse.

APPENDIX 2: Hadith and Sunnah

The Meaning of 'Sunnah' and 'Hadith' –
A Brief Explanation

Sunnah (lit. 'custom,' 'wont,' 'usage,' pl. *sunan*) is a general term that may be applied to nations' customs and usages. The predominant meaning of 'Sunnah' is that of the spoken and acted example of Prophet Muhammad (pbuh). It includes what he approved, allowed, or condoned when, under prevailing circumstances, he might well have taken issue with others' actions, practices or decisions; and what he himself disapproved of or refrained from.

The Prophet's Sunnah is the crucial complement to the Holy Quran. Thus the Quran enjoins prayer, but not how it is to be performed: the form of canonical prayer (*Salah*) is based entirely on Sunnah.

The importance of the Sunnah arises from the function of the Prophet (pbuh) as the Messenger, and hence the inspired and far-sighted nature of his acts, and the Holy Quran's injunction to pattern oneself after him: "You have a beautiful example in God's Messenger." (Q 33:21)

The Sunnah falls into several categories: *as-sunnah al-mu'akkadah*, which is 'confirmed' by being demonstrably repeated in the lifetime of the Prophet (pbuh) so that it has assumed an almost obligatory character, sometimes legally binding when it concurs with clearly essential aspects of ritual and law. And the *as-sunnah al-za'idah*, the supplementary or elective Sunnah in matters less essential. Emulation of the Sunnah is clearly commendable.

The applicable aspects of the Sunnah form an element of the *usul al-fiqh* ('basis of law'), after the Quran, and along with *qiyas* ('analogy'), and *ijma'* ('consensus'), which determine the religious law of Islam.

Hadith (literally 'speech,' 'report,' 'account') are, specifically, Prophetic Traditions relating to the deeds and utterances of Prophet Mohammad (pbuh) as recounted by his Companions. Hadith are divided into two groups: *Hadith Qudsi* ('sacred Hadith'), in which God Himself is speaking through the Prophet (pbuh) and *Hadith Sharif* ('noble Hadith'), the Prophet's own utterances. Hadith are the basis, second only to the Holy Quran, for Islamic law (*shari'ah*).

The most respected collection of all is the Jami' as-Sahih of Muhammad Ibn Isma'il al-Bukhari (d. 256/870). This has 7,397 Hadith under 3,450 subject headings. Next is the *Sahih* of Abu al-Husayn Muslim ibn al-Hajjaj (d. 261/875), usually called 'Muslim'). The *Six Musannaf*, the principal canonic collections (i.e., those accepted as authoritative) also known as the 'six books,' are the *Sahihayn*, and the collection of Abu Dawud as-Sijistānī (4,500 Hadith) (d. 261/875), Abu 'Isa Muhammad at-Tirmidhi (d. 279/892).

The collection of at-Tirmidhi and Abu Dawud are *kutub sunan*, or collections of Hadith specifically relevant to the practices of the Prophet (pbuh). Finally, there are the collections of an-Nasa'i (d. 303/915), and Ibn Majah (d. 273/886), another *kitab sunan*. These collections include sayings of some of the Companions. Abu Hurayrah is the Companion cited as the primary source of the greatest number of Hadith.

Equally famous is the *Muwatta'* of Malik ibn Anas, the first collection ever written down. Another kind of collection is the *Musnad*. *Musnads* are collections grouped around the primary source, that is, the transmitter. The most famous (of four well-known *Musnads*) is the *Musnad* of Ibn Hanbal, founder of a school of law (d. 241/855). Ibn Hanbal's Musnad contains 30,000 Hadith. That of At-Tayalisi (d. 202/818) is the first Musnad with 2,767 Hadith from 600 authorities.

The *isnad* is the chain of transmission. Distinctions are made according to whether the Hadith was 'heard,' 'reported,' 'disclosed,' 'found,' and other categories relating to the circumstances of transmission. The transmission is the *riwayah*; the transmitter is a *rawi*, who, it was admitted, could edit the Hadith and improve upon its form and style, whence the same Hadith is found reported in different degrees of amplitude. The *matn*, meaning 'letters' (mutun), is the actual text of the Hadith.

The canonical collections grade Hadith according to indices of authenticity. The highest grade is *mutawatir*, which is 'recurrent' or reported by many different sources. Then there is *Sahih* 'reliable,' *hasan* 'good,' *da'if* 'weak,' and *mawdu'a*, or 'fabricated.' When collections of Hadith began to appear, scholars also studied what they considered to be fabricated Hadith. There was a saying "that there is no more reprehensible act than the fabricating of Hadith," which shows awareness that many Hadith were not historically authentic.

The collections of Bukhari and Muslim were scrupulously compiled in the first two and a half centuries of Islam. Their authenticity was assured by the criterion that the people of the time found most valid, that of an authoritative *isnad* or chain of transmission.

Bibliography

Translations of the Holy Qur'an used in this book:

Abdel Haleem, M.A.S., *The Qur'an: English Translation and Parallel Arabic Text*. Oxford University Press, Oxford, U.K., 2010

Asad, Muhammad, *The Message of the Qur'an*. The Book Foundation, 2003, reprinted in 2012 by Oriental Press, Dubai, U.A.E.

Nasr, Seyyed Hossein, et al, *The Study Qur'an*: *A New Translation and Commentary*. HarperOne, New York, U.S.A., 2015

1. Samᶜani, Ahmad, *The Repose of the Spirits – A Sufi Commentary on the Divine Name*s. Translated and with an introduction by William C. Chittick, SUNY Press, 2019

2. Chittick, William C., *In Search of the Lost Heart: Explorations in Islamic Thought*. SUNY Press, 2012

3. Muhammad, Ghazi Bin, *Love in the Holy Qur'an*. Expanded 7th Edition, The Islamic Texts Society, Cambridge, U.K., 2013

4. Glassé, Cyril, *The Concise Encyclopaedia of Islam*. Third Edition with extensive Chronology, Stacy International, London, U.K., 2008

5. Al-Uthaimeen, Muhammad, *The Beautiful Names and Attributes of Allah*. Darussalam, Riyadh, Saudi Arabia, 2010

6. Khawaldeh, Samira Fayyad, *The Most Beautiful Names of Allah*. Goodword Books, New Delhi, India, 2004

7. Samat, Talib & Brigitte Bresson, *The 99 Most Eminent Names of Allah.* Utusan Publications, Kuala Lumpur, Malaysia, 2001

8. Abdel Gawad, Ahmed. *And Allah, the Most Beautiful Names invite him to it.* Reading: Abdel-Halim Mahmoud. Cairo: al-Azhar, College Library of al-Azhar, 1985.

9. Abu Dawood, *Sunan Abi Dawood.* Commentary by Ahmed Muhammad Shaker, Abdul Aziz bin Abdullah bin Baz, Muhammad Nasir al-Din al-Albani, Muhammad bin Saleh al-Uthaymeen, Muhammad Hamid al-Faqi, Abdullah bin Abd al-Rahman al-Bassam, Salih bin Fawzan al-Fawzan, Abd al-Muhsin bin Hamad al-Abbad and Abdul Aziz al-Rajhi. Egypt: Al Falah Publishing and Distribution, First Edition, 1439 AH – 2018 AD.

10. Ahmad ibn Hanbal. *al-Musnad.* Edited by Ahmad Muhammad Shakir. Published by Dar al-Hadith, Cairo. First Edition 1416 AH – 1995 AD.

11. Albani, Muhammad Nasr al-Din al-. *Sahih al-Jami` al-Saghir and its Increases.* Published by Islamic Office, 1408 AH – 1988 AD.

12. Ansari, Ibn Manzoor al-. *Lisan Al Arab.* Beirut: Dar Sader, Third Edition, 1414 AH – 1994 AD.

13. Bukhari, al-. *Sahih Al-Imam Al-Bukhari.* Edited by Muhammad Fouad Abdul-Baqi. Egypt: Imam Muslim Library for Publishing and Distribution, First Edition, 1436 AH – 2015 AD.

14. Damishqī, Abu al-Fiḍā ‘Imād Ad-Din Ismā‘īl ibn ‘Umar ibn Kathīr al-Qurashī al-. *Al-sīra al-Nabawiyya.* Edited by: Mustafa Abdel Wahid. Beirut: Dar Al-Maarefa for Printing and Publishing, 1396 AH – 1976 AD.

15. Damishqī, Abu al-Fiḍā ‘Imād Ad-Din Ismā‘īl ibn ‘Umar ibn Kathīr al-Qurashī al-. *Tafsir ibn Kathir.* Edited by M. H. Shams al-Din. First Edition, 1419 AH – 1998 AD.

16. *Facilitated interpretation* - the authors are a selection of professors of interpretation - King Fahd Complex for the Printing of the Noble Qur'an - Second Edition, 1430 AH – 2009 AD.

17. Ibn Majah. *Sunan Ibn Majah.* Commentary by Sheikh Ahmed Muhammad Shaker, Abdul Aziz bin Abdullah bin Baz, Muhammad Nasir al-Din al-Albani, Muhammad bin Saleh al-Uthaymeen, Muhammad Hamid al-Faqi, Abdullah bin Abd al-Rahman al-Bassam, Salih bin Fawzan al-Fawzan, Abd al-Muhsin bin Hamad al-Abbad and Abd al-Aziz al-Rajhi. Egypt: Al Falah Publishing and Distribution, First Edition, 1439 AH – 2018 AD.

18. Ma'afri, Abdul Malik bin Hisham bin Ayoub al-Humairi al-. *Sirat Ibn Hisham.* Commented by and published its hadiths, and made their indexes Omar Abdel-Salam Tadmari. Beirut: Dar al-Kitab al-Arabi, Third Edition, 1410 AH – 1990 AD.

19. Maḥalli, Jalal ad-Din and as-Suyuti, Jalal ad-Din al-. *Tafsir al-Jalalayn.* Cairo: Dar al-Hadith, 1422 AH – 2001 AD.

20. Mahmoud, Abdel Halim. *"Remember me, I remind you.* Cairo: Dar al-Maaref, 1981.

21. Mubarkpuri, Safi-ur-Rahman al-. *Ar-Raheeq Al-Maktoum.* Qatar: Ministry of Endowments, 1428 AH – 2007 AD.

22. Nasa'i, al-. *Sunan Al- Nasa'i.* Commentary by Ahmed Muhammad Shaker, Abdul Aziz bin Abdullah bin Baz, Muhammad Nasir al-Din al-Albani, Muhammad bin Saleh al-Uthaymeen, Muhammad Hamid al-Faqi, Abdullah bin Abd al-Rahman al-Bassam, Salih bin Fawzan al-Fawzan, Abd al-Muhsin bin Hamad al-Abad and Abdel Aziz al-Rajhi. Egypt: Al Falah Publishing and Distribution, First Edition, 1439 AH – 2018 AD.

23. Nassafi, Abu Al-Barakat Abdullah bin Ahmed bin Mahmoud Hafez Al-Din al-. *Madarik Tanzil Wa Haqaiq al-Tawil (Tafseer Al-Nassafi)* Edited by Youssef Ali Badawi - reviewed and presented by Mohiuddin Dib Mesto. Beirut: Dar al-Kalam, First Edition, 1419 AH – 1998 AD.

24. Nawawi, al-. *Sahih Al-Imam Muslim Sharh Al-Nawawi.* Edited by Muhammad Fouad Abdul-Baqi. Tanzania: Abi Suhail Library, Egypt: Manarat Al-Islam for Publishing and Distribution, First Edition, 1441 AH – 2020 AD.

25. Othaimeen, Muhammad Bin Saleh al-. *The supreme saying in explaining the characteristics and names of God the Most Beautiful.* Collected and prepared by Irfan Bin Salim Al-Asha Hassouna Al-Dimashqi. Beirut: Dar Al-Fikr, 1426 AH – 2005 AD.

26. Radwany, Mahmoud Abdel Razek al-. *Allah's Most Beautiful Names in the Book and the Sunnah.* Cairo: Salsabeel Library, First Edition, 1426 AH – 2005 AD.

27. Tirmidhi, *Sunan Al-Tirmidhi.* Commentary by Ahmed Muhammad Shaker, Abdul Aziz bin Abdullah bin Baz, Muhammad Nasiruddin Al-Albani, Muhammad bin Saleh Al-Othaimeen, Muhammad Hamid Al-Fiqi, Abdullah bin Abdul Rahman Al-Bassam, Saleh bin Fawzan Al-Fawzan, Abdul Mohsen bin Hamad Al-Abbad and Abdul Aziz al-Rajhi. Egypt: Al Falah Publishing and Distribution, First Edition, 1439 AH – 2018 AD.

28. Baldock, John, The Essence of Sufism. Arcturus Publishing, London, U.K., 2004

قائمة المراجع

1- أسماء الله الحسنى الثابتة في الكتاب والسنة – المؤلف محمود عبد الرازق الرضواني – الناشر مكتبة سلسبيل – القاهرة – الطبعة الأولى 1426ه.

2- ولله الأسماء الحسنى فادعوه بها – جمع وترتيب: أحمد عبد الجواد – قراءة: عبد الحليم محمود – الناشر مكتبة الكليات الأزهرية – الأزهر – القاهرة – 1985.

3- فاذكروني أذكركم – المؤلف عبد الحليم محمود – الناشر: دار المعارف – القاهرة – 1981.

4- تفسير الجلالين (جلال الدين محمد بن أحمد المحلى – جلال الدين عبد الرحمن بن أبى بكر السيوطي) –دار الحديث – القاهرة – 1422 هـ – 2001 م.

5- تفسير القرآن العظيم (ابن كثير) –المحقق محمد حسين شمس الدين – الطبعة الأولى 1419ه.

6- التفسير الميسر – المؤلف نخبة من أساتذة التفسير – مجمع الملك فهد لطباعة المصحف الشريف – الطبعة الثانية – 1430 هـ –2009 م.

7- صحيح الجامع الصغير وزياداته – المؤلف محمد نصر الدين الألباني–الناشر المكتب الإسلامي سنه النشر 1408 هـ – 1988م.

8- سنن أبي داود – تعليق الشيوخ أحمد محمد شاكر وعبد العزيز بن عبد الله بن باز ومحمد ناصر الدين الالباني ومحمد بن صالح العثيمين ومحمد حامد الفقي وعبد الله بن عبد الرحمن البسام وصالح بن فوزان الفوزان وعبد المحسن بن حمد العباد وعبد العزيز الراجحي –الناشر شركة الفلاح للنشر والتوزيع – مصر – الطبعة الأولى – 1439هـ –2018م.

9- سنن الترمذي – تعليق الشيوخ أحمد محمد شاكر وعبد العزيز بن عبد الله بن باز ومحمد ناصر الدين الالباني ومحمد بن صالح العثيمين ومحمد حامد الفقي وعبد الله بن عبد الرحمن البسام وصالح بن فوزان الفوزان وعبد المحسن بن

حمد العباد وعبد العزيز الراجحي – الناشر شركة الفلاح للنشر والتوزيع – مصر – الطبعة الأولى – 1439هـ – 2018م.

10 – صحيح الإمام البخاري – المحقق محمد فؤاد عبد الباقي – الناشر مكتبة الامام مسلم للنشر والتوزيع – مصر الطبعة الأولى – 1436هـ – 2015م.

11 – صحيح الإمام مسلم شرح النووي – المحقق محمد فؤاد عبد الباقي – الناشر مكتبة أبي سهيل – تنزانيا – منارة الإسلام للنشر والتوزيع – مصر – الطبعة الأولى – 1441هـ – 2020م.

12 – القول الأسمى في بيان صفات وأسماء الله الحسنى – المؤلف الشيخ محمد بن صالح العثيمين – جمعه وأعده عرفان بن سليم العشا حسونة الدمشقي – الناشر دار الفكر – بيروت 1426 هـ – 2005م.

13 – مسند الإمام أحمد بن حبل – المحقق أحمد محمد شاكر – الناشر – دار الحديث – القاهرة – الطبعة الأولى 1416 هـ – 1995م.

14 – سنن ابن ماجه – تعليق الشيوخ أحمد محمد شاكر وعبد العزيز بن عبد الله بن باز ومحمد ناصر الدين الالباني ومحمد بن صالح العثيمين ومحمد حامد الفقي وعبد الله بن عبد الرحمن البسام وصالح بن فوزان الفوزان وعبد المحسن بن حمد العباد وعبد العزيز الراجحي – الناشر شركة الفلاح للنشر والتوزيع – مصر – الطبعة الأولى – 1439هـ – 2018م.

15 – سنن النسائي – تعليق الشيوخ أحمد محمد شاكر وعبد العزيز بن عبد الله بن باز ومحمد ناصر الدين الالباني ومحمد بن صالح العثيمين ومحمد حامد الفقي وعبد الله بن عبد الرحمن البسام وصالح بن فوزان الفوزان وعبد المحسن بن حمد العباد وعبد العزيز الراجحي – الناشر شركة الفلاح للنشر والتوزيع – مصر – الطبعة الأولى – 1439هـ – 2018م.

16 – لسان العرب – ابن منظور الأنصاري – دار صادر – بيروت – الطبعة الثالثة – 1414 هـ – 1994م.

١٧- مدارك التنزيل وحقائق التأويل (تفسير النسفي) -المؤلف أبو البركات عبد الله بن أحمد بن محمود حافظ الدين النسفي-المحقق: يوسف علي بديوي - راجعه وقدم له محي الدين ديب مستو - الناشر دار الكلم - بيروت - الطبعة الأولى -1419هـ -1998م.

١٨- الرحيق المختوم - صفي الرحمن المباركفوري - الناشر وزارة الأوقاف القطرية -قطر - 1428هـ-2007م.

١٩- السيرة النبوية - أبو الفداء إسماعيل بن عمر بن كثير القرشي الدمشقي - المحقق: مصطفى عبد الواحد - الناشر: دار المعرفة للطباعة والنشر - بيروت - 1396هـ - 1976م.

٢٠- السيرة النبوية - عبد الملك بن هشام بن أيوب الحميري المعافري - علق عليها وأخرج أحاديثها، وصنع فهارسها عمر عبد السلام تدمري - الناشر دار الكتاب العربي - بيروت - الطبعة الثالثة -1410هـ -1990م.

٢١- الجامع لأحكام القرآن (تفسير القرطبي) - أبو عبد الله محمد بن أحمد بن أبي بكر بن فرح الأنصاري الخزرجي شمس الدين القرطبي - تحقيق أحمد البردوني وإبراهيم أطفيش - الناشر دار الكتب المصرية - مصر - الطبعة الثانية - 1384هـ -1964م.

٢٢- الفروق اللغوية - الحسن بن عبد الله بن سهل بن سعيد أبو هلال العسكري -المحقق محمد إبراهيم سليم - الناشر دار العلم والثقافة للنشر والتوزيع - مصر - 1418هـ-1997م.